D0921048

Crooked Zebra

by

Bob Weltlich

authorHOUSE™

1663 LIBERTY DRIVE, SUITE 200
BLOOMINGTON, INDIANA 47403
(800) 839-8640
WWW.AUTHORHOUSE.COM

First published by AuthorHouse 10/13/04

ISBN: 1-4208-0846-X (sc)

Printed in the United States of America
Bloomington, Indiana

This book is printed on acid-free paper.

About the Author

Robert (Bob) Weltlich Jr. is no stranger to the game of basketball having coached twenty-nine years at the NCAA Division I level, twenty-two as a head coach. During his coaching career, which has transcended five decades, Weltlich has won three hundred games, conference championships and "coach of the year" awards in four different leagues and is one of a handful of coaches to take three different teams to the NCAA Tournament. He has witnessed such changes in college basketball as the adoption of the shot clock, the three-point line and three man officiating crews.

Weltlich was born November 6, 1944 and grew up in the small town of Orrville, Ohio. He graduated from Orrville High School in 1962 and Ohio State University in Columbus, Ohio in 1967. After two years of teaching and coaching in Rittman, Ohio, Weltlich enlisted in the Army and joined Bob Knight as an assistant coach at the United States Military Academy at West Point, New York. He then followed Knight to Indiana University in Bloomington, Indiana, where from 1971 through 1976 the Hoosiers won four Big Ten Championships, compiled a 63-1 record during the 1975 and 1976 seasons and became the last undefeated National Champions.

His success as an assistant coach resulted in Weltlich being named head coach at the University of Mississippi in Oxford, Mississippi in 1976. During his six-year tenure, the Rebels won the school's only Southeastern Conference Championship in basketball and played in three straight post-season tournaments for the first time in school history. For his efforts Weltlich was named SEC Coach of the Year in 1981.

In 1982 Weltlich accepted the head coaching position at the University of Texas at Austin, Texas. During the next six years the Longhorns would win the conference regular season championship in 1986 and play in the National Invitation Tournament. A second league Coach of the Year Award would come his way after the 1986 season.

After being out of coaching for two years, while serving as a college basketball color analyst for radio and television, Weltlich returned to the hardwood in 1990 as the head coach at Florida International University in Miami, Florida. During the next five years the Panthers would have their first winning season as a Division I program, win the Trans America Athletic Conference regular season and tournament championships and play in their only NCAA Tournament, losing to eventual national champion UCLA. These accomplishments would lead to Weltlich's selection as the 1993 TAAC Coach of the Year.

After another break from coaching, during which Weltlich once again served as an analyst for radio and television, he once again returned to coaching as the head coach at the University of South Alabama in Mobile, Alabama in 1997. During the next five years the Jaguars would win three regular season Sun Belt Conference championships, one conference tournament championship and appear in both the NCAA and NIT Tournaments. Weltlich would be selected in 2000 as the Sun Belt Conference Coach of the Year.

Weltlich is also no stranger to international basketball, having served in numerous capacities with the United States national teams during a period spanning three decades. He coached the U.S. team to a silver medal in the 1982 World Championships and served in the selection of the 1979 gold medal Pan American team, the 1984 gold medal Olympic team and the 1990 Goodwill and World Summer games team. He has also been active as a National Association of Basketball Coaches member for twenty-five years, serving in numerous positions.

Forward

It is worth noting a recent study entitled "NCAA Division I Officials: Gambling with the Integrity of College Sports?" authored by Ann G. Vollano and Derrick L. Gragg, both compliance staff members at the University of Michigan. This report collected from 640 Division I football and men's and women's basketball officials, released in March of 2000, revealed the following: 84.4% of these officials have gambled since becoming a college official with approximately 40% admitting to sports betting, including 2.2% who admitted to betting through a bookie. Two officials reported they had been approached about fixing a game, while twelve indicated they knew other officials who had not called a game fairly due to gambling considerations.

It is also worth mentioning that the NCAA (National Collegiate Athletic Association) considers gambling and even legalized betting to be one of the biggest problems facing intercollegiate athletics today. This concern is best reflected in seminars conducted by the NCAA as well as recent legislation outlining penalties for athletes and athletic personnel found to be involved in gambling, even in states where betting is legalized. In fact, not only did the NCAA hired a person, Bill Saum, Director of Agent, Gambling and Amateurism Activities, to lead their anti-gambling campaign, but the NCAA Tournament Committee mandated FBI background checks on selected officials who are assigned to work the NCAA Basketball Tournament.

Of further note, during the year 2001 the NCAA supported legislation introduced in both the House and Senate. Bills S. 718 sponsored by Senators McCain (R-AZ), Brownback (R-KS), Edwards (D-NC), Jeffords (I-VT) and Fitzgerald (R-IL) in the Senate, and H.R. 1110 introduced in the House by Representatives Graham (R-SC), Roemer (D-IN), Kind (D-WI) and Osborne (R-NE) were aimed at banning sports gambling on college games in Nevada.

But with the extent of legalized gambling, the Nevada's Gaming Control Board estimated legal sports betting at approximately $2.3 billion in 1998, the real problem lies in illegal sports betting throughout the U.S., estimated between $80-$380 billion annually. As the above referenced report indicated, "more than $300 million was bet on sports online in 1998 through more than 280 online gambling sites. In 1999, about 2.5 million people were estimated to be playing National Collegiate Athletic Association (NCAA) basketball tournament pools online with that figure expected to grow to 10 million by 2001 (Lowry, 1999). The FBI estimates that as much a $2.5 billion is illegally bet on the NCAA Division I men's basketball tournament alone – in addition to the $80 million wagered legally in Las Vegas (Harden, 1998)." With the money involved, scandals of the past will pale in comparison with point-shaving and fixing games in the future if such should occur.

This book is dedicated to my wife and children,
loves of my life and the inspiration for all that I do.

Special thanks to Tommy Hicks for his time, effort and writing
expertise in helping to make this book a reality.

By Definition

The word Zebra is a slang term in sports describing a referee or an official because of the black and white striped shirt they wear as part of their uniform. Therefore, a <u>Crooked Zebra</u> is an official or referee who cheats and/or is dishonest in the dissemination of his or her duties as they relate to their particular sport or event.

Prologue

Does it get any better than...wait a second: "Bob, hey man, wait a minute!" What's he running from? "Bob, slow down." That can't be him. "Hold up, we need to talk." But he sure looks familiar. Is it the walk, his build, clothes or baseball cap that stirs my interest? No, it can't be. "Please excuse me," as I force myself out of line and hurry down the corridor searching for a guy that looks familiar and brings back so many memories. Damn it, he's gone. Just disappeared. Are my eyes playing tricks on me or have I just witnessed something so bizarre I can't explain it? Who am I kidding? Too many times these past few months I've seen this guy, only to find I mistook him for someone else. He's dead, or at least that's what everyone believes. No way would he show his face in such a public venue if he were alive. The risk is too great and could cause too many problems for too many innocent people. Let it alone Jim. Go back to your lovely wife and enjoy a very special day.

And what a great day it is. As I walked into the United Center in Chicago, I couldn't believe this day had finally arrived. Betty and I are guests to see the Chicago Bulls play the New Jersey Nets in the opening game of the NBA (National Basketball Association) season from court level seats. While Betty visits the ladies room, I think I'll buy a bag of popcorn and a couple of beers. We still have plenty of time to get to our seats for warm-ups. Even though we're early, it's amazing how many people, mainly autograph seekers, mingle around the concourse areas. No one puts on a better pre-game show than the Bulls, and with the cost of tickets most people want to take in all the festivities. To think our son is part of this.

As Betty and I walk to our seats, we both have a chance to speak briefly with Chad. Most of the players are out early to warm up and work on their shooting. Many just enjoy renewing friendships and visiting with each other since they have either played in college together or were once on the same NBA team. This being the first game of his professional career, I don't want to distract Chad and yet I know his mother wants to give him a hug and a kiss and wish him good luck. A few minutes won't hurt and this time will give me a chance to find our seats. While they visit I can't help but think about the guy I saw earlier. One thing about Bob, you could always depend on him doing the unexpected. So, if somehow it was Bob, it should come as no surprise he would be at this place at this time. What a wild journey he and I have traveled these last couple of years.

Chapter One

My name is Jim Stanton, and I have been a FBI (Federal Bureau of Investigation) agent most of my adult life. During my career I have had the opportunity to work investigations in almost every area of law enforcement, and I cannot get over the senseless crimes committed by people that destroy relationships, shatter families and often times result in death. This is a story about one such case. I cannot help but reflect on that particular investigation and the events leading to its tragic ending.

It all began in the early 1980's in Orrville, Ohio, a small Midwest community located in the northeast portion of the state near Akron and just south of Cleveland. Orrville is a typical close-knit community with an unusual amount of industry nestled in the middle of an agricultural area. This town of approximately eight thousand people is best known as the home of Smucker's, the world famous jam and jelly company.

Bob Girard was a local sports hero who graduated from Orrville H.S. and went on to Kent State University, approximately forty-five minutes from his home, where he had a less than distinguished college career in basketball. After graduating from college, he began teaching continuing education in the small community of Rittman, Ohio and coached basketball while assisting with football and baseball. A bachelor, Bob was a tall, handsome, athletic guy with dark hair and baby blue eyes. He carried himself with great self-confidence and was known to party with the best of them. Finding

1

women to date was the least of his problems, but staying single and enjoying the rewards of multiple relationships was another story. He enjoyed the benefits of single status and had no intention of settling down or getting married.

During that period he met Nancy Champion at a basketball game. As the action on the court headed in one direction, Bob noticed Nancy, a tall, leggy, blue-eyed, blonde haired beauty walking in front of his bench. It was impossible for his peripheral vision to ignore this athletic looking gal. Her stride was as perfect as her shape. Cheerleading advisor for the opposing team, Nancy's upbringing was the opposite of Bob's, growing up in the large city of St. Louis and attending the University of Missouri where she was a world class swimmer and the darling, if not the ace, of the tennis team. Through a friend, and with a desire to get away from home, she became aware of a teaching job in physical education in the tiny community of Doylestown, Ohio, a league rival of Rittman. She was much a one-guy gal but had found no one of interest in this small community. It was not uncommon for her to take weekend trips back to her old stomping grounds hoping to find some excitement.

As so often happens in small towns, Bob and Nancy were introduced and a brief but intense courtship followed. They were married six months later. It was a small wedding but an event people who attended still talk about. There was no question in anyone's mind this was a marriage that would last. After all, they had so many things in common. Here were two responsible, independent, active people with great love and respect for one another and a genuine interest in sports and outdoor activities. Both were in the early stages of their respective careers and neither had an immediate timetable for children. For now they would just enjoy themselves and the moment.

Shortly after their marriage Bob and Nancy decided to move to warm weather. Nothing is more depressing, especially for warm-blooded, outdoor, athletic types, than spending five months a year in cold weather. Through letters and phone calls their prospecting proved successful. Bob found a job as a vocational education director in Florida at Miami High in the inner city, while Nancy became a substitute teacher and part time fitness trainer on South Beach. They bought a small house in the South Miami area, and Bob supplemented his salary by officiating high school basketball games during the school year while running a series of small but well attended summer basketball camps.

As Bob's camps continued to grow, he was making as much money in three months of the summer as with his nine-month teaching job. Life was good for the popular and attractive couple and this was probably the most enjoyable time of their lives. They had time together, freedom to travel, great weather, surroundings to enjoy their outdoor activities and enough money to pay the bills. Their situation also allowed for an occasional spur of the moment adventure that often involved a short drive to the beach, bottle of wine at a local restaurant and the ensuing marital eroticism. They were blissfully happy and content with their simple existence and uncomplicated lives. Neither Bob nor Nancy had any idea how quickly and undeniably their lifestyle could change.

Chapter Two

It was the third year of camp when Bob ran into a youngster named Chad Payne, an eleven year old boy from a single parent family who needed a male companion and role model in his life. His father Tom was a drunk and had abused both Chad and his mother. Tom and Betty Payne were married at an early age after Betty became pregnant with Chad. Feeling forced into marriage, Tom made no attempt to be a responsible husband or father. Things deteriorated so badly Betty served divorce papers when Chad was only two years old and the boy had very little involvement with his father, which was fine with both Betty and his father. On the other hand, Bob and Nancy loved children but had no real desire to start a family. So it was only natural Bob would take an interest in a young boy filled with enthusiasm and optimism about sports, especially the game of basketball.

For a couple of weeks that summer Chad hung around Bob's camp, constantly sneaking into the gym to shoot baskets whenever the other campers went to lunch or were on break. Busy with administrative duties, Bob didn't notice this young interloper. It was Nancy, who helped with the camp, that constantly made mention of this youngster. Chad was not a registered camper and thus not covered under the camp's insurance. This led her to approach Bob about the situation.

"Bob, have you seen the scruffy little kid that's hanging around?" she asked.

"Not really. What's the problem?"

"Well, he's not registered and yet he continually sneaks in and plays with the balls. Not only do we have a liability problem if he gets hurt, I'm also concerned he may steal something."

"What do you want me to do about him? He's just trying to have some fun."

"You need to talk with him and tell him he can't play while camp is going on unless he is registered. After all, if we allow every kid to come without paying, then we won't have anyone who will pay. Remember, this is how we make our living."

"Okay, I'll talk to him," Bob replied. "Which one is he?"

"Don't worry, I'll point him out the next time I see him."

The following day, with Nancy's help, Bob cornered Chad while he was shooting at one of the baskets. It was during lunch and Chad did not see Bob coming.

"Hey young man, what's your name?" Bob asked.

"Who wants to know?" the boy answered defiantly.

Bob stared at him, "the owner of the camp."

"So why do you need to know my name?"

"Because you're not supposed to be here if you're not a registered camper, so you can either tell me your name or I'll call the juvenile authorities and they'll find out who you are."

"Don't worry big man, I don't care about your camp anyway," Chad shouted as he ran from the gym.

Bob and Nancy felt they had seen the last of this ill-mannered boy, but much to their surprise that would not be the case. This young boy would continue to show up at the most unexpected times and although Bob would corner him, Chad would always seem to escape Bob's grasp. After each incident he would stay away from the camp for a couple of days before returning. Bob was intrigued by this youngster and began to develop an appreciation for his persistence. He seemed different than many of the tough kids Bob came into contact with.

Then one day it happened. Instead of running Chad introduced himself to Bob and Nancy. It was almost like he was relieved to be caught.

"My name is Chad."

"Well, what's your last name and where do you live?" Nancy asked.

"Payne and I live about a half mile from here."

Bob scratched his chin. "Where are your parents and why do you come here?"

"My mom works and I don't have a real dad. There's nothing to do around home so I come here to see some of my friends and play ball. Anyway, what business is it of yours?"

Bob thought what a belligerent attitude for a little kid, but he was not about to back off. "Anything that involves this camp is my business. With your attitude you may need to find another place to play. We don't allow smart-ass kids in our camp. So, until you learn how to act, why don't you go home and not bother us."

Chad slammed down the ball and stormed out of the building, but he would stay away from camp for only a couple of days. As Bob found out more about this boy, he was reminded too much of himself as a youngster. Bob talked to Nancy about involving Chad in some of the camp activities like getting water, racking the basketballs and running errands for the coaches, assuming the young boy would improve his attitude.

"So, I see you're back," Bob said when Chad returned a few days later. "You still got a chip on your shoulder or have you adjusted your attitude?"

"Maybe I have and maybe I haven't," Chad shot back. "Its not like I need this dumb camp, but nothing was going on around home so I thought I'd come see my buddies. Don't worry, I won't mess with any of your camp balls or get in the way."

"Well tough guy, since you don't need this dumb place I guess it would be out of the question to ask if you're interested in helping around the camp. That way I won't have to run you off and maybe we can keep you out of trouble," Bob replied.

Bob and Nancy both noticed a sudden softening in Chad's demeanor but could tell he still wanted to play the part of a tough guy.

"I guess I could help, but it depends on what you want me to do."

"Don't worry, it won't be hard. Now go get some lunch with the other campers and report to me at the start of the afternoon session."

That afternoon Chad carried water to the coaches and picked up the loose balls at the end of each session. He also helped keep score during the games and proved to be a very good helper. Chad would not miss a day of camp the rest of the summer, and Bob worked out a pay scale to reward him. Their relationship grew in a positive way, but the Girards still wondered about Chad's mother and his home situation.

Chapter Three

Betty Payne was a wonderful person, but a mother often times overwhelmed by raising a rebellious son without a father. Each year became increasingly more difficult as Chad hung around with the wrong group of kids. The first time Bob and Nancy met Betty they sensed she was suspicious of their involvement with her son. But knowing how happy Chad appeared in recent weeks, and seeing the sincere interest for her son exhibited by the Girards, Betty was quickly convinced he had found people that could provide positive direction in his life.

Bob and Nancy on the other hand were extremely impressed with Betty. For a lady of few words and slight build, she had a toughness and protectiveness about her that stood out. Although not especially pretty, Betty exhibited an inner strength and warmth that drew people to her. She was friendly, witty and very giving even though she had very few material things. But when all was said and done, she was like a mother bear protecting her cub. Heaven help anyone who mistreated or tried to take advantage of her son.

As time passed, Bob and Nancy became second parents to Chad and involved him and his mother in many of their activities. Christmas and Chad's birthday were always spent together, and Bob began to work with Chad after school and during weekends with homework and basketball. As a result Chad's attitude softened and he began improving in school, not only academically but also in his personal relationships with other classmates and teachers. No one was prouder than Bob when Chad made the Westwood Junior High School basketball team as a seventh grader. In the Girards' minds Chad's athletic accomplishments were surpassed only by his success in the classroom. Bob was now involved in basketball officiating, working NACA (National Athletic Collegiate Association) Division II and junior college games. As much as he enjoyed this diversion, the real excitement was yet to come.

By the time Chad was a junior at Miami East High School, Bob was working in some of the best leagues in the country, including the SEC (Southeastern Conference), Big East and the ACC (Atlantic Coast Conference). In fact, Bob was making as much money officiating college basketball as he was teaching and was able to do both thanks to a flexible schedule. His teaching position involved placing young people in jobs around the community and monitoring their progress. This gave him immense freedom to come and go as he pleased, and from November through March he was officiating as many as fifty games.

Bob and Nancy continued to treat Chad and Betty as extended family, and during Chad's senior year it was rare if both would miss one of his games. An example of Bob's interest took place the night Chad's team played for the district championship. Bob made arrangements to miss a big ACC game between Duke and North Carolina, a prestigious game as well as a big payday, to see Chad play. It was a good decision since it would be Chad's final game as a high school player. As the captain, leading scorer in the county and first team all-state, Chad was the main reason for the Miami East Arrows' success.

He had really developed into an outstanding player and years in the weight room had served him well. If there ever was an All-American kid, this was the guy. Six foot, three inches tall, dark hair, olive skin, blue eyes and a smile that could charm the pants off almost any girl, Chad had a sensitivity not found in many young men his age and a deep respect for women as well as his elders. He inherited his mom's toughness and focus and was charismatic to the point that people of all ages were drawn to him.

9

As a player Chad had an uncanny ability to get the ball to the open man, create and score off the dribble, anticipate his opponent's next move and elevate all those around him to play at a higher level than many of them thought possible. At any point Chad could single handedly take over a game, yet, as good as he was, he never allowed himself to act superior to any of his teammates. He was the consummate team player with an appreciation and understanding of the game and others' feelings.

Although Chad played well in his final game, scoring twenty-eight of his team's fifty points, gathering eight rebounds, dishing out seven assists and committing only two turnovers, his team was beaten by city rival and perennial power West Miami High School. Chad was heartbroken after the loss, but Bob helped put things in perspective.

"Tough game kid," Bob said.

"Yeah, especially to lose to those guys," Chad responded.

"They're a very good team with a great tradition."

"I know, but to get this far my senior year and not be able to get to the state playoffs is disappointing. I wanted so badly to win this game for my teammates and coach," Chad replied as tears welled in his eyes. "We worked too hard to have this happen. It's just not fair."

"Well, no one said it was going to be fair. Just don't let this one game cloud all the success you've had during your high school career. After all, it's not the end of the world," Bob replied, trying to comfort a distraught young man.

"Maybe not, but it doesn't make it any easier to accept the loss. We've always been in West Miami's shadow and this was the year to break the jinx."

"Listen, if this is the worst thing that happens to you, then you're in store for a pretty good life. Everyone knows how hard you tried. Now you've got to put this game behind you and get ready for bigger and better things. There are still a lot of goals to accomplish. The worst thing you can do is live in the past." Bob had never seen Chad so visibly upset. "Let's catch up to Nancy and your mother."

Bob had never felt more like a father and Chad more like a son. It was times like these that Bob wondered what would happen when Chad went off to college and was no longer an everyday part of their lives.

But Chad was not just successful at basketball. He was elected class president, most likely to succeed and was valedictorian of his class. As educators, nothing pleased Bob and Nancy more than Chad's attention to his studies and his involvement in Bob's camp as a counselor and role model for the younger kids. Betty Payne couldn't believe her good fortune to have a son like Chad with friends like the Girards. All the hard work was paying dividends and the future looked extremely bright.

Chapter Four

As an outstanding player and student, Chad's college choices were virtually limitless. He leaned heavily on Bob during the recruiting process, relying on Bob's contacts as well as his familiarity with the coaches and their programs. Bob decided early on not to tell Chad where to go to school, but instead to simply advise him what programs to consider. Once they narrowed the list to five schools, Bob stayed in the background as Chad advised him of the nature of the phone calls, home and campus visits.

Chad visited Indiana University of the Big Ten Conference, Duke University and the University of North Carolina out of the ACC and the University of Florida and University of Kentucky of the SEC. Each was a top academic school, rich in basketball tradition and members of high profile conferences that appeared on national television, all competing for the national championship on a regular basis. Chad enjoyed all his recruiting visits, but displayed remarkable maturity and patience in evaluating each of these programs.

After the visits Bob and Nancy sat down with Chad and his mother to discuss the pros and cons of each school. It was important for Chad to make a well thought-out decision based not on emotion, but on which school best suited his needs.

"How are you going to decide which school is the right one for you?" Bob asked Chad.

"I don't really know. I like them all."

"Well then, let's keep this simple. Let's make a list and rank those things that are important to you and your mother."

Betty was confused and asked, "What do you mean?"

Bob responded. "What's the most important things for you and Chad as he gets ready to go off to college, is it the distance from home, academics, weather, opportunity to play or what? Some things will be more important than others, but we need to remember ultimately this will be Chad's decision on what is best for Chad."

"I want to go where I can play right away. I also want to play in an established program and compete for a national championship."

"What about your education?" Betty interrupted.

"Mom, you know that's important but all these schools have great academics."

"Is that right Bob?"

"Yes Betty, they are all solid academic schools with great alumni support that will be important to help Chad after he graduates."

"Well, I just want to be sure Chad has a chance that I never had and that involves graduating from college."

"That makes sense," Bob replied, "so what else Chad, how about style of play?"

"That's important. I'd like to play up and down but I think I can play any style. The big thing for me is we win and there's real interest and support for basketball. I don't want to go to a football school where basketball isn't appreciated."

Nancy asked her first question, "how about distance?"

"That's real important too. I want to be close enough so mom can see me play and I can get home if something happens. But I also want to start being independent."

"Don't worry about me son."

"Look mom, no one knows or appreciates more how hard you've worked to give me this chance and I'm not about to let you down. I love you."

It was here a single tear slipped down Betty's cheek, running right past the corner of a smile of pride.

Bob too was proud. "Then let's keep working on your list, taking time to ask and answer questions and coming to a decision in the next few weeks."

Following continued discussions and soul-searching, not to mentions hundreds of phone calls and letters from recruiters, Chad accepted a scholarship to Duke University, a school that offered the best mix of things Chad wanted. Chad's decision was made difficult since he was recruited by all the top schools, but he knew at Duke he would have a wonderful opportunity to be involved in a great academic school as well as an outstanding basketball program. Also, it was not too far from home and he would see Bob from time to time when Bob officiated ACC games.

Two questions yet to be answered were whether Chad was really good enough to play for the Blue Devils and if Bob could justify in his own mind officiating Duke games based on his close relationship with Chad. The night Bob, Nancy, Betty and Chad and a small group of friends celebrated Chad's graduation and acceptance to Duke, it never entered anyone's thinking these two families would be linked in one of the most bizarre stories anyone could possibly imagine.

Chapter Five

With Chad moving forward with his life, Bob and Nancy talked about starting their own family. They had been trying to have a child for more than a year. On the Fourth of July Nancy told Bob the good news.

"Why don't we call another couple and go down to Bayside to watch the fireworks?" Bob suggested. "In fact, let's invite a couple of counselors from the camp. It'll be a party."

"Sounds like a great idea," Nancy responded. "You ask the counselors and I'll find out what Betty and Chad have planned. Also, be sure to go to the store and get some ice cream and cake for later. Maybe everyone can stop by the house for dessert."

"Why don't you make the calls so I can go to the store real quick? Is there anything else we need?"

"What about a jar of pickles, ice cream and some strawberries."

"That's an odd combination," Bob said with a surprised look.

"Not if you knew what I know."

"Oh, my God, you've gotta be kidding! Tell me it's true!"

"Well daddy, unless my doctor screwed up, we're going to have a baby."

Bob picked Nancy up above his shoulders, gave her a big hug and kiss and asked with a grin from ear to ear, "When did you find out? When is the baby due?"

"I found out late yesterday and it looks like we're going to have a bigger family sometime in late February or early March. I can't believe we're about to be parents."

"Well, maybe we should stay home and celebrate. After all, its not every day a guy finds out he's going to be a father. What do you think?"

Nancy laughed. "Let's go down to Bayside. What better way to celebrate than with fireworks on Independence Day. Anyway, I want to tell Chad and Betty the good news. I'm sure Chad will trip out."

Without having mentioned a thing about the baby, everyone returned to the Girards for cake and ice cream after the fireworks. After all had left but Betty and Chad, Nancy finally broke the news. "Chad, how would you like to teach a future camper to play basketball?"

Chad thought that was a strange request. "The summer's almost over and I don't know if I'll have time before leaving for school. Who is it you want me to work with?"

"Oh, it's not this summer. In fact, it will probably be a few summers down the road," Bob offered.

"We don't know yet whether it will be a boy or a girl," Nancy chimed in, "but we're excited it will be a Girard."

"Oh my God," Betty screamed as Chad looked on dumbfounded! "I can't believe it. When did you find out and when is the baby due?" Betty, more than anyone, understood how important this new addition would be with Chad going away to school. She was also in a selfish way looking at this as an opportunity to help repay the Girards for what they had done for her son. Although she could only afford to give time, she knew there would be many a night when Bob and Nancy would need a break from the new baby.

"Way to go," is all Chad could say as he embraced both Nancy and Bob. "You can count on me to help anyway I can. This will be like having a little brother."

"Or sister, but thanks Chad. By the way, Nancy and I would like very much for Betty to be our child's godmother. I hope that's okay with you?" Bob asked Betty.

"I would have been insulted and disappointed if you hadn't asked," Betty responded.

When the euphoria of the impending birth subsided, the reality of the life change hit Bob. As a natural first step in expanding and raising a family, it would be important for he and Nancy to find a larger house in a better section of Miami. Bob would contact a real estate friend and ask him to look for something suitable.

But what Bob didn't think about in this moment of excitement was what all of this would mean financially. After all, with the new house would come a significant increase in mortgage payments as well as city and county taxes, not to mention insurance costs. Also, each summer more camps sprang up and the competition for kids was intense. Bob's camp had experienced a slight decline in numbers and that naturally impacted their income. Nancy had lost hours at her fitness club as the South Beach scene exploded with the advent of larger but fewer fitness centers staffed by younger fashion-oriented trainers.

Bob and Nancy wanted so much to realize their vision of the 'American Dream,' and yet through all of their work and planning they were experiencing nothing more than an increase in expenditures coupled with a cutback in income. If sacrifices needed to be made, then so be it. How could anyone be discouraged with all the good fortune the Girards had experienced in their relatively young lives together?

Chapter Six

It was about this time Bob ran into Gary Branson, a friend and fellow basketball official. One night while Bob was having a beer at a South Beach bar waiting for Nancy to finish up at the health club, he was approached by Gary and a stranger. Gary was one of those GQ guys who tried to be politically correct. A former player himself, he had a good grasp of the game but was not considered one of the elite officials, although he and Bob had worked well together in what few games they officiated. He had networked himself into the better leagues, but was known to be a real ladies man and had a mysterious, secretive side to him. No one seemed to be able to get close to Gary and much of his background was unknown to Bob.

"Hey Bob, what brings you in here?" Gary asked.

"I'm just waiting for my wife to finish up at the health club and then we're going to have dinner and catch a late flick," Bob responded. "So what brings you to south Florida this time of year? No one comes to this heat in the summer."

"I'm just visiting my buddy Mario," Gary replied as he introduced Bob to his friend. "We're old friends and I thought I would spend a long weekend on South Beach and look at all the beautiful people. In fact, we're talking about jumping on a weekend cruise to the Bahamas. I wouldn't mind a couple of days of wine, women and lying on the beach. So what have you been up to?"

"Plenty, Nancy's pregnant and we've moved into a new house since I saw you last."

"Are you still working with the school system?" Gary inquired.

"Yeah, and it won't be long before we get cranking again. I swear the summers seem to get shorter each year. So Mario, how do you know Gary? You must not care much about your reputation if you're hanging around with this guy," Bob said jokingly.

"Gary and I go back quite a ways. He was always a real ladies man and I hung around him just to get his rejects," Mario said with a wink. "We've known each other since high school and I usually pick him up when he's in town to officiate a game. I love sports, especially basketball, so it's great for me since Gary gets me tickets to the games."

"And what do you do for a living?" Bob asked Mario.

"I run a small trucking business down by the docks. It was my dad's until he retired. My two brothers and I bought him out and I'm involved mostly in the marketing and advertising part of the business. Did I hear Gary say you're a teacher?"

"Yeah, I run a vocational placement program for one of the local high schools. I don't know about you, but if you know anyone hiring people please refer them to me so I can help place my kids. The kids do a great job and we can use all the help we can get. Unfortunately, there's talk the program might be discontinued because of a lack of funding."

"What a shame that would be," Mario chimed in.

Bob responded, "They'll probably use the money they save on our program to buy computers for the rich kids in advanced classes. Education just isn't what it used to be."

"I know exactly what you're talking about," Gary added. "They have gifted, advanced, EMR's and every other pigeonholed group you can think of. Hell, we're creating our own monsters by stereotyping and separating kids. We ask them to perform to a minimal level and then wonder why they don't perform better."

Mario interrupted, "You couldn't get me to teach for all the tea in China. Teachers don't seem to teach anymore. They're just babysitters, psychologists and prison guards. If I was teaching today I'd probably kill a kid or he would kill me, but I guarantee you one

19

thing, no smart-ass kid is going to tell me to 'kiss off' and walk away untouched."

As Bob shook his head he said, "I know where you're coming from. Unfortunately, until we regain control of our classrooms, the teacher and students who want to learn have no chance. We need to go back to spanking their ass. I can remember the teachers who gave me whacks and I guarantee you I didn't screw around in their class again."

As the conversation continued, Mario began to show an unusual amount of interest in Bob. Bob attributed that to Mario's interest in sports. So many times in the past people would ask Bob about officiating, leading to questions about different coaches and teams. People seem to gravitate towards sports and those who know the key players. Bob knew the coaches and players and in fact had developed some close relationships with many coaches through his officiating. Some of those relationships grew as Bob took on more primetime games and earned the trust of the coaches themselves.

"So I understand you and Gary officiate games together," Mario stated. "Can this guy officiate worth a damn?"

"Gary does okay. If he ever figures out the difference between a block and a charge he'll really be dangerous," Bob joked.

"Give me a break," Gary laughed. "No one has messed up that call more than you."

"Who are the easiest and toughest coaches to work for?" Mario interrupted. "Is the guy at Indiana as tough on officials as people say, and how about the coach at North Carolina?"

Bob was the first to respond. "Well, they both have completely different demeanors, but both will let you know in no uncertain terms when you miss a call. That's the way most of the really good coaches are. The worst thing you can do with any coach is to blow a call and then try to bullshit your way out of it. Most appreciate you just admitting you 'blew it.' Any coach understands officials are just like players and coaches in that they make mistakes. Gary and I have been around long enough to be trusted. We really don't have many problems anymore."

"I agree with that," said Gary. "If the coaches feel you're working the game as hard as they're coaching, they'll generally cut you some slack. But with the two guys you asked about, you better not come unprepared or not work hard. If you do they'll eat you up and spit you out. These guys know the rules better than some of the officials."

"And why shouldn't they get upset," Bob added. "After all, they work their ass off getting their teams ready to play and expect their kids to play hard, so why not us?"

Nancy walked into the bar looking tired but happy. As she joined the men, the conversation quickly turned to her day and what she and Bob had planned for that evening. Trusting his friend Gary, Bob thought nothing of Mario's offer to set them up at Clarity's, a popular restaurant in Coral Gables. Living on a tight budget, why not take advantage of such a generous offer. After additional small talk, Bob and Nancy excused themselves and enjoyed a rather expensive night at one of the city's great eateries.

Chapter Seven

Chad's first year at Duke was a real learning experience. He did not receive extensive playing time at first, which is characteristic of freshmen in high profile programs, although he did play more minutes than most first-year players. With the exception of limited playing time, he thoroughly enjoyed everything else about the situation. Duke proved to be everything he hoped academically, and the social life for a guy from Miami was actually better than he anticipated. But he did miss mom and South Beach.

The atmosphere for basketball was truly amazing in the Atlantic Coast Conference, a real hotbed for college hoops. Playing at North Carolina, Wake Forest and other ACC schools was a dream come true. There was the added benefit of a competitive non-conference schedule, which included the likes of the University of Michigan, UCLA and other nationally ranked, top ten teams. Every game was a battle in front of a packed house with national title implications. Everyday Chad found himself competing against other former high school All-State and All-American players from around the country. As a point guard, Chad was just one in a line of previous great players at his position who benefited from Coach Pankowski's (affectionately known as Coach P) knowledge of the game. His challenge was to continue to play hard, maintain a positive attitude and work to get stronger and improve his game. He was excited about the prospects of his sophomore year, knowing the guy ahead of him was a senior and the starting position would be open. Chad also knew things would be easier since he now understood the system and there would be new players Coach P could yell at.

Bob and Chad had the opportunity to see each other on numerous occasions that first year. But as close as they had grown, they both knew they had to maintain distance and act indifferent towards each other during games. Except for family and intimate friends in Miami, few people knew of the special relationship between these two friends.

One game in particular that reflected this awkward situation was a Duke home game against Florida A & M, a non-conference game in late November. Chad was especially excited when he got the opportunity to play extended minutes in a fifteen-point win. As he checked into the game, he thought he caught a glimpse of Bob winking at him. Chad would find the friendly look to be short-lived. As he drove the ball to the basket Chad felt contact and heard the whistle blow. Confident the foul was on his opponent, Chad bounced to his feet in anticipation of shooting free throws. Out of the pack Bob appeared, pointing at Chad and signaling a charging foul.

"Charging foul on #12 white," Bob announced in a firm voice. "Player possession foul. Green ball out underneath the basket."

Chad couldn't believe what he was hearing and muttered under his breath, "That was a block. There's no way I charged."

Bob overheard Chad's comment as he was moving toward the scorer's table and responded in a low voice, "Give it a rest #12. It was a charge and I don't want to hear anymore about that call or any others. Just play."

Chad could see Coach P on the sideline questioning what was going on. He did not allow his players to question calls, feeling that kind of behavior distracted from the player's focus and created an adversarial relationship with the officials.

"Chad, forget the call and get back on defense," Coach P yelled.

Chad also overheard Coach P tell Bob he missed the call. But that was small consolation, although he appreciated his coach defending him. Chad now realized with Bob officiating he would be held to a higher standard. Although Chad did not agree with that kind of reasoning, he accepted it and played on. After all, nothing could impact their friendship.

Bob, on the other hand, knew he needed to be careful not to punish Chad because of their relationship. It was unfair to hold Chad to a higher standard because it not only would hurt the boy but would also penalize the Duke basketball team as a whole.

. Bob made the decision not to call many Duke games in the future since Chad was about to become a prominent player on the team. He would try to limit himself to non-conference games. This could be easily accomplished because Bob was working other conferences and could pretty much pick and choose his games. Since the Southeastern Conference had always been his first priority, and the University of Miami was in the Big East, it would be easy to reduce the number of ACC games he worked without anyone noticing or suspecting a conflict of interest. Bob felt this decision would eliminate a lot of problems for himself and Chad.

Chapter Eight

Aside from a great season of officiating, things at home were not going well. With Nancy's delivery time drawing near, she was no longer able to work at the fitness center. Her lack of work was compounded after the first of the year when Bob was notified by his school principal, with state tax cuts and reduced budgets, his position would be eliminated and he would have to return to the classroom next year in another capacity. Bob knew what that meant to his officiating. He would now be punching a clock, confined to the classroom and relinquishing the flexibility to control his time away and travel schedule during the week. This would surely result in fewer games, a drop in his ratings and less earnings. Bob had a difficult decision to make. His life was teaching and working with young people, but his future was dependent upon increased income as he and Nancy eagerly awaited the arrival of their baby. Fortunately, he had some time to make a decision on what to do.

Nancy encouraged Bob to consider alternatives to teaching. As she explained, "You don't need to do something you really don't want to do. After all, you know enough people who could help you find another job. With your people skills and reputation, there's a bunch of people who would like you working for them."

"Maybe, but you know how much I like working with kids. I've always felt I could make a difference and just can't see myself doing anything else."

"Well honey, you need to give this some serious thought. We can cut back on things and still make ends meet, but with the baby due next month we need to make some long range decisions."

"I can always go back to the classroom, but if I do I'll have to give up a lot of my officiating," Bob replied. "You know how much I enjoy that and how well it pays. I just don't know if I can afford to give that up right now."

"What's the alternative?" Nancy asked.

"That's the problem, I don't know. I can look into officiating full time in the pros, but that would mean a bunch of time away from you and the baby. Plus, I'm not sure I'm cut out to deal with some of those high-priced superstars."

"When do you have to give your principal an answer?"

"Fortunately not until the first of July, so we'll just have to see how the camp goes this summer. Who knows, maybe we'll have to sell it."

"I sure hope not," Nancy interrupted. "You've worked so hard to build the business and the kids would be broken hearted if they didn't have your camp to go to. In any case, it's not something we have to make a decision about right now. We'll work something out."

Realistically, with the baby due it was not quite that simple. Nancy hoped to spend time with the baby and not have to return right away to work. Finding a decent job should not be a problem for Bob, but would it pay the bills while providing him with the chance to be happy? Both could only hope so.

Chapter Nine

Bob's future decision would be influenced in a strange way through a chance conversation with his friend Gary Branson. Their conversation took place at Mo Joe's, a sports bar and restaurant in Coconut Grove, after both men worked a University of Miami versus Central Florida game in early February. Bob's friend was not flying out until the next morning, so they decided to stop and have a beer.

Much to Bob's surprise, Mario, the man he met with Gary the previous summer, joined the two men at the bar. Bob couldn't help but wonder who and what this guy was all about. A Danny DeVito look-alike, the guy was short and balding with unruly hair and a mix of Italian and Hispanic ancestry. His demeanor was harsh and he was constantly looking around, avoiding eye contact and making him difficult to communicate with. Yet, Mario appeared to grasp what was being discussed. His attire was outdated and sloppy but he was not unclean. If one didn't know better you would think he was someone's lap dog or gopher. He and Gary had something going on besides friendship, but Bob had no idea what that could be.

After discussing the game and additional small talk, Gary and Mario began to question with unusual interest Bob's thoughts on what he had planned for the future. Gary was aware of Bob's financial concerns since they had discussed them at length during a previous road trip. They both talked about applying to the NBA for permanent officiating jobs as well as other ways to increase their income.

27

"So is it my understanding you may be changing jobs and if so do you know what you want to do?" Mario asked.

"Not really. I would like to continue to teach but I don't want to be restricted to the classroom. The NBA is a long shot and I don't want to be gone that much with a new baby on the way. Things are tough right now."

"How important is the college officiating?"

"I really enjoy it. Gary and I have both worked hard to get where we are and the money is great. Also, I would love to have a chance to work the Four Final."

"Well," Gary jumped in, "it sounds like you're going to have to find something else to do to make more money that will allow you to still officiate. After all, another mouth to feed is not going to make it any easier to pay the bills."

"You got that right," Bob answered. "With the new baby, Nancy will be limited in what she can do job wise and I don't want her working for awhile anyway. My gut reaction is I'll have to find another job. But what kind of job is going to pay enough and still allow me to control my hours so I can officiate?"

Bob was somewhat surprised when Gary suggested they move to a table located in the corner of the bar. Mario, on the other hand, saw this as the right time to broach a subject he and Gary had discussed at length. What he was about to discuss could be risky, especially since he was unsure how Bob would react. He was about to propose "point-shaving" (controlling the scores of games), a form of racketeering and a crime.

"Gary, this might be a good time to talk to Bob about our idea," suggested Mario as a lead in. "Maybe you could explain what we do. Who knows, this might help Bob solve his problem."

On cue Gary proceeded. "Bob, I was in much the same situation as you a year ago when Mario approached me about making some extra money. All I ask is you don't say anything until you hear us out."

"Don't worry, I'm interested in anything that will help solve my problem."

"You know about my marital problems. Well, most of the problems were money related. My wife has always lived beyond our means and the spending finally caught up with us. As we cut back on spending, and I was forced to spend more time on the road to make more money, our marriage started to come apart. To make a long story short, Mario approached me about a way to increase my income. Basically, what we do is control the point spread on college basketball games."

Bob interrupted, "What do you mean control the point spread? What games and who's we? What are you talking about?"

"Slow down," Gary insisted. "It's not what you think, and it's also not important right now who 'we' is. The fact is we influence the points scored in a game, not the outcome."

"Come on Gary, how can that be?"

"Simple, we don't decide who wins or loses, we just ensure the number of points the game is decided by. In any event, this plan saved my marriage and helped me have some of the things my wife and I always dreamed about."

"But isn't that illegal," Bob asked rather apprehensively.

"Not really," Mario lied. "Remember, we're not determining who wins and loses, only the margin of victory. That way no one gets hurt."

When Bob fully grasped what was being proposed, he abruptly got up from the table. "This is frickin nuts!" he exclaimed as he rushed out of the bar.

On the drive home the conversation replayed in his head. Bob could not believe what he just heard or how Gary could be involved in such a scam. How could anyone suggest they could impact the outcome of a game and that not be illegal? Bob was now torn between reporting the incident to the commissioner of the Big East Conference and pretending the conversation never took place. As much as Bob knew what he should do, his friendship with Gary and financial problems kept him from taking that first step.

Mario was not overly concerned by Bob's possible actions. It would be his word against Gary's, and both Gary and Mario were convinced Bob needed a financial windfall to get him out of the money problems he was encountering.

"Don't worry about Bob," Mario assured Gary. "He's reacting normally."

"How can you say not to worry? If he reports me to the league commissioner, I'm in a shit-load of trouble, and what about the operation?"

"First, he can't prove a thing and who would believe him anyway? Bob's no dummy, so he won't act without thinking first about what we discussed."

"Are you sure about this? How about I give him a call?"

"Yeah I'm sure, and no, don't give him a call," Mario responded. "A call now would create more questions. Let's just let him think about things for a couple of days. I think you'll be surprised. If it makes you feel any better, I'll put a tail on him that he's fully aware of. That should give him second thoughts about doing something he might regret."

"Don't do anything to force his hand."

"Let me take care of this," Mario said in an irritated voice.

"Okay boss." Gary knew he had nearly crossed the line and Mario was not someone you wanted to upset.

"Well, it's time for me to get home. Let me know the next time you'll be in Miami. Give your wife a hug. By the way, how did you get stuck with such a bitch?"

"Just plain bad luck, but I do love her," Gary replied as they departed the bar.

The next day at school Bob faced a real dilemma and was totally distracted from teaching. As much as he knew the implications of further discussing the previous night's proposal, he tried to convince himself there was no harm in finding out more about what was suggested. After all, the bills continued to mount and he could see no immediate relief from his financial problems. It was obvious he could not discuss this matter with anyone, including his wife. But how and when would he learn more about this proposal and how far should he pursue this idea? He would wait until the next time he and Gary were scheduled to officiate together and then make the necessary arrangements to visit with him and find out just how involved his friend was in this point-shaving plan. Meanwhile, he would discreetly ask around and find out more about Mario.

Chapter Ten

It was two weeks before Bob and Gary worked together during a game. Because the game was a night game in Oxford, Mississippi, both men would have to stay over after the game before returning home. This would give Bob the opportunity to speak with his friend about Mario and his proposal.

Bob's research linked Mario to some very suspect people, including those with ties to the Cuban Mafia, but he had not been charged with any illegal activities. He was also very successful in business but seemed to live beyond his means. No one seemed to be able to put a handle on Mario's personal life or outside activities. That being said, Bob had trouble believing Gary was involved with unscrupulous people or anything illegal. He decided to hold judgement until after they had a chance to talk.

The days prior to the game with Gary seemed like an eternity. Not only did Bob find himself easily distracted and seemingly uninterested in school but he also appeared distant to Nancy. She asked if anything was wrong but he merely explained he had a lot on his mind with the teaching change and prospects of developing a new career.

"Have you decided what you're going to do?" Nancy asked.

"Not really, but I'm looking seriously at two or three things," Bob lied.

"Anything you care to discuss or want an opinion on?"

"No. It's too early to bother you with this. You've got enough to worry about with the baby. When I get closer to making a decision I'll want your input."

"Well, you know whatever you do will affect all of us. I don't want you doing something you're going to be unhappy with. It's not worth it to me and the baby if you're miserable."

Bob nodded his head but thought, "That's easy for you to say." He couldn't help but wonder if he was doing the right thing waiting to meet with Gary.

After all these years, striving so hard to develop a reputation as one of the hardest- working, honest and consistent officials in college basketball, could he afford to show any interest in something so contrary to everything he believed in? Maybe it's not what he thought it was. Other questions were how deeply his friend was involved, what kind of relationship had Gary developed with Mario and who else was involved and ultimately responsible for what went on in this scheme?

Bob and Gary finally hooked up at the Kentucky versus Mississippi game in Oxford. Gary approached Bob and the game as if nothing had happened. Bob was amazed at Gary's demeanor and began scrutinizing the other two officials as the game progressed. The game was closely contested and the officiating was very forthright and consistent. Bob could not detect any real questionable calls and felt much better about Gary after the game, which the Rebels won by five points.

Since the three officials arrived at the game from different locations, no one had much time for casual pre-game talk. After the game was the first real chance for the officials to discuss the game as well as personal things. The third official was driving back to Jackson, Tennessee and seemed in a rush since he was scheduled to be at a meeting first thing the next morning. He was also scheduled to officiate in Knoxville the next night.

After their normal post-game evaluation, Bob and Gary drove back to Memphis, the city with the closest airport for them to fly out of the next day. They both were staying at the Airport Hilton and agreed to follow one another and meet for a drink at Bombers

Restaurant near the airport before calling it a night. Just like players and coaches, officials also needed time to wind down after games.

The drive back to Memphis seemed unusually quick and Bob found it extremely difficult to piece together his thoughts. How should he initiate the conversation and what questions should he ask? Would Gary make the first move? Bob suddenly had a thought the whole thing could be a setup. But with Gary's admitted involvement with Mario, he didn't really think that was possible. He should have his answers shortly.

At the restaurant the two men settled in for a couple of drinks and some casual conversation. After a short time, because it was getting late, Bob prepared to broach the subject when his friend initiated the conversation.

Gary had notified Mario he would be working the game with Bob and Mario advised him to study Bob and see where he was coming from. Mario's tail had uncovered no unusual activity with Bob and Mario felt Bob might just be willing to find out more about their operation. If Gary felt comfortable with the situation, he was to engage Bob in a conversation regarding their last meeting, but be careful not to go too far. If Bob was genuinely interested in pursuing their plan, Gary should refer him to Mario for specific details. If he was uncertain with Bob, break off the conversation and go to his room.

"Listen, I apologize for Mario's behavior the last time we were together," Gary began. "I've known him all my life and he can be a pain in the ass sometimes."

"Oh, don't worry about it. I like the guy but I couldn't believe what he was saying. After all, I really don't know Mario well enough for him to assume anything, let alone discuss a point-shaving scheme."

"Well, you know what they say about alcohol," Gary added as an excuse for Mario while he sat back in his chair. "Mario is a classic example of what can happen when a guy has too much to drink. Needless to say, we left right after you did and I took him home while he could still walk. He's been known to be a bad drunk."

"It's no big deal but how did you get involved with him in this point-shaving scheme?"

Gary seemed hesitant about talking further but sensed Bob might be interested in what he was doing. Maybe Mario was right.

"At first I was like you," Gary went on. "I just couldn't believe anyone, let alone a friend, would ask me to be party to such a crazy plan. In fact, I was downright pissed off. Yet the more I thought about my situation the more I wanted to know."

"So, what did you do next?"

"I made arrangements to talk with Mario the next time I was in Miami much like we're talking now. I explained on the front end I was opposed to fixing games but felt it couldn't hurt to find out what all was involved."

"Then what happened?" Bob asked.

"Mario took me through the plan and the more I heard the more interested I became. The way he explained it I didn't feel I would be doing anything too bad."

"How can you say that and what do you mean not too bad? That's like saying a woman is only a little bit pregnant. There's no such thing. She's either pregnant or not and this is either right or wrong."

"That may be, but when your marriage is coming apart and you need money things take on a different look. Anyway, it's not like we determine who wins the game, only the points involved. It really isn't such a bad thing."

"So what you're confirming is you're part of a point-shaving scheme involving college basketball games you work in?"

Bob's head was spinning. He was confused because he did not know where to go with this conversation or where it might take him. Here was a guy Bob trusted and regarded as one of the top officials. Bob's expression must have given him away because Gary's next action was to ask for the check. He explained any further conversation concerning this matter would have to take place back at the hotel. It was now very evident the two men were probing one another and it would be interesting to see how this played out. Both men respected each other as people and officials and had grown to be good friends. They also had much in common. Upon returning to the Hilton Bob joined his friend in his room, only to be frisked so

Gary could determine whether Bob was wired and this was a setup. Shocked, Bob in turn asked the same of Gary. Bob was reasonably sure of the answer to his last question but waited for Gary's response. That response would determine the direction these two men would follow. Further discussion would not only affect their relationship as officials but also as friends. Bob was careful with his next question and in fact really wasn't sure he wanted to hear the answer.

"Now that we've searched each other, will you answer the question? Are you involved with Mario in fixing games?"

"No, not in fixing games," Gary responded. "You know I wouldn't fix a game. I love and respect the game as much as you but I don't see any harm in making some much needed money if it doesn't mean cheating on who wins."

"Isn't that what you're doing?"

"Absolutely not, the team who deserves to win will win. I just make sure the points are in line with the bet."

Gary went on to explain that after his immediate rejection of the proposal he then thought about all the ramifications of such a plan. This led him, much like Bob, to seek more information about what was expected and involved. It was explained to him that shaving points was not fixing games but just helping determine the final score of those games. In other words, the favored team would never be required to lose. Only the point spread on the game would be impacted. Gary made it sound like he was not really doing anything illegal but his response sounded rather hollow.

Bob knew they were discussing point-shaving and was knowledgeable enough about the scandals of the 1950s to know this type of activity was not only illegal but bad for the sport. Yet, Gary led Bob to believe he was asked very infrequently to participate in this activity and was never asked to throw a game.

What Bob heard next was truly shocking. Gary confessed he was involved in point- shaving that evening with the Ole Miss/Kentucky game. Bob was literally dumbfounded since he had purposely looked for anything out of the ordinary but felt the game had been well officiated. How could the game be fixed and an experienced official like himself not notice anything wrong? Gary explained it

36

was because Ole Miss had played so well and was able to win the game on their own merits, thereby covering the nine-point spread of the favored Wildcats without any interference from the officials.

Bob's next question, "what if Kentucky played well early and shot out to a double-digit lead? Then what happens?"

Gary explained, "I get involved early so the game won't get away."

"But how can you be so sure things will work out? You and I both know games don't always go the way they're supposed to. There are just too many variables."

Gary was best able to explain how it worked when he replied, "After all, who is to say whether it's a block or charge, a blocked shot or goal-tending, a clean steal or a reach-in foul or any other of a number of judgement calls? A call at the right time will go a long way in determining the way the game is played and the eventual score."

"But tonight, not only did Ole Miss cover the spread, Kentucky lost the game."

"I understand that, but at no time was I obligated or inclined to cause Kentucky to lose. Tonight they just got their ass kicked from the get go. Remember, the money was still on the winner to win, just not by the projected margin."

To hear Gary explain it, an important call would be construed by most observers as nothing more than an equaling out process giving both teams the opportunity to win the game. The key was not to allow the game to get inside the last thirty seconds with the spread still in doubt. One must always remember there are two other officials and a group of players of whom you have very little control on a play at the end of the game. In other words, do not allow yourself to be surprised.

After listening to his explanation, Bob could not believe how nonchalant and composed Gary was with this activity. Gary assured Bob he was not always this way. The first couple of games he was scared something would go wrong and he would be exposed. He then came to realize how easy and foolproof the plan was. As Gary explained it, the officials are the last ones suspected of any illegal wrongdoing. All publicized scandals of the past were a result of illegal activities by players and coaches, thus perpetuating the myth that officials were above reproach.

Gary seemed humored by the reality of the situation. As he further explained, the coaches and players operating independently would have the least control of fixing a game. Just think he told Bob, common sense suggests if a player played badly the coach would take him out and put him on the bench, thus eliminating his impact on the game. The player might also get into foul trouble or get hurt and become a non-factor in a particular game. Likewise, if the coach juggled players, especially his best players in an unusual manner, there would be too many questions from the fans, administration and news media. Furthermore, a player off the bench might on any given night contribute more than the starter or so called star player. Another problem for the coach is the better players if benched would leave the program since they were not receiving adequate playing time. In the final analysis, the players in high profile programs are basically interested in what is going to happen to their careers as they prepare for the NBA and the future big dollar contracts. Conclusion, the one constant in this scenario is the unsuspected official who is present and in a decision making position for the entire game.

"So what you're telling me is the official controls the outcome of the game and as long as nothing bizarre happens he is never really questioned?" asked Bob.

"Bingo. History tells us it has always been public perception the greed lies with the coaches and players, especially in the big programs, and that has led to questions regarding the integrity of the game."

"Why do you think this hasn't been done before?" Bob asked.

"It has," replied Gary. "Back in the 50s and even in the last couple of years."

"No, I mean by officials."

"Who's to say it hasn't? I'll bet somewhere along the line an official has fixed a game or at least altered the outcome. We just haven't heard about it. After all, who would he tell?"

Bob was reminded as the game progressed, and coaches and players were being held to a higher standard by their respective institutions and fans, the unquestioned power base in college basketball had swung to the officials. Bob merely shook his head as he realized the ultimate truth of Gary's statement.

"Well, you've got a point. If I couldn't detect anything in tonight's game, how would a novice notice or suspect anything in any game?"

Bob's curiosity was now running at full throttle. The questions were running rampant in his head but he sensed he would get nothing more from Gary. In fact, as he asked Gary the next question he knew it would be the last of the evening. Bob wanted to know how long his friend had been involved in this scheme. Gary explained this was only his second year and the games were few and far between. He was asked to work games perceived to be nondescript and with decided favorites. Games closely monitored because of their national ranking implications, league championship games and NACA (National Association of College Athletics) tournament games were not part of the equation. Those games were too closely scrutinized and the closeness of the betting spreads caused concerns for the people in charge. As was the case in the Kentucky at Mississippi game, there was little national interest and the spread was large enough to give an official some working room without risk of exposure.

With that Gary brought the conversation to an end. He trusted Bob but was not willing to get into more details of the operation. If Bob had any interest in pursuing this conversation, he would have to talk with Mario. The less Gary knew of Bob's involvement, the better for both of them. On the other hand, if Bob decided to expose this plan Gary would deny any knowledge of wrongdoing and those organizing the scheme would look unfavorably on such a decision.

"By the way, have you noticed anything unusual since we last met?" Gary asked.

"Like what?"

"Like someone keeping an eye on you?"

"Well, now that you mention it I did notice a guy kind of following me around. But I just thought I was imagining things."

"Be assured that was not your imagination. The guys I'm involved with have far- reaching tentacles and know just about everything that's going on."

"This is bigger than Mario isn't it?" Bob asked. "Is the Mafia involved in this?"

"Don't go there. Just let it be," Gary responded.

Gary assured Bob he was not threatening him but Bob needed to understand the seriousness of the situation. Bob indicated a desire to find out more about the plan and therefore had been granted access to confidential information. Any violation of this confidence would be interpreted as betrayal and would be dealt with harshly. Bob acknowledged the seriousness of Gary's warning.

"Look, I wish I could spend more time with you and answer questions, but it's getting late and I have an early flight," Gary said.

"When can we get together again and discuss this more?" Bob asked.

"Never. I've probably told you too much already. Anything more you want to know you need to ask Mario."

"How do I contact him?"

"Not so fast. First think over what we discussed. If you're interested in pursuing this, call my house and leave your name and number. Don't leave a message, just your name and number and the word 'callback'. I'll then arrange for a meeting with you and Mario. But let me caution you on one thing. Whatever you decide, in or out, don't talk to anybody about this. Mario and his bunch can be very tough to deal with if they sense they've been betrayed."

Gary stood up, shook hands with Bob and left. Bob returned to his room in a state of bewilderment. He could make partial sense out of what he had been told but still had a lot of questions. Could he actually bring himself to be part of such a scheme? What would happen if his wife and friends were to find out about such activity? How did the point-shaving scheme work and what kind of rewards were there for the officials that were involved? How many other officials were involved in this plan? Was point-shaving really not a crime? These were but a few of the questions Bob asked himself but knew he would only have answered by discussing the plan with Mario. Was he ready to take that next step?

Bob spent a sleepless night thinking about what he should do. This was not something he could easily accept or dismiss but would require some soul searching to determine whether he could be a part of such a plan.

The flight back to Miami was filled with anxiety but it was always good to get home. He seemed to think and function better in friendly surroundings and the company of his wife and friends. The next couple of weeks would be some of the most important in Bob's life as he mulled a decision that could impact the rest of his life.

Bob worked five more games over the next two weeks but none with Gary. He was now paranoid about who might be involved in the point-shaving scheme and was beginning to analyze every call made by every official. If there was any illegal activity going on Bob could not detect anything out of the ordinary. That is not to say there were no bad calls being made since that was normal for some of the officials now calling games. It was just not apparent the officiating was biased or unfair.

Chapter Eleven

During Bob's officiating career a number of rule changes had been made, including the thirty-five second shot clock and the three-point line, which he felt had improved the game. He had also been part of the evolution of two men officiating crews to three men crews and was not convinced that change had necessarily been for the best. There was no arguing the court had better coverage, but he was convinced at least three problems resulted from the adoption of this new officiating format.

First, older officials were being retained that could not previously keep up with the game when only two officials were involved. This resulted in more position officiating and much less running. Unfortunately, with the thirty-five second shot clock, up tempo play and bigger and better athletes, these older officials still could not stay up with the game. Still, as their skills diminished, they continued to work as beneficiaries of the 'good old boy network.'

Second was how 'area specific' officiating had become. Each official now seemed to watch an area of the court and was hesitant about making calls in the other officials' areas. Bob was sure this was a source of great frustration to both players and coaches. Nothing makes coaches more upset when they question a call than to have an official tell them the play was not his. This was one area of officiating in which Bob strongly disagreed. He felt when there was a foul or rule violation the official should make the call regardless of one's area of concern on the court. In Bob's mind this was the great 'copout rationale' officials had adopted in recent years.

The influx of a new breed of official that was more concerned about how he looked and the theatrics of calling the game than the substance of what was actually happening on the court and how it impacted the players and coaches was the third concern. Many of the young guys Bob worked with were in great shape physically but could not administer the game nor communicate with the players and coaches. In fact, some were not well versed on the rules. Often these officials hid behind the technical foul and misdirected mandates of the college presidents, athletic directors and conference commissioners who passed legislation in an attempt to improve sportsmanship.

If a coach was openly critical of the officiating, he could be suspended from coaching for one game or more. He had no other school or team to coach. On the other hand, if an official was negligent in calling a game, he could be suspended by a league but in all likelihood would find another league to work while serving that suspension. Although supporting the officials, the inequity of the situation really stuck in Bob's crawl.

Since there was a shortage of good officials, disciplining these guys was a problem for the conference supervisors of officials. On one hand they wanted to discipline the officials while on the other they were afraid they would lose the better officials to another league if they did. This apparent double standard created problems in the coaches' minds and often times resulted in an adversarial relationship between coaches and officials. Sportsmanship was important, but it could not be force fed or accomplished solely by gagging coaches and strapping them to a bench. It would also require improved training amongst the officials, better communication between the officials and participants (coaches, players and fans) and professionalism gained through mutual respect.

Chapter Twelve

Over a period of several days Bob digested everything he and Gary had discussed and decided he wanted to pursue the point-shaving scheme further. As instructed, he called Gary and gave the signal he would like to meet with Mario. Gary returned the call and told Bob he had spoken with Mario, and since Gary was calling a Miami Hurricane game in Miami at the end of the week asked if they could get together.

Bob volunteered, "I'm free later that night. I promised Nancy I would take her to dinner. She needs a night out, but I can run her home and meet you after the game."

"That sounds like it will work. Just to be sure the game is over let's plan to get together around 11 o'clock," Gary suggested. "That'll give both of us plenty of time in case something comes up. Where can we meet?"

"What do you know about South Miami?"

"Not much but I'm sure I can find my way around. Just don't make it too far off the main drag."

"Let's meet at Korbit's, a sports bar right off US 1 in a small shopping center around 128th Street. You can't miss it. It's right across from a park with lighted baseball fields and basketball courts."

"What kind of a place is it?"

"Don't worry, it's reasonably quiet and not crowded. That is once the bikers quiet down. We should be able to talk without anyone bothering us. Do you think you can find it?"

"If I have any problems, I'll pull in a gas station and ask."

"If I don't hear from you by 10:30, I'll see you at the bar. I'm only about fifteen minutes from the place. Oh, by the way, try not to screw up the game," Bob chuckled as he hung up the phone.

By the tone of the conversation Gary surmised Bob was not only interested in finding out more about the point-shaving scheme but also in becoming a participant. Gary would get a message to Mario advising him of the time and place of the meeting. Mario wanted to meet with Bob and explain more about what was involved. How much detail they would get into would be dependent on the questions asked and interest shown.

The next few days were agonizing for Bob. The biggest problem was his inability or unwillingness to share his concerns with anyone, especially Nancy. What he already knew, and his refusal to report Gary and Mario to the proper authorities, was enough to link him with the illegal operation. Would he be any less guilty after all this time without having taken the appropriate action? He didn't think so. Bob believed in his own mind he was committed to joining the operation regardless of what he learned at the next meeting. Until then it was important he continued his normal routine and not raise suspicion with Nancy or any of their friends. The next few days would be spent compiling a mental list of those questions he needed answered. If he was to be a part of the operation, he wanted to understand how it worked, feel sure it was safe and be assured it was worth his time and effort.

The day of the game finally arrived and Bob could not wait until he could meet with Gary. Usually local officials helped out by picking up visiting officials, but Bob could not pick up Gary because he was tied up at school. It wasn't a problem since Mario had already made the necessary arrangements to pick Gary up at the airport, drive him to the Airport Marriott and get him to the Miami Arena for the game.

What Gary and Mario did not know was Bob had made arrangements to attend the game. Bob was able to borrow a ticket from a friend and sit away from the court in an out of the way place. He hoped Gary would not see him at the game. If he did, Bob could always say his dinner plans had been cancelled because Nancy was not feeling well and he just wanted to watch the crew work. What Bob really hoped to accomplish was to objectively evaluate the three officials and see if he could detect any wrongdoing or suspicious activity. The game played out and Bob didn't notice anything out of the ordinary.

With the game well in hand, Bob slipped out of the arena with about five minutes left. This would give him plenty of time to get to Korbit's and find a table. By leaving early Bob would have a chance to get his thoughts organized. He was confident he had not been seen and made a mental note to ask Gary if the game was part of the point-shaving plan.

As Bob sat in a booth at Korbit's, he asked himself what he was doing in this smoke- filled bar waiting to meet with two guys who stood for everything he was adamantly against? Bob had visited Korbit's on numerous occasions but had never really noticed the kind of people that frequented the place. Considering this was in the heart of South Miami, there were very few Hispanics playing pool and the pinball machines. Smoke filled the place and there was the stench of spilled beer. The booths were disfigured with knife marks depicting the initials of those who had sat there before, and by the looks of things most of the patrons had arrived by motorcycle. This was as close to a 'redneck' hangout as you would ever find in South Florida and not a place for the 'faint of heart'. The television carried highlights of the Miami game, but no one seemed to care since Waylon Jennings was on the jukebox.

In the midst of these surroundings walked Mario. Bob knew this was not an accident but was somewhat surprised Gary was not with him. Mario went to the bar and ordered a drink, apparently oblivious to Bob. What was Mario doing? The only logical answer was he must be waiting for Gary, but at 11:15 it was apparent to Bob that

Gary was not coming. The game had ended more than two hours earlier.

Then it all became clear. Mario went to the men's room and upon his return stopped by Bob's table. As Mario invited himself to join Bob, it was obvious he wanted to feel comfortable with the surroundings before approaching Bob. Mario got right to the point and elected not to waste time with small talk.

"Good to see you again Bob," Mario began. "Nice choice for a meeting."

"Good to see you too, Mario," Bob replied knowing Mario's comment about the bar was sarcastic. "At least you won't have to worry about anyone knowing you. So, where's Gary?"

"I'm filling in for Gary. Something's come up and he won't be joining us. Anyway, as Gary told you, I'm the guy you need to talk to. Anything we do is done one on one with me and does not involve anyone else."

This turn of events troubled Bob, but in reality he knew all along he would be dealing with Mario and not Gary as he pursued the point-shaving scheme. Before any further conversation took place, Mario asked Bob to follow him to the men's room where he asked to frisk Bob to insure he was not armed or wearing a wire.

After making sure Bob was clean Mario apologized, "Sorry about the search but one can't be too careful these days."

"That's okay, I understand your concern. Anyway, this is not the first time I've been checked for a wire," alluding to Gary's search in the hotel. Bob wondered if this was going to be standard operating procedure every time they met.

After they returned to the table, Mario ordered a drink and asked, "What kind of questions do you have? I know you and Gary talked in Memphis, so what's left?"

Bob's stomach was churning but he decided this was the time to find out what he was getting into. "Well, let's start with how the games are picked?"

"We try to find rivalry games with minimal national interest that have sizeable betting lines. That way there's not much scrutiny and we can better control the outcome."

"So give me an example."

As the waiter dropped off menus, Mario replied, "As Gary mentioned, we stay away from major conference rivalries, conference tournaments and NACA final sixteen games. There is too much money involved in these games and the betting line doesn't always favor our position. A good example was the recent Mississippi/Kentucky game you did with Gary. Ole Miss has not been a high profile basketball program but the people in Kentucky sure do like to bet on their Wildcats. On the other hand, North Carolina versus Duke would be a problem. Those games are normally a pick, and with the scrutiny surrounding two top ten programs it would not make much sense for us to risk the exposure."

Now it was Bob's turn to look over his shoulder to see if he recognized anyone. He was just short of coming apart at the seams. He was afraid Mario would order something to eat, knowing anything he would try to eat he would probably throw up. Mario did not seem too concerned about who else might be in the bar and appeared anxious to continue the conversation. The guy mauling the girl in the corner while they danced was not much of a distraction, and Bob wondered if he was the only one in the place that was sweating.

"So, how long have you been involved in fixing games?" Bob continued.

"Let's get one thing straight Bob. We do not fix games nor do we determine who wins the games," Mario lied but replied with great conviction. "We merely control the scoring margin in the game." This was a ploy to convince and assure Bob that he was not getting involved in anything illegal. A 'fix,' as regarded by the general public, was illegally determining who won a game and was considered criminal in nature. Mario wanted to convince Bob that point-shaving did not fall into that category.

"Pardon me," Bob replied, feeling better about this arrangement. "How long have you been involved in shaving points with college basketball?"

"Just a couple of years which means we're right on the edge of a great opportunity. Only a small group of people are involved and

48

there are millions of dollars out there for the taking, provided we select the right people to help seal the deal."

"Well, just how many guys are involved?" Bob inquired.

"If you mean other officials, that's none of your damn business. What makes this work so well is the secrecy we have and the protection we afford each guy."

Bob sensed he was pushing a little too hard and elected to back off a bit. After all, Mario apparently was not a guy to mess with and there must be others much tougher and more powerful involved in such a plan.

"But I know Gary is part of your operation," Bob added.

"That's only because we elected to let you know. Sure he was the contact guy, but even then you wouldn't have known for sure he was involved if we didn't want you to."

"What's the big deal if another official knows?"

"Put yourself in his place. How would you like it if guys you were working with knew you were involved in point-shaving. Some guys just don't deal well with that sort of thing. Hidden identity allows each official to do his job without concern about who knows what or whether someone is looking over his shoulder. It just keeps it clean and simple."

Mario suddenly excused himself to go to the men's room. As he walked past the bar, Bob noticed Mario stop and talk with a large, baldheaded man. This guy was huge, had a tattoo at the base of the back of his neck, wore an earring and looked like the character out of the old 'Mr. Clean' ads. Why Bob didn't notice him before was strange since his suit was out of character for Korbit's. Suddenly it dawned on Bob that this guy was Mario's watchdog. He had been in the bar before Bob arrived watching to make sure everything was in order. You had to give Mario credit. He sure left nothing to chance.

Upon Mario's return Bob asked, "How are the officials contacted and how far in advance do they know which games they'll be involved in?"

"We work out a system with each guy based on his situation. Everything we do is on a secured phone line and we only involve people in our organization who are extremely dependable and loyal." Mario went on to say, "As far as the games, as you well know each official gets his assignments from the conferences nearly two months before the start of the season. This gives us plenty of time to look at the match-ups and decide which ones we want to be involved in."

"So you're saying each official knows that far in advance?"

"Not exactly, we target certain games, but whether those games will actually end up on our books will depend in great part on how the betting goes and what kind of season the teams are having. If a surprise team begins to draw undo attention, we may have to back off them. So we won't know until the week of the game if certain teams will remain on the board. In that situation the official on that game may only have two or three days advance notice."

Mario went on to explain other variables that could affect the games selected. These were things beyond their control. The team they wanted to bet on might not be playing well, a key player got sick or hurt, someone quit the team or a coach was suspended. All of those things impacted the game and many times these things happened just before game time. Also, if they noticed unusual betting activity they might lay off that game.

"Have you had any problems in the past with anyone being exposed?"

"Do you think I would be talking with you right now if we had? This plan has operated for two years without a hitch." Mario went on to explain the expansive network of his people involved in this operation and how different bookies from different areas under Mario's umbrella bet on different games. Thus there was no real pattern or location that could be detected in the betting that would alert law enforcement agencies or legalized gambling operations to question what was going on.

"So how much can an official make?"

Bob was shocked to find out the minimum was $5,000 per game and dependent on the betting and profit involved there were additional bonuses available. Apparently the higher profile the game, the more at risk and the better the compensation.

Last, but certainly not least, Bob just had to know, "Why me?"

"Partly because Gary recommended you, but mostly because you have a solid reputation, you work the major conferences and you get a lot of the kind of games we are interested in," Mario responded, not quite revealing the whole truth.

Actually two of the major requirements of the mob in selecting their participants was each official be married and have a living family. Needless to say, this afforded Mario and his henchmen a lot of leverage in controlling those involved.

Bob wanted to know what the next step. Mario explained he should digest what they had discussed and he would contact Bob in the next couple of days. Mario was also emphatic about not contacting Gary concerning the nature of this meeting. Bob's involvement would be with Mario, who acted as the sole contact unless otherwise instructed. Bob was not to ask nor would he know the identity of those at the top. He was only to know the operation was of a national nature and not limited to South Florida. Mario also forewarned Bob that regardless of his decision his people would not allow for anyone or anything to get in the way of what they were doing. The tone of Mario's voice accentuated that last point.

Realistically, once it reached this level both Bob and Mario knew there was no turning back. After all, Bob had further inquired about the operation after having met with Gary, thus opening himself up to real problems if he did not follow through. If he were to back out now, Mario was someone who could make life miserable, assuming he would allow Bob to live at all. This operation was large and profitable enough not to allow anyone to betray or expose what was now considered by the mob a 'money-making machine.'

Mario finished his drink and excused himself from the booth. Bob, who was visibly shaking and sweating profusely, as instructed left the bar fifteen minutes later. On the way home he couldn't help wonder what he had just gotten himself into.

Chapter Thirteen

As the season was drawing to an end, Bob thought it improbable he would be asked to participate in the point-shaving scheme until next season. Little did he understand it was not by chance Mario and his group wanted to be sure Bob was one hundred percent committed to the program. Involvement immediately would allow them to observe his commitment and officiating now that he understood what was at stake.

Like players and coaches, officials respond differently to different forms of pressure. After being approached by Mario, some officials did not handle things well. Not only did their officiating deteriorate but they became suspicious in their behavior, thus disqualifying them from further consideration after only a couple of games. Those few who did not make it had received the equivalent of severance pay, but also had their lives threatened as well as the lives of loved ones if they discussed the operation with anyone. With loved ones at risk, the mob had very little trouble controlling matters, especially with the limited number of people involved.

Getting Bob immediately involved in a point-shaving game would set the hook and prevent an off-season of second thoughts as to whether he was doing the right thing. Mario wasted little time contacting Bob and scheduled a meeting two weeks later at the Valley Pub on SW 184th Street. At this meeting Mario confirmed Bob's involvement and presented a system to provide for future contacts. This would ensure secrecy and safety for all parties involved.

Although the meeting was scheduled for 8 o'clock in the evening, Mario had a trusted friend arrive at the restaurant an hour beforehand to secure the area and look for anything or anyone suspicious. When Bob arrived he was instructed to sit at a table in the corner near the television. This would allow them to talk without worrying about someone overhearing their conversation. Mario would join him after a few minutes. Mario's bodyguard at the door would ensure neither man had been followed nor would they be interrupted.

Mario's friend arrived at the designated time. There were only two couples eating dinner and three people sitting at the bar. Fortunately no one was sitting in the corner booth, although Mario had reserved the table just in case there was a crowd. Being a regular at this bar, Mario's friend recognized most of the people and did not notice anything or anyone out of the ordinary. There was only the customary chatter and activity surrounding friends talking and people watching TV.

Promptly at 8 o'clock Bob walked in and took a seat at the designated booth. The waitress brought him a menu and he ordered a drink as he had been instructed. About thirty minutes later Mario walked in and received an affirmative nod from his friend indicating things were okay. Mario then joined Bob at the table. As in the past, he ordered a drink and exchanged small talk.

"It's good to see you," Mario started the conversation. "How's it going?"

"Everything's just fine," Bob responded.

"I see you've worked a couple of big games since we last talked. Have you seen or talked to Gary?"

"No, but there's a good chance we'll see each other in a couple of weeks at the Big East Tournament. I'll tell him we visited."

"There's no reason to do that. As I emphasized before, what we do is between you and me and no one else. Can you join me in the men's room?"

Bob knew this was precautionary and Mario would once again check to ensure he was not wired. He wondered if once he worked a game this procedure would stop or was Mario the kind of guy who would always be suspicious and error on the safe side.

Upon returning to the table Mario went right to the heart of the matter. "Well what's it going to be? Are you in or out?"

Bob replied, "I'm in. Based on what you've told me I can't see not doing it. What now?" Bob was amazed at how relieved he felt having finally voiced this decision.

Mario wasted no time outlining the plan. The game was the University of Kentucky at Louisiana State University, a bitter Southeastern Conference rivalry. Both teams had been dominant during the 80s and 90s and both coaches were especially charismatic. Rick Green at LSU had taken the word 'motivation' to a new level. His teams were especially difficult to play against in big games at home. Kentucky on the other hand was lead by Dick Galino, a coach many thought was revolutionary with his up tempo, full court pressing and three-point shooting style of play. The Wildcats were the defending national champs, in first place in the conference and a favorite to defend their national championship even though they had lost a number of key players from the previous year to the pros. This was a very heated rivalry, but LSU had not been as strong since it lost its dominating center as an underclassman to the NBA.

"Look, this could be a tough game," Mario pointed out. "Remember, the game's in Baton Rouge and the Tigers always plays well at home, especially against the Wildcats."

"What's the spread?"

"Kentucky's favored to win by fifteen points."

"Surely you jest. That's a bunch of points in a game like that. I had LSU earlier this year and they're not that bad."

"Well I hope you're right. The early money is on the Wildcats but we're going to bet on LSU to cover the spread. Kentucky embarrassed Rick Green's team the last two times they played and I just have to believe Green will have his guys ready."

"I would tend to agree," Bob added. "But the biggest problem is how explosive Galino's guys can be and how LSU will react if the Wildcats get off to a big lead. LSU's young players could lose confidence and things get ugly."

"That's your job. Don't let the damn game get ugly. Fifteen points should be plenty of points to work with. You should be able to control things without too many difficult calls."

"So let me be sure I understand. With a fifteen point spread, what exactly do I do?"

"You need to make sure if Kentucky wins they do so by less than fifteen points. Remember the magic number is really fourteen. On the other hand, if LSU wins or loses by fourteen or less points, we're home free."

"Let's just hope those Tigers are ready to play."

With an icy stare Mario responded, "You need to be sure they are."

Bob thought to himself how simple the plan sounded but in actuality how hard it would be to carry out. He knew there could be a problem since Kentucky was clearly the better team and its style of play could create havoc. The Wildcats' scoring spurts were legendary and it would be difficult to control the outcome if the LSU players became dispirited.

Then unexpectedly Mario slipped Bob an envelope. Mario instructed Bob to open it later but explained it was an advance on the game. Before Bob could say anything, Mario exited the restaurant leaving Bob to his own thoughts. When Bob got to his car he was stunned to see the envelope contained $2,500. The hook was now set, money had changed hands and both men understood there would be no turning back.

Chapter Fourteen

Bob could hardly sleep and was actually relieved the next day when he left for the airport and the trip to Louisiana. Fortunately he did not have to leave until after work since he was able to get a direct flight and gain an hour going west. With the game scheduled for an early Saturday afternoon tip-off, the officials normally arrived the day before to eliminate any possible travel delays. The day of the game they would leave for the arena at least two hours before game time. This would enable them to beat the crowd and go over their pre-game instructions. Bob was anxious to see who the other two officials were and wondered if either one was also involved in the point-shaving plan.

Bob arrived in Baton Rouge around six o'clock that evening and went directly to the Hilton Inn located near the campus. Before dark he was able to get in a quick walk although the temperature was rather chilly. As usual, he called Nancy to tell her he had arrived, then showered and went to the hotel restaurant for a light meal and a chance to relax.

After a nightcap he returned to his room, read the newspaper and watched television until he turned off the light at 11 o'clock. Sleep was out of the question, and after about an hour of rolling around in bed Bob finally took a sleeping pill and dozed off around midnight, but not before being plagued by all the same questions Mario already answered. Did he really want and need to go through with this? Money was still a concern but was point-shaving the answer?

Problem was, as Bob realized, he had already crossed the line and had no real options. He had accepted the $2500. There could be no turning back or questioning his decision. He could only hope he made the right choice. Little could he know or want to think about the long-term consequences of that decision.

The next morning he ate a light meal, checked out and located the other two officials who were also staying at the same hotel. As expected, Bob knew both men and they immediately began to talk about the season, although most of the discussion centered on court coverage, the rules designated by the rules committee as points of emphasis and what to anticipate from the two teams.

Because it was Kentucky the crowd was in a fever pitch. The students had waited outside overnight to be the first in line to get tickets for the game. They had arrived at the game two hours early and continually chanted "Tiger bait, Tiger bait" at the Kentucky players. It was always a mystery to Bob there had not been any fights since the opposing players had to file through the students to get to and from the locker room. But the Kentucky players were used to playing games in hostile environments and they just went about their business, paying little attention to the fans. The LSU players, on the other hand, were emotionally charged and appeared to be ready to redeem themselves for the previous two losses.

One of the officials was very well respected and a good friend of Bob's, but the other one was young and not quite ready for this kind of game. Bob realized the young guys needed a chance to get some experience but would have preferred a stronger third guy for this game, especially with the point-shaving scheme in place. You could count on the more experienced guys not to make any unexpected calls, whereas the new guys were sometimes 'thrill a minute.' As Bob and the other officials made their way to the respective teams' benches to greet the coaches, Bob was nervous to the point he felt slightly light-headed. It was becoming increasingly more difficult for Bob to hide his emotions.

LSU jumped to an early lead and seemed to feed off the spirited crowd. But after a brief double-digit deficit, the Wildcats settled into their game plan and began to take over. Their press and up-tempo style of play began to take its toll and by halftime the Wildcats led by five points. There had been no incidences in the first half and both teams went to the locker room with no real foul problems. The young official had struggled, but the two veterans had stepped in and helped carry the load.

"You okay?" Bob asked the young man.

"I guess so. Man, this game is sure physical and the crowd's crazy."

"Welcome to the SEC," the other veteran official added.

"Look, you're doing fine," Bob reassured him. "The hard part is over. Just take a deep breath, collect your thoughts and you'll be okay."

"That's easy for you two guys to say. Both of you are used to this."

The older official added, "You never get used to this. If you do, it's time to hang up the whistle. Anyway, we're here to make sure things go okay and give both teams a chance to win the game. Like Bob said, just continue to do what you did in the first half. You'll be fine."

"I'll do the best I can," the young official replied with not much conviction.

"That's all we can ask," Bob responded, but he wasn't sure the young man's best would be good enough. Bob had too much riding on this game to have some rookie screw it up. "Now let's get back out there and finish the game. Remember, we're all in this together."

As the score ballooned to double digits in Kentucky's favor early in the second half, Bob became concerned and began to second-guess his ability to control the point spread. What was happening to him? He knew, just like the young official, he would have to work through this situation, but his confidence he could carry out the plan was diminishing. He tried to remember what Gary had told him after the Ole Miss game. "Impact the game early so there would be no surprises," but had the game gotten beyond that point? He better hope not.

With less than two minutes to play, a Wildcat guard hit one of his team's trademark three-point field goals to push the lead to seventeen points. Bob began to feel nauseous. His only hope was the Kentucky substitutes, now in the game with the big lead, would force the action and make the same mistakes most bench players make when they are given a chance to impress the coach. Rather than play within the system, subs usually tried to do more than they should and that thought process usually led to bad shot selection, turnovers and mental mistakes. Sure enough, LSU scored on a put back as a result of a missed blockout on a rebound and the lead was cut to 15 points. They then intercepted the inbounds pass to get another possession with twenty seconds left in the game. The Tigers immediately called their last timeout. The game was decided for all practical purposes, but Coach Green, like any good coach, wanted his players to understand the importance of competing until the final horn. At this point Bob knew he had to control the action in these last few seconds of the game, even though he felt as though he was about to vomit. He prayed nothing would happen that came as a surprise. This was no time for one of the other guys to make a crazy call.

As LSU worked the ball inbounds underneath its basket, and with the outcome of the game already determined, one of its guards drove the ball to the basket and missed a layup. Suddenly there was a late whistle. Bob called a foul on a Wildcat player. Bob was the trail official and basically out of position to make the call, but there appeared to be enough contact by a defender to erase any questions regarding the whistle, especially with the game already decided. The young man made the first of two free throws before missing the second with approximately ten seconds left to play.

As the Kentucky rebounder dribbled the ball into the frontcourt, he spotted a teammate on the wing making a cut toward the basket. He passed the ball to the cutter who fumbled the ball before laying it in the basket as the clock expired. Just when it appeared the basket would count, Bob rushed out of the pack, signaled a traveling violation and disallowed the basket. It was a late whistle but not one anyone would question. The final score was 90 to 76 in favor of Kentucky, a fourteen point victory for the Wildcats. As was normally the case, the officials rushed off the court to the dressing room.

After the officials returned to the locker room and conducted their post game discussion, Bob knew the other two guys were wondering what went on in those last twenty seconds of the game. He decided to defuse the situation.

"Good job," Bob said to the young official.

"Thanks, but I need to do better. I must admit I was scared shitless to start the game. I've never had a game with this kind of atmosphere. Man, that crowd was nuts."

"But you hung in there and worked through your first-half jitters. This should be a good learning experience for you. We've all had to go through this."

The older official winked at Bob and then added, "Just be glad the game wasn't close at the end. I've been in games like this where all hell breaks loose. Neither one of those teams has any lost love for the other."

"Man, that's and understatement," Bob added.

"By the way, what's the deal on the last call?" the older official asked Bob.

"It was an obvious violation and I just felt it was a call that needed to be made," responded Bob as he turned his attention to the young official. "Always keep in mind the substitutes at the end of the game deserve the same effort from us as the starters get. Did you ever play college basketball?"

The young official shook his head, 'no.'

"I did and nothing pissed me off more than officials at the end of the game just trying to get the game over. I wasn't a great player and a lot of times I would go in at the end of the game to mop things up. The problem was I worked just as long and hard in practice as the regulars and I felt I should get the same coaching and officiating as those guys. I couldn't help I wasn't good enough to start and play the whole game, but I guarantee I tried just as hard as the next guy."

"I can appreciate that," chimed in the older guy.

"In any case, I promised myself I would never do that to anyone if I became an official. And by God, I've kept my word. I just hope you'll do the same."

But in the back of his mind Bob knew he was rationalizing his last call. He had done a poor job controlling the game and had allowed the outcome to be determined in the last few seconds. There was no way he could have imagined how nerve racking and difficult this would be. Needless to say, he was relieved with the outcome and vowed to learn from the experience.

He flew back to Miami that night and stopped by a local bar on the way home to wind down. All of his pent up emotions surfaced and he needed time to relax and put into perspective what he had just done. Had his officiating impacted the game? Was either of the other officials involved in the point-shaving plan? What could he expect now in the form of a payoff? How many times would he be asked to carry out this plan? These were all questions running rampant in Bob's mind, but only time would provide the answers. For now he needed to quit worrying about things he could not control or for which he had no answers.

The answer to one of his questions was forthcoming. On Monday Bob received a phone call from the father of one of his students indicating he would like a to schedule a conference to talk about his son's progress academically. On Tuesday the father arrived at Bob's room after school. He was not someone Bob recognized, but that was not unusual since most of the parents showed little interest in their child's education. But instead of a conference, the parent simply made a delivery. He handed Bob an envelope.

"What's this?" Bob asked.

"Something from a mutual friend," replied the father who then turned to walk away.

"What about the meeting regarding your son?"

"Don't worry. Everything's been taken care of."

The meeting was of course a hoax and Bob wasn't sure the man was who he said he was. In fact, he doubted this man had a student in school. After the man left, Bob discovered $10,000 in cash in the envelope. There was no note or any indication where the money came from except the man's parting comment, "I'm a big LSU basketball fan and was disappointed they lost to Kentucky this past weekend."

Bob sensed this was just the beginning of a long and profitable relationship and the beauty of this arrangement was the money was tax-free. He found it somewhat hard to believe he could walk away with a net profit of $12,500 for one game. On the other hand, it had taken him almost two days and a muscle-relaxing pill to settle down after the LSU /Kentucky game. He found himself constantly looking over his shoulder to see if anyone was following him. This was going to be a tough way to live, but the most difficult thing now was to find a way to hide and shelter the money so no one, especially Nancy, would ask questions.

With the newfound income, Bob decided to open a separate account under his name in a small bank in Homestead, Florida. Living in South Miami, it was only a twenty-minute drive whenever he needed to make a deposit or withdrawal. At the same time, he began to wonder what to do with the money and how to invest it. Should he seek help from Mario or invest on his own? Bob's concern was his link to Mario since he was now convinced Mario was nothing more than a front man for the Cuban Mafia, a powerful underworld group located in South Florida. If something went wrong with the operation, there would surely be a trail leading to Bob and the others involved. On the other hand, Bob was feeling greedy and could only envision the return on his dollars if he invested with Mario's group. The investment would not only yield a high return but would also be tax-free. Bob decided he would talk with Mario about this possibility after the season.

Chapter Fifteen

A few days later, on February 26, the most wonderful thing happened to Bob and Nancy. Late that morning Bob received a call at school indicating Nancy needed him to take her to the hospital. Upon Bob's arrival home, Nancy was already experiencing severe labor-pains.

Nancy greeted Bob, "Honey, I think we better get to the hospital and the faster the better. The contractions are coming really fast."

"Do I need to call the doctor?" Bob asked.

"No, I've already called his office and told them we're on our way. Let's just hope we get there in time."

"Don't worry, we'll get there in time. I'm not about to deliver our baby. What do we need to pack?"

"Nothing, just bring the bag on the table. I've already packed everything I need."

"Let's go," Bob said as he picked up the bag and helped Nancy to the car.

After several hours at the hospital, Nancy was moved to the delivery room. The delivery went smoothly and it was but a short time before Bob was able to be with his wife and newborn son. They were now the proud parents of Scott David Girard, eight pounds, three ounces and twenty-one inches long. This blond-haired, blue-eyed boy could not have been healthier and mother and son were doing well.

After mother and son rested, Bob was able to join the two of them during Nancy's first feeding. The smile on Nancy's face told it all. Bob could not be happier. This was the most emotional thing he had ever experienced.

"Honey, you done good," was all Bob could say.

"He is beautiful isn't he?" Nancy asked.

"He couldn't be more perfect," Bob said as he leaned over to kiss his wife and son. "Now I'm going to let you get some sleep. I'll be just outside in the waiting room if you need anything."

Nancy chuckled, "Oh silly, you can stay in here with me. Things have changed since your mother had you. But why don't you go home and get some rest? The nurses can handle things on this end. When I come home, then I'll expect you to help."

"You don't have to worry about that, but you'll have to teach me how to change diapers."

The nurse returned. "It's time for you to get some sleep," she said to Nancy. "I'll take the baby back to the nursery. Is Mr. Girard going to stay?"

"I guess not," Bob replied as he turned to leave. When he got to the doorway he turned to say, "I love you more than you know. Now get some sleep and take care of that son of ours."

On the drive home Bob decided to earmark $5,000 of the original $12,500 game payoff for Scott's college education. If there was ever a time the Girard's needed money, this was the time. Bob was a proud and caring husband and father and he would do almost anything to provide for his family. Any questions or doubts Bob had concerning his involvement with Mario were now dissipating, if not indeed put to rest. The future would present new challenges and additional bills and he only had to look at his newborn son to justify his involvement with Mario and his group.

Chapter Sixteen

With conference tournaments just around the corner, Bob was rewarded for his solid season by being invited to referee the Big East Tournament. This was considered the next step toward being selected to participate in the NACA Tournament, college basketball's national championship. The Big East Tournament was played at Madison Square Garden in New York City and was always sold out. Bob would have a first-round game and advance through the rest of the tournament as evaluated. Based on his ratings during the regular season there was no reason to think he would not be in the final game, but that wasn't a given.

Fans don't understand how the process works and what little control one has as an official. It took only a poorly officiated game or incident to disqualify one from additional games and many times the situation was beyond an official's control. Good officiated games and positive evaluations could also be impacted by Mario's request to possibly fix Bob's first-round game. Bob would not know until mid-week which game he drew.

As it turned out his game was Providence College versus West Virginia University, two teams that finished the season with a rush. Both teams were dark horses to win the tournament and both needed to win a first round game to have any chance to earn a NACA or NIT berth. Bob did not think there would be much betting on this game, but realized in the tournament, with such a short amount of time between games, the Mafia was betting on the best of the guaranteed match-ups. After all, who knew which teams and officials would move on to the next round? Therefore they elected to get involved with Bob's first-round game.

Mario contacted Bob the day before he departed for New York, "congrats on working the Big East Tournament."

"Thanks, but I hope this is just the first step to the Four Final."

"So you've got Providence and West Virginia."

"Yeah, and it should be one hell of a game. Both teams need a win badly to get to post- season play."

"That's what we figured. There should be above average betting on this game. We're going with West Virginia and the points."

"You mean West Virginia to win," Bob responded.

"That's right. The Mountaineers are favored to win by six points, so seven is the magic number. Anything above seven gets us to the bank."

"I'll do the best I can, but this should be a nail-biter."

"Do better than that," Mario said in a joking but threatening tone of voice. "Make it happen. Good luck and I'll talk to you when you get back."

Bob was excited about the tournament and left for New York the next day. In the officials' meeting the night before the opening round, Bob looked around the room trying to guess who else might be involved in the point-shaving scheme. The only one Bob knew for sure was Gary and they both went out of their way to avoid each other. All of the other officials at the tournament were his friends and people he held in high regard.

As usual, game day was wild. Bob had the second game in the afternoon and the first game went into overtime, delaying the start of his game. The afternoon games were not as crowded since it was during the week and many of the local fans worked, but still there was a better than average crowd for such a game. The first game delay only added to Bob's anxiety level.

Much to Bob's surprise, his game went smoothly as West Virginia rushed to an early lead and never looked back. Its open floor play and three-point shooting proved too much for the Providence Friars, as did its suffocating zone defense. The game went without incident and the Mountaineers held a double-digit lead throughout most of the second half. Bob was relieved he did not have to make any last second calls to impact the game outcome. The final score found West Virginia winning by eleven points, and Bob was on his way to another good payday. Equally gratifying, Bob was asked to move on to the second round of the tournament with one of the other officials in his crew. This also placed him in good position to call the tournament final, a major step in being selected to continue on to the NACA Tournament.

Bob was not surprised when he didn't receive another call from Mario. After all, there was such a short amount of time between games. Without knowing who would play the next day until the previous games were completed, it was difficult even for the Mafia to mobilize their people in time to lay the necessary bets without raising a red flag with the legalized gamblers and law enforcement authorities. Bob welcomed the opportunity to work the rest of the tournament without having to look over his shoulder.

The remainder of the tournament went without incident and Bob called the final game between Villanova College and Georgetown University. Villanova featured a high scoring offense, while the Georgetown Hoyas relied on their suffocating defense. These teams presented contrasting styles of play, but it was a rather easy game to work. Players from both schools were somewhat fatigued having played the three previous days to get to the finals, but all played extremely hard. Both teams were destined to play in the NACA Tournament and both programs possessed a lot of tradition and pride. In the end, Georgetown's defense prevailed and the Hoyas carried off another Big East championship.

The stay in New York had been delightful, although it was not a city where Bob would like to live. As hectic as Miami could be, New York was twice that all the time with too much cold weather. Bob was glad to return to Miami and the warm sun. Two days later one of Mario's people delivered an envelope containing $15,000. This was more than Bob expected, but he would later find out the post-season tournaments paid more, something of a reward system for advancing beyond the regular season.

In a couple of days Bob was notified he was to work in the NACA Tournament. He was extremely pleased and proud. His first-round game was to be played in Boise, Idaho, one of the West Regional sites. Bob felt this would expose him to people outside his normal officiating area and thus improve his chances to advance in the tournament. The games were scheduled for Friday and Sunday, so he did not plan to leave for Boise until Thursday.

On the flip side, Duke had been seeded number four in the East and its games would be Thursday and Saturday. Bob called Betty Payne to extend his congratulations to Chad and to find out whether she would be able to go to the tournament since it was being held in Winston-Salem, NC. Betty indicated she did not think she could get off work on such short notice and wanted to wait in hopes Duke would make it to the Four Final which was scheduled for the RCA Dome in Indianapolis. Bob was happy for Chad and his mother, but particularly relieved he was not in the same region. For the first time he realized, even with his reduced ACC schedule and avoiding Duke's regular season games, there was still no guarantee he would be able to avoid Chad and the Blue Devils in the tournament.

Bob could now officiate in a relaxed manner since Mario had indicated the NACA Tournament was a bit farther than the Mafia wanted to venture at this time. Too much scrutiny and security associated with such an event. Too many last minute bets would raise a red flag. The first-round games went without incident, and Bob advanced on to the West Regional Super Sixteen the following weekend in Los Angeles. At his relatively young age this was something to be proud of. He hoped to referee the final game of the West Region but realized his short time in officiating would probably preclude him from receiving that opportunity. The further one went down the tournament road, the more age, experience and politics became factors. His gut feeling proved accurate. He was not assigned additional games. Still, Bob had a great season and was determined to get to the NACA Four Final next year.

Bob received many favorable comments about his officiating and attributed his success to being more mature, happier and for the most part more relaxed than he had been in years. He knew these feelings were the result of financial security, a job he enjoyed, a new baby and a loving wife.

Meanwhile, Chad finished his first year of basketball as Duke advanced to the NACA Tournament after finishing second in both the ACC regular season as well as the conference tournament. Unexpectedly, his playing time increased near the end of the season as a result of an injury to the starting point-guard. Chad was both physically and emotionally more mature than most players his age, but still struggled in making the transition from a substitute to a starter in such a competitive league. The experience in the NACA Tournament would prove invaluable to him in the future, although there was no way for him to understand that now.

Unfortunately for Betty and Chad, Duke was beaten in the first round of the NACA Super Sixteen in a stunning upset. The year had been a long one, and with two key players injured Chad tried to shoulder too much of the burden of producing in an effort to make up for the loss of the veteran players. He did not play poorly as much as he tried to do things he really wasn't comfortable doing. Chad was a player who ran the offense, distributed the ball to others, keyed the defense and made free throws at critical times. Now he was trying to score and it was impacting his ability to get the ball to others as well as running the team. Playing within one's limitations is sometimes hard to achieve, but something Chad would need to learn if he was to be successful in the future.

Bob, with an off day, watched Duke's final game on television and his heart went out to Chad. It's one thing to play poorly because you don't care, but it's another thing to fail as a result of trying too hard. Chad's problem was the latter. As a freshman it would prove to be an invaluable lesson and Chad would have three more years to chase that illusive national championship. Being selected first team All ACC freshmen team and being named Duke's most improved player were honors enough for this young man. The loss would do nothing more than make Chad work harder and become more determined in his approach to improving his game.

Even with his late-season success, Chad was anxious to return home for the summer, see his friends and work on his game. As much as he enjoyed Raleigh-Durham, it was a long cry from South Florida. The weather, South Beach, Coconut Grove and the social activities in Miami were far superior to anything he had experienced anywhere else. To 'add icing to the cake,' he had done very well academically and did not have to attend summer school. Thus he anticipated another summer working in Bob's camp, lifting weights and relaxing with his mom.

Chapter Seventeen

With school out Bob and Nancy prepared for the start of camp. Nancy's work was limited while caring for Scott but she could handle much of the paperwork. Unexpectedly, Betty Payne proved to be of great help. She was constantly looking to make extra money and was able to relieve Nancy of some of her administrative duties. Chad was now at the age and had the experience to basically run the camp. Camp enrollment was still down but not as much as the previous year thanks in great part to Chad and his growing popularity. Many of the young people in Miami had followed Chad's career and looked upon him as a sports hero. He served as a role model and many parents wanted their kids to be around such a person. Others mistakenly believed if Chad could make it, then surely their children could too if they just attended a camp like Bob's.

Part of being a frustrated former athlete, or uninformed parent, is the lack of understanding concerning sports camps. Most camps provide great personal learning experiences for the campers but going to a camp does not necessarily guarantee immediate success in the future. If success could be accomplished that easy, every kid would go to a camp of his or her interest and immediately become a star. In any case, both Nancy and Bob were finding additional income was necessary for them to continue their lifestyle.

Mario had maintained an at length relationship with Bob of which Nancy was not aware. During the off-season Bob had very little contact with Mario. With the entire summer ahead, Bob had time to reflect on his involvement in the point-shaving operation and had reached the point where he was convinced this plan was a good way to have the things he and Nancy always wanted. He was now oblivious to the possible consequences of his actions.

Mario stopped by the camp once merely to see how Bob was doing and to make sure Bob received his money. To deflect suspicion he visited the camp under the pretense of enrolling a camper. When alone Mario asked, "How's my favorite college basketball official?"

"Great," Bob replied. "I can't thank you enough for your generosity. The payoffs were more than I ever expected."

"We try to take care of those who take care of us," Mario responded. "But if you think that's big money, wait until next year."

"I'm just sorry I didn't get started sooner."

Part of a crook's mentality is the belief he has the perfect plan for the perfect crime. I know of no one who committed a crime thinking he would get caught and punished. Furthermore, Bob had convinced himself the scheme was fail-proof. A big part of this rationalization was the belief that since you are not going to determine who wins or loses, but merely the margin of victory, you are not doing anything wrong.

"As I explained, this program is still in its infancy," Mario said. "We have to be very careful whom we involve. But my people like your work and this should be the beginning of a long and profitable relationship."

"Is there anything I can do for you?" Bob offered.

"Just continue doing what you're doing. Community activities like this camp and your work at school help create positive feelings and place you above suspicion," Mario replied as he looked at his watch. "Well, if you don't have anything else on your mind it's time to get back to work. Let me know if I can help with anything."

As Mario walked away Nancy approached and asked Bob, "Who was that man?"

"No one in particular, he's interested in enrolling his nephew in our camp and just wanted to find out more about what we do," Bob lied. "He also seemed interested in buying our camp if it ever was for sale."

As the summer wore on, Bob became increasingly aware of how much Chad had matured and how special he was. With all the attention from the campers during the day and girls after hours, he still was the same solid kid Bob and Nancy had grown to know. Not a week went by he did not make time for the Girards as well as his mother. The four of them would have dinner or just spend an evening together reflecting on the past and what the future might hold. Many times Chad would stay over at the Girards and talk basketball with Bob. He would then go into work with Bob the next morning.

In one of those conversations Chad exposed himself in a way that nearly brought tears to Bob's eyes. "We really haven't had much of a chance to talk seriously," Bob said. "How was your first year at Duke? Are you happy there?"

"I really like it," Chad responded. "I wish I could have played more, but I understand I was only a freshman. When I did get to play at the end of the season, I didn't play nearly as well as I hoped."

"You must have played pretty darn good. After all, you made the all conference freshman team. That's no small feat."

"Yeah, but I could have done better. Anyway, Coach P and the assistants are great and the players really get along well. It's like a family."

"How does your mom feel about you being that far from home?"

"She wishes I was closer but realizes my other choices out of high school were even farther away. She also knows how much I like it there. I'm hoping she'll get a chance to see me play next year. With all the distractions here, she's glad I'm not in Miami."

"Have you thought about any long range goals?" Bob inquired.

"My primary goal is to graduate. Mom would be so proud since I would be the first one in my family to do so. I also want us to win the national championship and after graduation play in the NBA or overseas. If I could do those three things, I would be the happiest guy in the world. Not only could I take care of myself but more importantly I could take care of mom."

Trying to hide his feelings, Bob said, "If you keep working the way you are, all of those goals are very realistic. Watching you play at the end of the year I couldn't get over how much you improved."

"Probably because we got better officiating," Chad joked while trying to lighten the conversation. "I still can't believe that charge call."

"You're probably right, but you're lucky I didn't give you a technical for mouthing off. All kidding aside, your mom, Nancy and I could not be any prouder of you."

"A lot of what I am can be directly attributed to you and Nancy. If you hadn't taken me under your wing, one only knows where I might be now, probably in jail."

"I seriously doubt that. Anyway, it's time to go to bed," Bob said misty-eyed as he tried to change the subject.

Very few young people today understand sacrifices their parents make for them. Kids take for granted things their parents felt were special when they were young. Many times Chad's mom worked a second job late into the night to pay for things Chad felt he needed that other kids already had. Betty had gone the extra mile so her son could be involved in extra school activities and athletics, and Chad knew she had paid a price with her own lifestyle. How many times had she driven to one of his games, rejected a date so she could take him somewhere or passed on something she wanted so she could buy him a new pair of basketball shoes. She was a great mother and Chad was committed to repaying her many times over. Bob sensed with Chad's discipline and determination he would fulfill his goals and dreams.

During this time Chad had very little contact with his father. Tom had remained single and had bounced from job to job. Infrequently he found his way to one of Chad's games when he was in high school. Even with television, Chad's father had not seen him play in college. The phone calls at Christmas and on his birthday meant little to Chad who reserved his parental love and concern for his mother. He had spent most of his life without a father and could see no reason to worry about Tom at this point in his life. After all it was Bob, not Tom, who had been there when he needed a male role model.

Chapter Eighteen

As the July 1st deadline approached for Bob renewing his teaching contract, things became confused and hectic. Bob knew he needed the regular income of teaching to support his family, but on the other hand he knew he could not give up the joy of officiating and the additional income he had grown accustomed to having. Nancy had expressed concern about how tight money had gotten in paying their bills, but was still not aware of Bob's involvement with Mario. That money in Bob's separate account was used discreetly and only when needed since it would cause Nancy to ask too many questions if he began to flash it around. The NBA had rejected him as a full time official but indicated they would be evaluating him for the future. Nancy and Bob agonized over what to do. With the addition of Scott to the family circle, Bob needed to explore every possible avenue.

On a whim, and actually against his better judgement, Bob contacted Mario to see if there was anything he could do to help. Bob's concern centered on his already increasing involvement with Mario and what he was convinced was the Cuban Mafia. How much longer could he hide this association from Nancy? What would she say if she found out? Yet, to Bob's surprise, Mario was able to help beyond his wildest imagination. What Bob did not understand about the mob was its intolerance to allow something as simple as an individual's job to get in the way of making millions.

"So what can I do for you?" Mario asked during their conversation.

"I need help with a new job."

"What happened to your teaching position?"

"As I told you and Gary, they're changing the program as a result of budget cuts and I'm going to have to go back to the classroom fulltime," Bob responded. "If I do that, I won't be able to work as many games and at some point I'll be dropped from some of the leagues."

"We sure as hell can't have that. So, fill me in?"

"I'd like to stay in education, but I also want to continue to officiate. It just doesn't look like I can do both. You got any suggestions?"

"What are you willing to do? With your education you should be able to get plenty of jobs," Mario replied.

"Maybe so, but I just haven't been able to come up with anything with the flexibility I need. I'm just not sure what I'm qualified to do. Teaching has been my career. I guess I'd be interested in anything that doesn't require me to sit behind a desk all day. I need to be able to somewhat control my schedule."

"Let me work on this and I'll get back to you in a couple of days. We can't allow something as simple as this to get in the way of a good thing, if you know what I mean."

"Thanks. The sooner you can let me know the better. I've got to give my principal an answer by the first of July."

"I said I'll let you know," Mario repeated in an irritated voice.

Two days before the July 1st deadline Bob interviewed and was appointed the head of social and recreational activities at one of the local companies, and with a substantial increase in pay. Once again Mario had come to the rescue. These kinds of programs had become commonplace with the growth of unions and the emphasis on improved national healthcare. Who said the mob no longer had influence with the unions?

Bob knew he would miss the everyday associations with the kids at school, but also knew he would still be involved in teaching while working with kids during his summer camp. Not only did this new job offer more flexibility with hours, but also paid better with improved benefits. He would turn the everyday operation of his summer camp over to Nancy, although he would still be able to make selected appearances during each week. Chad and his mother also proved they could help. More importantly, he would be able to ensure the future of his family.

Little did Bob realize the mob's hooks were now implanted even deeper, and what little resistance he might have offered, if he had second thoughts about the point-shaving scheme, were now out of the question. There was no backing out now.

Nancy did not question Bob's good fortune in finding a new job. She did notice a sense of relief in his attitude and was delighted he was happy. Maybe now they could afford to pay off some of their debt. Nancy not only managed the summer camp, she had also resumed work at a local health club on a limited basis. She was always one who took great pride in her appearance and the additional income would come in handy.

Contact with Mario had been minimal since he helped Bob get the job. That was how both preferred it. He did not dislike Mario, but always felt a little uncomfortable around him as a result of their involvement in the point-shaving operation. Maybe it was also because of Mario's alleged associations and the secrecy with which he conducted business.

Bob and Mario finally met the last session of camp, once again under the pretense Mario was checking on his nephew. The meeting was a follow-up to one of Bob's earlier questions concerning investment opportunities. Bob had earmarked the money from games to be used for Scott's education, retirement and any unexpected expenses he and Nancy might incur. The separate account had served its purpose, but that money needed to do more than grow at the bank's normal interest rate. Bob wanted the money to make considerably more money.

Much of what Mario's group did with the money collected from gambling, union influence, prostitution, etc., was laundered and invested abroad, mainly in South America through private accounts. As they sat in Bob's office, Mario explained what investment opportunities existed and was very straight forward in explaining his group had no interest in being involved with an individual at such a small level. Not only was it an insignificant amount of money, they feared a trace and did not want to risk disclosure. Mario's advice was to invest in mutual funds with a local broker, preferably someone Bob knew and trusted. Mario also cautioned it was absolutely necessary Bob's broker and bank had no idea where this money originated. Tell them it came from the summer camp.

As the conversation turned to the future, Mario indicated how pleased he was with Bob's job performance and asked if Bob had any questions or second thoughts. Bob said he was pleased with the new job and felt things were going well. His biggest question was the number of games he would be involved in next season. Mario explained his bosses wanted to further evaluate Bob to make sure he could carry out their plan before they dramatically expanded his schedule. After all, millions of dollars changed hands each game and there was no room for error. But if last year was any indication, he could expect more games in the upcoming season.

"I think you can understand our position," Mario explained. "After all, you've only been involved in two games and neither of those was particularly difficult."

"So how much more difficult can this point-shaving get?" Bob asked. "Since I delivered those games, why the questions as to whether I can do it in the future?"

"There's really no question. As I told you before, my bosses were pleased with your work. We just can't give you a definite number for next year until we see your schedule."

"Mario, just so you understand, I'm committed to this deal. You and I both know how much I need the money. I didn't risk my neck to make a few bucks working only a couple of games a year."

"Don't worry. You're one of our top guys. As long as you do the job you'll get the games. Keep in mind, we evaluate each guy on a game-to-game basis and you're no exception, so anything else?" Mario asked in a definitive manner.

Bob could sense Mario was irritated and tried to change the mood by saying, "I just wanted to thank you again for your help with the new job."

Mario's look softened. "I'm glad I could help. How's it going?"

"Good. I think they're pleased with my work and I like the company. If you hear anything to the contrary, please let me know."

"Don't worry, you'll be the first to know," Mario said as he got up to leave. "I'll touch base with you when you get your schedule. See you later."

With the conclusion of the summer, the Girards' were back to normal, or as normal as a couple could be with the presence of a six-month-old baby. Fortunately, Scott was a good baby and did not fuss much. Nancy had elected to breastfeed for only a short time before placing Scott on the bottle. This was due in part to her personal beliefs and because Scott's nursing was very painful. Nancy was not one for discomfort or lack of sleep. Like any good father, Bob took his turn during the night feedings and even in changing diapers. As much as he fussed about doing 'woman's work,' he thoroughly enjoyed the involvement with his new son.

Bob and Nancy decided to have a small party celebrating Scott's baptism and Chad's returning to school. The party was enjoyable and Nancy and Bob were amazed at how many friends made the effort to attend. Bob couldn't imagine being happier and was convinced the future held nothing but good things for him and his family. It was a bit too early, but Bob and Nancy were already beginning to talk about having another child, hopefully a girl. They had even discussed names if that should happen.

Bob and Nancy decided with the arrival of Scott, and Bob's job going well, she would cut back on work at the health club and stay home more to devote time to raising their son. Bob had already earned a pay raise, and with the basketball season just around the corner surprised Nancy with a new car on her birthday.

"Happy birthday, honey," Bob said as he handed her a small box while they drove to Curio's, her favorite restaurant on Miami Beach. "I hope you like your present."

"Oh Bob, you shouldn't have," Nancy responded not knowing what to expect.

Just as Nancy opened the box Bob pulled into the restaurant's parking lot.

"What are these?" Nancy asked as she looked in the box at a set of keys.

"What do you think they are?" Bob replied as he pulled in a parking space next to a new car. "Why don't you try the keys on that," he said, pointing to the silver, 4-door Honda Accord.

"This can't be!" Nancy exclaimed. "It's beautiful, but can we afford it?"

"With my new job and increased salary, sure we can."

"I can't tell you how much I love you," Nancy said as she leaned over to give Bob a kiss. "Since Scott arrived and you started your new job, I've never seen you so happy."

"That's because I've never been this happy. I've got it all, a lovely wife and mother, a beautiful son and a job I enjoy that allows me to take care of both. What else could a man want? Now let's eat dinner so you can drive your new car home."

Needless to say dinner went well. The wine, the chef's special and the flaming dessert, all things Bob had pre-arranged, were perfect for the occasion. As they gazed into each other's eyes during dinner, both reflected back to the young, wild romantic years of their early marriage.

"Can you believe what a great relationship we have?" Bob started the conversation. "My feelings for you have only grown stronger throughout the years."

"When I look at so many of our friends and their problems, I thank God we share a love that has kept us together and produced such a beautiful child," Nancy replied. "Through the few tough times I have never doubted once the strength of our marriage."

"I could never have found a better partner or soul mate," Bob said. "You have always been there for me and I hope that I will never let you or Scott down."

"Don't worry, you won't," Nancy responded misty eyed.

It was one of the few times they had been away from Scott, and they decided to dance the night away to commemorate this wonderful evening. Yet Bob and Nancy could not wait to get home to make love. By the time Bob returned from taking the babysitter home, Nancy was already in a low cut negligee, listening to soft music and sitting on the sofa with a glass of champagne in her hand, a glass awaiting Bob' attention and the room draped in candlelight. It didn't take long for both to finish the champagne and become participants in wild sex, reminiscent of what they experienced when they were first married. As they lay in each other's arms, it was impossible to consider dark clouds were forming on the horizon.

Chapter Nineteen

Summer changing to fall signaled the start of the school year with basketball soon to follow. Bob continued to do well at his job and was thankful his work allowed him time with Nancy and his son, to watch in awe the growth of Scott on a daily basis and to view the wonder of it all. Nancy cut dramatically her hours at the health club and was enjoying her time as a mother. She had never been happier.

This would be an important year for everyone involved. How was Bob going to handle the point-shaving scheme? Would Nancy detect any difference in Bob or ask questions concerning their recent financial good fortune? How much would Chad play and would he make the starting five at Duke? These were but a few of the questions yet to be answered.

What kind of a schedule Bob would have for basketball was not yet finalized although he had been involved in some preliminary talks with the supervisors of officials for several conferences. Bob felt he should and would be receiving more nationally prominent games. Mario and his group felt the same way.

Bob still did not realize his selection to participate in the point-shaving plan had not been a lucky break. Like anything the Mafia was involved in, this had been an on-going process over a period of years. The evaluation process began years before and had culminated in the selection of a few good men. Gary Branson had been one of the early ones and became the operations point man for the mob. Early on Bob was identified as a bright and upcoming official with unlimited potential. Working the major conferences was a prerequisite for selection because that's where the money was bet and Bob had access to three of the best leagues. The door was opened when Bob mentioned to Gary the financial problems he was experiencing and the need for extra money. Little did Bob know his first meeting with Gary and Mario was not by chance. Mario had flown Gary into Miami specifically to make the contact, and they had tracked Bob and knew where and when he would be available for what they hoped would appear to be an accidental encounter.

September seemed to fly by, and Bob received his final officiating assignments for the upcoming basketball season in early October. The assignments were always sent out early enough so each official could clear his schedule, scratch games he could not work and have time to make travel arrangements. Although he had the opportunity to work in all the major conferences, Bob narrowed his choices to the SEC, the ACC and the Big East Conferences.

The Big East was his first choice since he could do many of the local games with Miami University, thus eliminating much of the unnecessary travel and time away from home and his job. The Big East was recognized as a premier basketball conference, the league only recently having begun football. Being a basketball purist, Bob realized the significance of the Big East in relation to college basketball, especially during an earlier time when the National Invitation Tournament was recognized as the national championship of college basketball. Back then, all the big games were played at Madison Square Garden in New York City, and when one thought of Clair Bee, Joe Lapchick and all the other great coaches from the east one thought of basketball at its best.

The Southeastern Conference was his second choice because he started his major college officiating in that league, plus he liked the coaches and the supervisor of officials, John Guthwin. Guthwin had been a coach himself in college and had a great sense of what it took to be a good official. Travel in this league was also relatively easy.

The ACC was also a high-profile conference and one Bob enjoyed working because of the fan excitement for basketball. But Bob made them his third choice and limited his games because of his friendship with Chad. Of the few games he requested, none of those involved the Duke Blue Devils. There was still no connection between the two and Bob did not want to bring their relationship into question. That eliminated a lot of problems, and yet with Bob's extended schedule should not create any shortage of games to work.

Bob truly enjoyed officiating and was excited to be assigned a number of high-profile games, especially early in the season. The non-conference schedule proved better than expected. Villanova College at the University of Arizona, Syracuse University at the University of Utah and Indiana at North Carolina were huge games with national championship flavor. These were all top twenty teams with rich basketball traditions and outstanding coaches. Bob was smart enough to know at least one, possibly all three games, would be on Mario's schedule. Only time would tell, but if he had to bet he would pick Syracuse at Utah and Indiana at North Carolina for sure. Those two games had great story lines.

Rod Majic at Utah was one of the more colorful coaches in all of basketball and had developed a very strong program in the southwest part of the country. Syracuse of the Big East was a perennial power and Coach Jay Heimer, although greatly under-appreciated, always seemed to have a trick up his sleeve. They had nearly beaten Kentucky and Indiana in recent years to win the national championship.

On the flip side, the Indiana Hoosiers coached by Rob Day and the North Carolina Tar Heels under the leadership of Dean Thomas had met on only a couple of occasions, but each game solicited widespread attention. There were no two coaches more recognizable in college basketball than Day and Thomas. Both were in the basketball Hall of Fame and amongst the top ten in college winning percentage. A match-up of this magnitude was something to behold. But these games were more than a month away and Bob had other concerns, especially with his job. He was relieved he had no Duke games, but that came as no surprise since he had listed the ACC as his third choice. Duke had also decided to play non-conference games outside its immediate area, thus journeying more into the Midwest and West to expand its recruiting base. Those were not areas and leagues Bob worked and therefore it was unlikely he would be assigned such games.

Bob was determined this would be the year he would make it to the NACA Four Final. It would not be easy but he felt confident he could realize his goal if he worked as hard as the previous year. Being assigned several big games would also help in his quest. The excitement was building from within.

This was also the time of the year Bob would begin his conditioning routine, much like the players themselves. The training included lifting weights three days a week, some distance running for aerobic conditioning and playing in his company's recreational basketball league. All of these things enabled him to get into basketball shape while also providing activities for his company's employees. Management seemed pleased with Bob and he was delighted to be making more money, although he did miss the kids at school.

College basketball officiating began in earnest the last week in November, but Bob would work some scrimmages and exhibition games before then to get in game shape and sharpen his execution. Thanksgiving weekend is generally the starting date for the college season and from then until early April was an official's payday. There was nothing Bob could do to supplement his salary while enjoying the work like basketball officiating. Each year it was becoming increasingly more difficult to get into game condition, but with the nature of his new job it would be easier this year than some in the past. Basically the company was paying him to get in shape while conducting activities for others.

In late October Mario contacted Bob about a meeting. The two men got together at Denny's Restaurant in Homestead over an early morning cup of coffee one Saturday. The same arrival and meeting procedures applied, only this time Mario arrived early and was joined by Bob at a corner booth. Bob was intrigued by what Mario wanted considering the games were more than a month away. This time Mario did not check him out to see if he was wired. Was he beginning to trust Bob or was this designed to create uncertainty in the future? Mario wasted little time getting to the point of the meeting.

"Look, I know you think I want to talk about your schedule, but actually I've got something else on my mind. What other officials do you know that can be trusted and might want to join our team?"

"Right off hand I don't know of any, but I've not given it much thought," Bob said with a surprised look.

"Don't act so surprised."

"I guess you're right. After being recruited by Gary, I guess it makes sense you might want me to recruit someone. It just happened a little quicker than I expected."

"Well, we need some new faces. Guys like yourself who we can trust. Why don't you give it some thought and let me know if you think of anyone."

"No problem. I'll look through my officials' directory. I'm sure that will jog my memory. When do you want me to get back to you?"

"Obviously, the sooner the better since it will take us some time to check these guys out. Just be sure they can be trusted," Mario emphasized.

The irony of that statement almost made Bob laugh. Mario wanted someone he could trust who was willing to lie and cheat. Bob also wanted to know the specific criteria for picking a candidate for this operation.

"The guy needs to be bright and an up-and-coming official," Mario went on. "He should be involved in good conferences. After all, that's where we make our money. And it helps if he's living beyond his means and has financial problems."

"What about his job and marital status?"

"Those things are no big deal," Mario lied. This was not the time to let Bob know how important the family situation was in maintaining leverage. He didn't want Bob worried about Scott and Nancy as he began the new season.

"Like I said," Bob replied, "give me a couple weeks and I'll let you know."

"Oh, one last thing," Mario added as he asked for the check. "We're looking for someone who works out west. That's the next area we want to explore."

The mob was pleased with their coverage in the East, Midwest and Southeast but had yet to tap into the major conferences west of the Mississippi. Bob would be asked only to make the introduction much like Gary had done with him. Mario would then handle the rest. Such was the case with Gary who to this day was not one hundred percent sure Bob was involved in the operation. Mario explained he wanted to move on this by sometime after the first of the year in anticipation he could bring one or two officials on board by midseason and no later than the conference tournaments. This gave Bob sufficient time to do his homework and he told Mario he would give him the names in plenty of time.

October meant the start of practice, and Bob as a veteran official was asked by the Big East and SEC supervisors of officials to evaluate the younger officials during preseason scrimmages and exhibition games. This was becoming increasingly more difficult since Bob felt many of the new guys were not competent, ill-prepared or just plain in it for the money and not the love of the game.

This new breed of official was disturbing for many of the veterans who had paid their dues and were just beginning to realize some of the rewards of officiating at a high level. Nothing could mess up a reputation quicker than a couple of bad games as a result of other guys not doing their jobs. Fortunately, the top conferences were pretty solid and added very few new guys from year to year. It also helped that the new guys were given a reduced schedule that included numerous non-conference games. Financially, there was never a better time to be a college basketball official.

Bob wondered how Chad was doing. Practice had begun and he had not heard from Chad or Betty concerning Chad's progress. At a mandatory meeting between coaches and officials in Atlanta regarding rules interpretations, Bob had the opportunity to visit with Coach Pankowski and was told Chad was doing well. Coach P, as he was referred to affectionately by his players, spoke very highly of his team and Chad in particular, saying the sophomore was having a great preseason and had worked himself into the starting lineup. With three starters returning plus a great recruiting class, the season looked solid for the Blue Devils, a team many picked as serious contenders for the national championship.

Bob kept his questions general, not wanting the coach to recognize he and Chad were friends. Bob was proud of Chad knowing how determined and hard he had worked for this opportunity. For Chad, playing at Duke was a dream come true and Bob knew he would make the most of this chance during the season ahead.

Bob believed this would be a pivotal season for Chad who would have to show marked improvement over last year if he was to someday play in the NBA. He had gotten stronger over the summer, concentrating on weight training while playing in the local summer league. But his improvement could only be evaluated under fire at a competitive level like the ACC. Coach P seemed to think this could be a breakout year for Chad, but thoughts of the NBA were way off in the future. Playing on a championship team in the ACC and playing against the best players in the world were completely different obstacles.

Chapter Twenty

The pre-season went well and now the regular season games were about to begin. Mario's call was not unexpected. The targeted game to start the season involved Villanova and Arizona. Both schools had excellent teams, were well coached and the game would be a big intersectional match-up. Mario placed the call under the pretense of thanking Bob for taking care of his nephew at the summer camp, when in reality it was to set up a meeting.

Arizona was a seven-point favorite playing at home, and a split crew was scheduled to call the game. Two officials were assigned by the Pacific 10 Conference, Arizona's league affiliation, and one official came from the Big East, a league that included Villanova. Bob was the Big East representative, although he knew most of the guys who worked in the PAC 10. Split crews were a common practice but one most coaches disliked. Each coach felt the other coach had his league official looking out for him and it put the officials in a difficult position with the fans, often leading to a perception of favoritism.

There was a move afoot in the NACA to have a national officiating bureau, but it had not materialized and was unlikely in the near future. There were too many supervisors and officials with big egos to get a consensus on the topic. The mindset was often to protect one's own and to hell with everyone else. The best way to staff these kinds of games was to request officials from a neutral league, but that seldom happened. The supervisors proclaimed the honesty and unbiased approach of their respective officials, but the coaches had real questions about this arrangement.

Bob's meeting with Mario was set for eight o'clock Wednesday evening at the New Cutler Inn, just off Old Cutler Road in southwest Miami. This was a restaurant that favored a local crowd and afforded good food, moderate prices and reasonable privacy. The drill was much the same as in the past. Mario's friend screened the place early and Bob and Mario arrived at slightly different times. Early dinner favored a small crowd and this night was no exception. Mario once again frisked Bob, creating a certain amount of uncertainty in Bob's mind but not coming as a particular surprise.

"Arizona is favored by seven and has really played well at home in the past," Mario said to begin the conversation.

"I realize that, but it's not like Villanova is a pushover," Bob responded. "They have a young team but one that's supposed to be very athletic. Also, it's the opening game and no one knows how either team is going to react."

"Yeah, but young teams always have early problems on the road."

"But Villanova played well in their two exhibition games and young teams have a way of improving very fast once they gain a little confidence," Bob argued.

"You're right and that's why we're betting on Nova."

"You're kidding me," Bob said, playing the devil's advocate. "Arizona is at home with an experienced team and you're going with Villanova?"

"Well, you can't have it both ways. A minute ago you were telling me how good Villanova is. Now you act like Arizona is unbeatable. Remember, we're not betting on Nova to win but just to cover the spread."

"Am I going to get any help in this game?" Bob asked, referring to the other officials.

"We've been over that before," Mario responded in an agitated voice. "Simply put, it's none of your damn business who else is involved in any game. You just take care of yourself."

"You can't blame me for asking."

"Yes I can, so don't ask again. You're starting to piss me off with this thing."

Sensing Mario was getting upset, Bob replied, "Okay, consider it a dead issue."

"Look, I don't mean to be short with you but you need to understand your only concern is to ensure the bet. Keep in mind the spread is seven and the magic number is six. We don't care who wins as long as it's not Arizona by seven or more points."

"Don't worry. I've got this thing figured out."

As Mario got up to leave, he handed Bob an envelope and whispered, "Have a good trip and I'll talk to you when you get back. Don't open this here."

This would be an average game betting wise and Bob could expect to earn anywhere from $7,500 to $10,000. Once again Mario had been instructed to give Bob $2,500 up front, which he did in a sealed envelope indicating the mob's growing trust in this partnership. Bob's only question was whether either of the other officials was involved in the plan. That question would likely go unanswered.

The trip to Tuscon was always an enjoyable one. Bob liked the Southwest and the cool, dry weather was a nice change. It afforded him the opportunity to eat good Tex-Mex food, something not often found in Miami. But Bob could not shake his concerns. This was a high- profile, nationally televised game, uncharacteristic of the low visibility the mob sought in most games. This seemed to indicate the Mafia was becoming more brazen in its approach to the point-shaving scheme. He hoped this aggressive attitude would not lead to trouble.

The next morning Bob met the other two officials for breakfast and was pleased he knew both guys. All three men left for the arena early and once there had a chance to talk about the rule changes and points of emphasis for the current season. Although they would never admit it publicly, officials talk about coaches much like coaches talk about officials. What disturbed Bob were guys who would brag about coaches they tagged with a technical foul. This was pretty much confined to the younger officials who were trying to impress the powers to be, although there were a few high profile guys who thought the game revolved around them. They would never admit to making a mistake and took offense if you questioned them. One of the guys in this group, Mike Ballard, exemplified a young, energetic and ego-driven official.

"So, have either of you guys had a game yet?" Bob asked.

Mike chimed in saying, "Yeah, I had Indiana two nights ago in their opener."

The third official said this game was his first of the year and then asked Mike, "How did that game go? I read where Indiana won by just a couple of points."

With a grin on his face, Mike replied, "They won no thanks to me. I made a call early that went against the Hoosiers and Coach Day got on my ass. I warned him, but he must have decided I was the guy he was going to stay after."

"He can be tough under those circumstances," Bob added.

"Well, I showed him who was boss. I waited near the end of the game and then nailed his ass with a technical. It was at a critical time and cost him two free throws and possession of the ball."

"I'll bet he really went off then," remarked the third official.

"That's an understatement," Mike replied. "It damn near cost him the game. If I had it to do over I'd give him the second tech and ship his ass to the locker room. Only problem, I want to do more Indiana games and I was afraid he'd blackball me."

"He can't do that," Bob responded.

"That's what you think. Maybe he's not supposed to be able to do it, but I wasn't willing to take that chance. Anyway, I got my money's worth with the first 'T,' and that should send a message to the other coaches I'm not someone they can screw with. After all, if I can stick Day with a 'T,' then you can bet I'm not going to take any shit from the other guys."

"As long as you feel his actions warranted the technical, then more power to you," added the third official in a questionable tone of voice.

"Let's make sure this game goes smoothly and avoid a similar problem," Bob interjected, trying to change the subject while wondering if the technical foul was merited.

The game was competitive and Villanova, in spite of its inexperience, played surprisingly well throughout the first half, building as much as a nine-point lead until a late rush by Arizona closed the gap to three points at half. With the score close there was no real reason for Bob to manufacture any calls, and the officials agreed at halftime the game had been both well played and officiated. The coaches seemed satisfied, and aside from the normal conversation the teams played minus any trash talking. Neither team was in foul trouble, although the Arizona point-guard had picked up two quick fouls and was forced to sit out much of the first half. His absence was probably a big reason for Nova's lead.

The second half proved to be much the same, although both teams made runs. One of Villanova's inside players picked up his fourth foul with nine minutes left, as did Arizona's small-forward and the team's leading scorer at the seven minute mark. With three minutes left and Villanova leading by a point, both players returned to the court. In the last two minutes Arizona's full court pressure defense created problems for Villanova's young guards, forcing three turnovers in four possessions. Still, Arizona was only able to convert on two of the turnovers. With less than fifteen seconds left, and Arizona clinging to a two-point lead, Nova fouled to get the ball back. Arizona's point-guard, to the delight of the home crowd, made both free throws to give his team what appeared to be an insurmountable four-point lead. Villanova desperately rushed the ball down the court and took a wild shot that was rebounded with about three seconds left, apparently sealing the win for the home team.

What happened next almost made Bob sick to his stomach. Thinking the game was over and the bet assured, Bob looked on in horror as the Arizona player upon receiving the in-bounds pass, took two dribbles and threw the ball at the basket from behind half-court as the clock expired. The ball hit off the back of the rim, falling innocently to the floor. Bob could only wonder what might have happened if that three point-shot had gone in and Arizona had won the game by seven points. He knew he had escaped and filed the incident in the back of his brain for future reference. Never again he promised himself would he allow the game to come down to such an improbable and potentially disastrous ending.

After the game the officials conducted their normal post-game review and then headed to the airport. Because of the early game all three officials were able to get home that same evening. At the airport Bob ran into a Villanova assistant coach who was catching the team flight back to Philadelphia. The assistant approached Bob and congratulated him on a good game. He indicated the coaches were pleased with the way the game was officiated, especially on the road, and felt they had had been given a chance to win the game at the end. Their problem was in their inability to make free throws and a couple of key plays down the stretch, but with a young team those things could be corrected.

His comments made Bob feel a lot better. If the coaches from the losing team felt the officiating was good, then it was doubtful anyone else would be suspicious or critical. The only thought still lingering in Bob's mind was whether one or both of the other officials were involved in the operation.

Mario was quick to make arrangements for Bob to receive the remainder of the money for his work in the Villanova/Arizona game. Bob was very aware his payoffs were always in unmarked bills so as not to leave a traceable trail. His biggest problem was deciding how to deposit the money on a regular basis without raising suspicion.

At the same time, the Duke Blue Devils were beginning their season with a relative easy non-conference home opener. Chad was expected to quarterback the team and proved up to the task as he led Duke to an impressive twenty point win, scoring fourteen points and handing out seven assists while committing just three turnovers. Equally impressive, he did a great job defensively and directed the team like a veteran.

Next up for Duke was a tough trip to the Hawaii Classic in Maui, Hawaii. Tough in the sense the eight-team tournament featured highly touted teams, but attractive because it allowed teams to get away to warm weather and beautiful beaches. Being from Miami, warm weather was less important to Chad than some of the other guys.

Many top schools played in Maui because it was outside the continental United States, yet approved by the NACA, so it would not count against the limit on the number of games a team was allowed to play during a season. Therefore, the Classic allowed Duke three additional games and often times one or two extra wins could mean the difference in qualifying for post-season play. Although tournament qualification was generally not a problem for Coach P and the Blue Devils, quality wins early in the season would go a long way in determining the seedings for the NACA Tournament. In any case, the trip to Hawaii was an excellent chance for Duke to be tested early and to establish itself as a national contender.

Ironically, Bob was assigned to the Maui tournament. It provided him an opportunity to see Chad and evaluate his progress, but could possibly create a conflict if Bob was assigned to work a Duke game. It would be good to see Chad and visit with him away from the mainstream of college athletics, yet it could be tricky. As it turned out, Bob only refereed one of Chad's games and it was a game the Blue Devils controlled from the opening tip. Chad played well, although he was somewhat erratic the rest of the tournament. That wasn't much of a surprise to Bob who had watched many sophomores and freshmen display similar traits throughout his officiating career. Duke won the tournament, improving its record to four and zero, but Bob and Chad had little opportunity to spend time together. With so many games and so little free time, things had been too hectic. It was a rewarding trip for both men and on a positive note Bob was able to bring Chad's mom a present from her son. The gift was nothing elaborate but showed Chad's thoughtfulness.

Meanwhile, everything on the home front was moving along smoothly. Nancy was still working a limited schedule at the health club, but was now talking more seriously about having a second child since the Girard's finances seemed to be in order. Bob's job was working out even better than he had anticipated, and Scott continued to grow and was beginning to crawl and mumble some words.

Under Bob's guidance, the fitness and recreational programs had grown so fast he was given the opportunity to hire an assistant. Randy Sanz had been one of Bob's best counselors at camp and over the years their relationship had grown very close. The compatibility between the two men made it easy and enjoyable for everyone. Bob felt good about the hire because it helped his friend and provided an assistant who Bob liked and trusted. No one was more appreciative than Randy for such an opportunity. It also freed Bob to spend more time with his family and do more officiating.

Bob was convinced he had been blessed. After all, only last year he was questioning where he would be working, where the money would come from to pay bills and whether he and Nancy could afford to have more children. Since meeting Mario and joining his venture, everything had fallen into place. With a better paying job and the security of knowing he could take care of and support his family, what else was there to worry about? Bob would soon discover the answer to that question. He would soon realize what effect meeting Mario would have on his life.

Chapter Twenty One

Next up for Bob was Indiana at North Carolina, a monster game with national implications. The Hoosiers were playing well by most accounts, but not by Rob Day's standards. Day was a perfectionist and it had been a number of years since one of his teams had won the Big Ten Conference, let alone contended for the national championship. Indiana was unbeaten after three games but would have that mark severely tested by the Tar Heels.

Dean Thomas had his North Carolina club poised for another run at the ACC crown and the national championship. After nearly self-destructing the year before, the Tar Heels had turned things around in time to make a run in the national tournament. Most of the starters were back from that team, leading to a preseason top five ranking, and the Tar Heels had played well in its first two games. Playing at home, the early line had North Carolina favored by seven points. Again the early betting was on Carolina, with the Mafia carefully placing money on the Hoosiers while taking the points.

Bob was surprised the Mafia would select another high profile game this early in the season, but felt good about the game because he sensed Indiana would be better than people expected. He had seen the Hoosiers at the end of the previous season and believed they had the talent and pride to produce an excellent season. A little young, only two seniors playing significant minutes, Day's team generally played older and more poised than expected, especially early in the season. The game was expected to be very competitive and attract a lot of national attention. With two nationally recognized programs, two Hall of Fame coaches and a national television audience, the stage was set for great drama.

Bob arrived in Durham the night before the game and was surprised when Chad phoned him at the hotel. "Hello Bob, this is Chad. I hope I'm not interrupting anything."

"What a surprise," Bob replied. "How did you know where to reach me?"

"I talked with mom last night and she said she thought you were doing the game tomorrow. So I had her call Nancy and get the hotel number. I hope you don't mind that I called?"

"You know better that that. Anyway, how are things going? Is your team as good as everyone thinks?"

"I hope so. We've had a good non-conference season so far and I'm playing a lot better than when you saw me in Hawaii. Also, the new guys are really giving us a lift."

"That's great. So what else is new?" Bob asked.

"I was hoping we could get together for dinner or is that not such a good idea. I would really like to talk with you about a couple of things."

Chad planned to go to the game, but knew there would be little time to visit with Bob at the game site nor would it be a good idea to do so. Bob normally would not fraternize with any player, but Duke was not involved in the game and Chad was not just any player. He felt he could justify dinner if they were discreet. They went to an out-of-the-way restaurant in Raleigh and thoroughly enjoyed catching up with each other's news. Bob updated Chad on what was happening in Miami and described how fast Scott was growing. Chad seemed quite happy and they talked more about his academics and social life than basketball. He appeared more confident and self-assured and it was easy to see the excitement in his eyes.

"I really enjoyed the company," Bob mentioned as they drove home from the restaurant. "Is there anything else we need to discuss or do you have any messages for your mother?" Bob sensed there was still something on Chad's mind.

"Well, there is one more thing. Is mom seeing anyone?"

"Not that I know of, but I don't keep close tabs on your mom's social calendar."

"I've been thinking I really would like her to find a good man. After all, I'm away at school and she has no one to share her life with."

"She's got us," Bob joked, thinking of Nancy and his relationship with Chad and his mom. "Seriously though, if you're looking for advice, just trust you mother's judgement. She can take care of herself. If she finds someone, so be it. Don't worry about her. She's old enough and wise enough to know what she wants."

"I guess you're right," Chad replied. "Just promise you'll keep an eye on her for me. If anything ever happened to her, I wouldn't know what to do. I worry, especially since I can't keep track of her."

"Don't worry, you and your mother are like family to Nancy and me. If anything comes up that I think you should know about, I'll give you a call. Now let's get you back to the dorm so we both can get some sleep."

As Chad got out of the car, Bob beamed knowing this young man, who was like a second son, was maturing and becoming an outstanding person. Once again he could only hope his own son would do likewise.

The rivalry and closeness of Duke and North Carolina was such the players played against each other in the off-season, and on occasion went to each other's games. This game was of special interest for Chad since he had been recruited by Coach Day at Indiana coming out of high school. In fact, he had attended Day's summer basketball camp when he was in junior high school, compliments of Bob who then believed the best basketball was played in the Midwest. At one time Chad thought he would play for the Hoosiers. His ultimate decision really came down to staying closer to home.

Even though things were hectic, Chad stopped by the bench before the game to say hello to Coach Day. He was surprised when the coach recognized him.

"Chad Payne," Coach Day responded. "Well, I'll be damned. What brings you into enemy territory?"

"I want to get an early scouting report on the Tar Heels and see your team kick their butts."

"I don't know about kicking their butts, but I can tell you they're very good. You know I'm still upset about you not coming to Indiana."

"Coach, if your school had been closer to home, I probably would have signed with you," Chad replied. "In any case, good luck today and the rest of the season."

"Thanks and congratulations on your success so far," Day responded as the teams returned to their benches for the introductions. "This should be a big year for you and you know you're playing for one of my favorite people. Good luck and give your mother my best."

A packed house and national television audience watched as Carolina's experience paid dividends in the early going. It jumped to an early eight-point lead, but the Hoosiers began to overcome the hostile environment and cut into the deficit. At halftime Indiana held a three-point lead with neither team in any kind of foul trouble. From an official's point of view these were the best games. Not only did you have two good teams well schooled in the fundamentals of the game, you also had an enthusiastic, knowledgeable crowd urging the teams to perform at a very high level.

The halftime was brief and to the point, and the officials were in agreement the first half had gone smoothly. Bob was working with two veteran officials and the three of them were consistently on the same page. The first half had gone better than Bob could have hoped, but he remembered his previous close call and vowed not to allow this game to get out of hand.

As the second half played out, the game went back and forth with more than ten lead changes. A critical call in the last two minutes unfortunately went a long way in determining the outcome. With the Tar Heels down one and the shot clock running out, the Carolina point- guard drove into the lane in an attempt to score or create a shot for a teammate. He was called for a charging foul right in front of the basket, soliciting groans and boos from the partisan home crowd. To Bob's relief the foul was whistled by an experienced official right on the play and it appeared to be a good call. This resulted not only in a change of possession but was the point-guard's fifth foul, disqualifying him from the contest.

"What kind of a call was that?" yelled the point-guard.

"Son, from what I could see, a good one," Bob responded, taking up for his partner as there was a break in the action while Coach Thomas made a substitution.

It was unusual for Bob to talk with a player but he felt this was an appropriate response to a tough call. He wanted the young man to know the call was the correct one and one he would have made in a similar situation.

"Bob, that should've been a block or at least a no call," Coach Thomas piped in as Bob came to the scorer's table to check in the new player. "Don't decide the game with a call like that at this time."

"Coach, I didn't make the call but it was a good one," Bob emphasized. "Anyway, you still have plenty of time to win the game."

"Maybe, but it won't be easy, especially without our floor leader."

"I can't help that but we need to get on with the game. Your time's up, so let's get a sub in the game."

What made Bob an excellent official was his ability to communicate with the players and coaches while supporting his fellow officials, especially during closely contested games. His approach was non-confrontational and yet he did not ignore or evade tough situations. He understood the frustrations of the players and coaches as well as the competitive nature of the sport. This was another example of his command of a tough situation.

Indiana was able to convert a three-point shot on the next possession, and without its point-guard North Carolina was not able to get back in sync. The game became a free-throw shooting contest for the Hoosiers down the stretch and they proved equal to the task. Day's team won the game, but not until a three point shot by Carolina to tie fell short with five seconds to go in the game. An ensuing foul resulted in the final two points for Indiana and the five-point margin of victory.

Once again everyone involved in the game, except possibly Dean Thomas, thought the game had been well officiated. This included the supervisor of officials for the ACC who was in attendance to evaluate the officiating and ensure the integrity of the game. Also, for the first time Bob did not have to sweat bullets in anticipation of the outcome of the game. What a relief for Bob when things worked so smoothly.

Chad left with about thirty seconds left in the game, attempting to beat the crowd and knowing Bob would be running late because the officials would shower and go over their post- game debriefing. Both Chad and Bob had already agreed it would be in everyone's best interest if they were not seen together. Although doubtful, it could raise questions down the road.

The flight home was uneventful and Bob was getting more comfortable dealing with the point-shaving plan. As long as he was not being asked to throw a game, Bob had convinced himself what he was doing was harmless. In denial, he began to rationalize and call what he was doing 'controlled scoring,' not point-shaving. He rationalized the teams were winning or losing as a result of their own play. What a great way for a guy who had paid his dues coming up through the ranks of officiating to earn a modest living. On his way home from the airport Bob made his usual stop at a local pub for a nightcap. This time he drank a premium beer to celebrate his good fortune. Life could be so good Bob thought.

When Mario's runner dropped off the next check for the Indiana/ North Carolina game, Bob realized there was nothing modest about the money he was making. The payoff was $15,000 cash. The past two games were his first real taste of point shaving with early non-conference games between high-profile basketball powers and the payoffs were much more than Bob anticipated. What Bob could not get over was the long arm of the Mafia. How was he to know who else was involved or might be watching him? It sure made it a lot easier knowing his family and friends were not aware of his involvement.

The hardest part for Bob was not being able to share his success with anyone, especially Nancy. It was becoming increasingly more difficult to look her in the eye, knowing he was not being open and honest in their relationship. Honesty and trust had always been the building blocks upon which their marriage was founded.

Another problem he would have to deal with soon was the investment of his discretionary cash. He was uncomfortable hiring a financial consultant, knowing questions might surface which could lead to exposure. Bob had always told Nancy he wanted to further his education and learn more about the intricacies of business with the summer camp. As a result, Bob used this as an excuse to enroll for the fall semester in a night course in investments at Miami-Dade Community College. The class would prove not only to be invaluable to Bob regarding investments of his bonus money, but would also give him a cover if he needed to meet with Mario. Toward that aim he purchased a laptop computer and a series of instructional business programs.

Although this conflicted with some of his games, he arranged a flexible schedule with his instructor to make up the missed class time. The teacher was a huge basketball fan and a couple of tickets to the University of Miami games went a long way to ensure Bob a lot of individual attention and flexibility. Furthermore, the majority of his games came after the first of the year, so he had to make very few adjustments with his assignments.

Chapter Twenty Two

With the season in full swing, Mario once again questioned Bob as to any officials who would be candidates for their point-shaving scheme. Bob had a couple of guys in mind but hadn't the occasion to work games with them yet. As such he couldn't gauge if they would be interested. One of the guys was scheduled to work with Bob the next game between Syracuse and Utah in Salt Lake City.

Bill Duncan was an official who worked the Western Athletic, the West Coast and the Mountain West Conferences. He was an older guy who had just gone through a messy divorce and was paying alimony and child support to his ex-wife and two kids. Bill had spent too much time on the road with his sales job and officiating trying to make ends meet and lost his marriage to outside interests. His wife started working and the relationship slowly deteriorated over a period of years. If the truth was told she had met another man, but that was a tough one to prove and the kids were too young to really know what was going on. One day she told Bill she wanted a divorce and there could be no reconciliation. Bill was shocked and terribly disappointed for the children, but had basically given up on the marriage and was relieved to get away from the daily fighting. Since he had no real proof of infidelity, he knew the kids would end up with their mother. The divorce was amicable but with child support payments he was on the books for more money than he could afford.

Bob visited with him last year shortly after the divorce and knew Bill would be a good candidate for Mario. His financial problems coupled with his reputation and access to the leagues on the West Coast appeared to be a natural fit.

Since Bill lived in San Diego, he would be arriving in Salt Lake the night before the game and the two men were slated to have dinner together. That would be an excellent chance for Bob to approach Bill but he needed to visit with Mario to find out how to handle such a delicate situation. Obviously one screw up could jeopardize the entire operation and put Bob at risk.

Two days before leaving for Salt Lake City, Mario and Bob met for lunch at Friday's Restaurant in the Miami Lakes Shopping Center. The nice thing about Bob's job was his ability to control his hours. A late lunch was never a question and gave him the flexibility to meet with people out of the office. This particular day Bob faked last minute Christmas shopping as an excuse. Lunch rapidly turned into a discussion about the upcoming game and what to say and do in Bob's initial meeting with Bill. Mario wanted to be sure Bill was a good choice and seemed pleased when Bob explained Bill's background and current situation.

"I'm telling you this guy would be great," Bob emphasized. "He has access to the leagues you need as well as enough financial problems to be interested."

"How long and well do you know him?"

"Enough to trust he'll jump at the chance to make some extra money. So how interested are you in talking with him?"

"We're always interested in quality people but we need to be damn sure this guy can be trusted and can deliver if we bring him aboard," Mario replied.

"Just let me know what you need from him and what my approach should be."

What Mario advised Bob to do was determine interest. This could be done in a variety of ways depending upon how comfortable Bob felt with Bill. They decided Bob would mention something in passing regarding the ability to make extra money and Bill's response would determine how far it would go from there.

"Feel him out without divulging what you're involved in."

"So, how do I do that?" Bob asked. "Give me some direction."

"Give me a break, you're not stupid," Mario said with a raised voice. "Just remember how we approached you and make sure no one else is around when you talk. The first thing is to find out how much trouble he's in financially. If for some reason you sense he's not reasonably desperate, then move on to something else."

Mario cautioned Bob not to present too much information and to be sure not to entertain any questions. Get a feel for the situation and get out. Bob's assessment of the situation would determine Mario's next step. Bob was beginning to sense Mario's trust.

The Syracuse/Utah game was sure to be a dandy. The Utes were coming off a great year but had lost a couple of key guys to the pro's and graduation. Their coach, Ron Majic, was one of the outstanding personalities in college basketball. This was a guy who ate even when he wasn't hungry and was not discouraged by multiple by-pass heart surgery. He was not a guy you would expect to find on the cover of GQ Magazine, but was a brilliant coach with a realistic and simple approach and a great teacher of the game of basketball.

On the other hand, Syracuse had struggled through a rebuilding season the previous year and was now putting the pieces back together. The Orangemen's coach, Jay Heimer, was a stoic and to-the-point kind of guy. There wasn't a lot of laughter and fooling around on his team, but he had always been underrated as a coach until he took his teams twice to the NACA final game. Jay wasn't afraid to try new things and that made his teams difficult to prepare for. Even then, the basketball critics and fans were not willing to give Heimer the credit he so richly deserved.

Playing in Salt Lake City was no picnic for anyone and Utah was a five-point favorite. Five was quite a few points but the Utes were playing at home where they were virtually unbeatable. With that kind of spread on a team with a basketball tradition as rich as Syracuse, it came as no surprise that some money was bet on the Orangemen against the points. Still, it was hard to believe a relatively young Syracuse team could win in Salt Lake. Mario instructed Bob their money would be on Utah to cover the spread.

Bob checked into the Salt Lake Hilton on Friday afternoon only to find Bill had not yet arrived. Bill's plane had been delayed but he was expected at the hotel by 7 o'clock. They had talked during the week and agreed to have dinner in the hotel. With all the traveling, the last thing most officials want is to run around town on a Friday night trying to find a place to eat. Dinner was scheduled for 8 o'clock and there was no reason to think Bill would be late.

At 8:15 Bill and Bob met in the bar for a drink before going to dinner. After some small talk they decided to move into the restaurant. The dining area was fancier than Bob was used to but the corner table allowed them the privacy needed to talk. Bill was taken back by the prices on the menu so Bob volunteered to pick up the tab. This insured Bob he would have Bill's attention and they would not be bothered. During dinner the talk turned to their personal lives as impacted by officiating. Bob could sense Bill was still struggling with how his frequent traveling had cost him his marriage.

"I just feel like if I had been home instead of away with officiating I might have been able to save my marriage," Bill explained.

"I can't tell you for sure one way or the other but I doubt very much officiating was the straw that broke the camel's back," Bob responded, trying to absolve Bill of much of the blame for a failed marriage. "Hell, if your marriage wasn't any stronger than that, then it was an accident waiting to happen."

"But I just don't know what else I did wrong." Bill was already ordering his fourth drink and beginning to slur his words.

"Probably nothing, in fact, officiating gave you extra income so your wife could enjoy the better things in life. It may have just been time for both of you to go separate ways."

"Well, I can't say I miss the day to day battles," Bill replied.

"So, how are the kids?"

"They've been great but that doesn't make it any easier. I only get them one weekend a month, two days a week and a month in the summer."

"That must be tough," Bob said compassionately.

"Real tough, but we try to make the best of what little time we have together."

The more he drank, the more Bob could sense the depression beginning to take hold of Bill. Through previous conversations he knew the kids meant the world to this man. It was evident Bob needed to bring this conversation to an end and get on with the business at hand. "Is there anything you can do to get more time with them?"

"Not really, although my ex-wife has been pretty good about allowing me to see them at other times when I really want to. I think part of it is because she wants to spend more time alone with her boyfriend."

Bob could only wonder what his world would be like if he lost Nancy and Scott. What made this even scarier was Bill's assertion he just did not realize his marriage had reached the point of no return until it was too late. Could Bob be overlooking something in his own marriage? He doubted it but it was food for thought.

Like Bob, there were few things Bill enjoyed more than officiating. But had the price been too high? Bob couldn't offer much support or advice and tried to convince Bill things had a way of working out for the best. It sounded like Bill had a good relationship with his kids and fortunately he and his ex-wife had remained friends. It could be a lot worse.

During after-dinner drinks Bob subtly inquired about Bill's interest in earning additional income. Bill seemed very interested, especially since he was in ring sales for Gemstone's Ring Company and basically on commission. This had been a good job for him for close to twenty years, but with increased living costs and tighter consumer spending things weren't what they had once been. Add to that the divorce and child support payments and money had gotten tight. Any reasonable way to make a few extra dollars would be welcomed.

"So, what are you doing to make extra money besides officiating?" Bill asked.

"The summer camp is still helping some, but I'm also doing some things with officiating to generate a few extra dollars."

"Like what? Are you working clinics?"

"Are you crazy?" Bob replied. "I can't stand those things. What I'm involved in takes too long to explain right now but I'm just interested to see if you want to make some extra money doing what you're already doing."

"As long as what I'm asked to do is reasonable, I'm always interested in making an extra buck. Lord only knows I can use it."

Little did Bill know 'reasonable' was in the eye of the beholder and what Bob was alluding too was more than a few dollars. Bill as one would imagine asked questions, but Bob would only tell him this was not a start-up business with normal overhead costs. Nor was it multiple level marketing. It was something new, exciting and could help Bill solve his financial problems. By now Bob was able to establish Bill was desperate to make more money and would do just about anything to improve his financial situation. He would only tell Bill the process was simple and someone would be contacting him in the very near future to discuss the details. After all, it was Mario's job to find out just how desperate Bill really was. The contact would use Bob's name as a reference.

The next day the game proved to be as good as advertised. The first half was a dogfight, with neither team leading by more than four points. Near the end of the half Bob made a big call on the Syracuse forward for his third foul. Coach Heimer went ballistic, but it was a block-charge call that was always subject to an official's judgement. Jay would not let up and Bob called a technical foul on him with less than two minutes to go in the half, resulting in a five-point swing and six-point Utah lead at half. Bob hated for this to happen since he would be doing a number of Orangemen games during the Big East season and did not want to go through the year with Coach Heimer constantly second guessing him. Jay was not one to let an incident like this go away. Fortunately, upon later review, the tape showed the call to be a good one and Bob could only hope Jay would understand he was merely doing his job.

This was another one of those split-crew games that led to more problems than solutions. As a result, the second half began under strained relations with Bob and Coach Heimer since Jay felt Bob was not protecting his interests. Protecting someone's interests at the expense of not making the correct call was not what officiating was about as far a Bob was concerned. As the game wore on it became apparent the rift between the two men was going to be a problem. The Orangemen started the second half with renewed determination and Utah was not as intense, perhaps as a result of the way the first half ended and their feeling of invincibility at home. At the ten minute mark the game was tied and Syracuse was gathering momentum.

Suddenly the game was impacted by a single, unforeseen incident. Utah's power-forward went up for a rebound, twisting his ankle when he landed on the floor. Not only was this kid the Utes leading scorer and rebounder, he was also the team leader. Now the plot thickened and Bob realized for the first time he was in for a long afternoon. There was still enough time to deliver the game but he would have to get overly involved and pick his spots. He was convinced things could still be worked out.

He was wrong. Inside the final three minutes the Orangemen built a four-point lead and controlled the game as they had throughout much of the second half. Both teams were aggressive at both ends of the court and both were now in the bonus free-throw situation. If the Orangemen continued to play with confidence, and the Utes could not shake the ball loose or come up with a couple of defensive stops resulting in easy points, then Syracuse not only would beat the spread, it was probably going to win the game.

Syracuse began to utilize the clock on offense, spread the floor while capitalizing on their quickness and forced Utah to extend its defense and take chances. On the other end, the Syracuse matchup zone created problems for the Utes. The Orangemen extended their perimeter defense, eliminated the three-point shot that was the strength of the Utah offense and dared the Utes' inside guys to score. Time was becoming a factor and Syracuse looked the cinch to spring the upset.

This was Bob's biggest nightmare. With the Orangemen comfortably ahead, the Utes having to chase on defense and rush on offense and Syracuse making free throws, there was little he could do to influence the outcome. Impacting a fast-paced game that was closely contested until the final whistle was greatly different from manipulating a game like this.

The decision inside the last minute was an agonizing one. Should he risk his reputation to impact the outcome of the game, which even he was not sure he could effect, or wait to fight another day? He decided to fight another day, although he could not imagine the consequences for not delivering the game. Syracuse went on to beat the point spread and win the game.

Afterward the officials went through their normal post-game routine. Both the other officials noticed Bob was pale and sweaty. When he excused himself to go to the restroom and vomit, Bill asked him if he was all right. Bob was beside himself and blew it off as something he must have eaten at breakfast. In all honesty, he was so shook-up he was having a difficult time breathing, in fact, so difficult Bill asked the arena manager to find a doctor to check on Bob. The doctor could find nothing wrong but did mention that Bob's blood pressure seemed a little elevated. He was cleared to go and the doctor recommended he visit his family physician when he got home if he was still experiencing any problems. Bob stayed in the shower for what must have seemed like an eternity, replaying the game in his mind and wondering how it got away so quickly. If he had a gun he just knew he would blow his own brains out.

Bill and Bob rode back to the airport together. Because of the afternoon tip-off, both men were able to get out of Salt Lake and back home that evening. At the airport Bob excused himself to go to the restroom where he vomited again. Just thinking about the outcome of the game made him sick. How would he explain to Mario what happened? Would Mario understand how this kind of thing could happen? Would he even care? What were the immediate consequences of this result? Talking to Bill about the aforementioned business opportunity was the furthest thing from Bob's mind. In fact, he was having second thoughts as to why he had gotten involved himself.

Chapter Twenty Three

The next forty-eight hours would tell the tale. It's funny how you don't think of the potential problems in any plan until something goes wrong and then you can't seem to explain what happened or fathom the end result.

Arriving home late, Nancy was still up and could detect something was wrong. Bob blew it off as just a tough game and long trip, but he knew he did a poor job convincing Nancy there wasn't more to this.

"Honey, are you sure everything is okay?" Nancy asked. "You look pale."

"Like I said, it's just the travel," Bob lied. "Trying to get out of Salt Lake after the game is always a hassle. Plus, I didn't have a real strong crew and didn't have one of my better games. The game was a battle and it wore me out but I'll be okay."

"Why don't you come to bed? You'll feel better after a good night's sleep."

"You go ahead. I'll be in as soon as I fill out my expense report and check on Scott. I'm just not tired right now. By the way, how is Scott?"

"He's been a little cranky but for the most part he's been good. Maybe tomorrow the three of us can do something. I'm sure he would enjoy spending time with his dad."

"That sounds like a winner," Bob responded. "Now go to bed and I'll be in as soon as I finish my report."

Bob slept poorly. Again and again the questions surfaced in his mind. What could he have done to ensure a favorable outcome to the game? Where did he lose control? Had any other of Mario's guys ever experienced this kind of a problem? Bob knew it wouldn't be long before he had the answers to these questions as well as quite a few more he probably hadn't even thought about. Morning couldn't come too soon. The waiting was killing him, although he hoped that wouldn't become the case literally. His personal strength when facing Mario would be severely tested.

On Sunday Bob spent quality time with his family, although his mind was somewhere else. The family went to early church and then out to breakfast, a tradition Nancy and Bob had established early in their marriage whenever Bob was not on the road. Although they took a few months off following the birth of their son, Scott was now old enough to go along without creating too much of a disturbance. Besides, their church had a wonderful infant care area. The afternoon was spent doing things around the house with Bob completing some neglected yard work while Nancy caught up with the laundry and other household chores. If it was Mario's intent to make Bob sweat, he was doing a good job. Each time the phone rang Bob felt it was Mario. But Mario never called and Sunday came and went. For Bob that meant another restless night.

It was not until Monday afternoon that Mario contacted Bob through one of his employees. They were to meet at Korbit's sports bar at 7:30 that evening. The message included the directive "don't be late." Fortunately, Nancy had nothing planned and Bob was able to leave the house without any questions. He told his wife he had to meet a guy who was a potential coach for his company's winter basketball team and this was the only time they could get together. As the lying became more frequent, the easier it got for Bob.

Bob arrived at the bar at 7:15. Taking no chances, he took his position in a booth in the far corner near the pool tables, away from the main traffic and out of earshot of the other patrons. Things were slow and Bob almost hoped for a big crowd, not knowing what Mario might do. Mario walked in about 7:40, followed shortly thereafter by someone Bob had not seen before. Although they came in a couple of minutes apart, Bob guessed they were together. After ordering a beer, Mario made his way to the pool tables where he pretended to notice Bob for the first time. Mario joined Bob while his friend carefully positioned himself in the next booth, thus preventing anyone from getting too close.

"Let's get to the point," Mario began. "What the hell happened?"

"It was a bad game to bet on and impossible for me to control the outcome," Bob responded. "Too many crazy things happened."

"Wait a minute! Don't give me that shit! I don't remember you saying anything about how hard this game would be. You don't seem to understand, anyone can handle the sure bets, but you're getting paid to handle the tough ones as well. So knock off the crap and give me a straight answer to the question," Mario said visibly upset.

"I told you from the start Syracuse would be all Utah could handle, and when the team's best player gets hurt it compounds the problem. When the bet is legitimate with no extenuating circumstances I can handle it. This wasn't one of those games." Bob went on to explain how limited his options became inside the last couple of minutes of the game and why he made the decision to just ride out the end result rather than expose himself and jeopardize future plans.

"Having said that, what do you suggest as a solution to this problem? What the hell are we supposed to do if our guys can't deliver?" Mario replied in a menacing tone.

Although basically scared shitless, Bob found the strength to answer. "First, let me look at the games so I can give you my insight into who should win. After all, I see most of these teams first-hand and I know who's good and not so good. Second, try to bet on games that favor teams winning by less as opposed to more than the spread, especially when the point spread is as great as it was in this game."

"I'll take that under advisement but you need to better understand what's at stake here. My bosses don't like to be disappointed and neither do I. Remember, when they're pissed off, then I'm pissed off!"

"So what happens now?" Bob asked.

After listening to Bob's depiction of what and how things happened, Mario surprised Bob with his analysis of the end result. Most important Mario explained, there was never justification for not completing the job with the desired results. Bob needed to be sure he understood that. On the flip side, some situations were more desperate than others.

Unknown to Bob, the Mafia had purposely set up this game to not cover the bet. The reason was simple. As they had gotten more and more involved in college sports, the FBI was becoming increasingly more interested in illegal betting patterns. Mario and his cronies had gotten wind the feds were snooping around college basketball. Although the mob spread its bets throughout the country through many different and diverse sources, it was time to completely derail the FBI's suspicions as to who might be involved. Whether it was this game or one in the near future, the Mafia would have to dump some money on a losing proposition to continue what it hoped would be a long and prosperous plan. If the FBI "bloodhounds" were not confused now, then they never would be.

"Look, there is no excuse for you not getting control of a game sooner, but the end result did not prove to be disastrous," Mario said.

"What do you mean?"

"We knew this would be a tough game, but we also know the FBI and legalized gaming establishments are curious about the betting from some of our sources. Not that they can identify them, because we're constantly changing, but rather the amount of money originating from certain locations. As a result, we needed to deflect some of the interest and attention from our activities, even at the expense of losing some money."

"You mean you knew the game was next to impossible to bet and you bet money opposite my instructions?" Bob asked in astonishment.

"Not really. The group I work for is quite a bit smarter than most people give us credit for. We merely wanted to create confusion for those who might be watching."

What Mario was alluding to and Bob didn't understand was the mob had placed a third official in the Syracuse/Utah game to ensure the outcome. No matter how hard Bob had tried, it would have been nearly impossible for him to control the outcome of the game. As much as the mob trusted Bob, they still weren't ready to sign over the farm to him or let him know everything that was going on.

"How could you do that?"

"Simple, if we continue to place large amounts of money on teams and always win, then someone is going to scrutinize our operation so closely we'll have to shut down and I guarantee you this scam is too lucrative to risk that happening."

"So you took a direct hit, but yet you're busting my ass."

"Yeah we took a hit, but this is nowhere close to busting your ass. Let me assure you, you don't want to know what busting your ass is really like," Mario said with an evil look in his eye. "These guys can get real nasty."

"So, what's the end result?" Bob asked.

"The end result is you've hopefully learned a valuable lesson and we lost only a minimum amount of money to ensure our long-range plans. Regardless of the outcome, we were in a win-win situation long term and the end result should deflect attention from us and you, which is important as you continue to work games for us. With that said, let me be the first to congratulate you on surviving your first screw up. On the other hand, let me caution you not to let it happen again."

The game had served as a test of Bob's abilities to handle a difficult situation. There had been occasions in the past when the official involved was so afraid of the end result he had destroyed his credibility at the expense of completing the deal. That official not only eliminated himself from future participation in the operation, he put the long-range plans of the mob at risk. That Bob had realized the final result was beyond his control and needed to maintain a sense of professionalism was viewed as a positive by the powers to be. The last thing the Mafia wanted was to deal with a weak and undisciplined person who would cave in at the first sign of pressure. What long-term goals the Mafia had for this plan was not something

Mario could discuss, but he assured Bob this was just the beginning of something very special.

After listening to Mario, Bob was stunned. In a period of a few minutes he ran the gauntlet of emotions; shock, relief, disbelief and plain mad. How could they put him on the end of a gangplank, allow him to cut the board and then expect him to swim to safety, all the time not allowing him to know what was really going on? How could they trust him to manipulate games but not trust him to know the real game plan? Where did Mario get off allowing him to worry about the outcome for two days without any indication of what he had just been told?

Through this entire conversation Bob was able to keep his head and elected to act in a civil way. He had been lucky and no one knew that better than he did. He had escaped a difficult situation and was not about to act stupid and create a problem.

Bob's only question was, "why me? Why hang me out to dry?"

And the answer, "because you're a key guy in what we're trying to do."

"So why jerk me around? The least you could have done was alert me to what was going on and not let me sit around all weekend with my stomach in my throat."

"That's just the reason we didn't tell you," Mario responded.

"What do you mean by that?"

"We needed to test you under fire. How would you handle yourself? Would you sacrifice the entire operation for fear of the consequences, run away, call the cops, over react or just deal with the reality of your mistake? These were all important questions to get answered to gauge your fitness to be our main guy in this operation."

"How did I do?"

Mario leaned forward. "You passed with flying colors. You maintained your cool under fire and you seem to understand the grave consequences of your actions. Most important, you did nothing to compromise the operation. Consider our actions toward this screw-up as a bonus, but don't let it happen again."

Without getting into details, Bob could sense the threat in Mario's statement. What Bob didn't understand was how far the Mafia would go if they sensed betrayal or disloyalty.

On an additional note, Bob told Mario about his conversation with Bill Duncan while they were together in Salt Lake City. Bob was convinced Bill was a player and encouraged Mario to follow-up on their conversation. Mario indicated someone would contact Bill in good time but also advised Bob there would be no further discussion about this matter. As was the case with Bob's initial exposure to Mario and Gary Branson, the matter was now out of Bob's hands and he would only be involved if the mob decided it was appropriate. Mario explained this minimized the chance of implication and exposure by others. The less number of people who knew those that were involved the better the chances of the plan succeeding. That proved to be the case in Bob's last game.

Needless to say, Bob was a completely different person when he returned home that evening. The baby had already gone to bed and Nancy had purposely stayed up to greet her husband. She was concerned by his strange behavior over the last couple of days and could sense almost immediately Bob was much more calm and relaxed. Christmas was nearly upon them and Nancy wanted things to go well.

"So, did everything go okay tonight?" Nancy asked.

"Better than expected," Bob replied in a smug way.

"You sure sound and look better than you have the last couple of days."

"I'm sorry if I've been a pain in the ass to be around, but with the games, travel, my job and being away from you and Scott things have been hectic and stressful. I hope you understand."

"Don't I always?"

"Most of the time but let's not get carried away," Bob joked. "But I do miss you and Scott when I'm gone. I hope to cut back on travel next year."

As the conversation continued, Bob lied about meeting a guy who would be the new basketball coach for his corporate league. Nancy updated Bob on everything that was happening on the home front, especially Scott's day to day experiences. Bob just wanted a moment to relax and have a beer.

"By the way, where is Scott?" Bob asked. "Is he asleep?"

"You've really been out of it. I put him down over an hour ago."

"I guess I just lost track of time. What say you and I find something to do."

"Like what?" Nancy asked sheepishly.

"Well, we could always work on giving Scott a playmate," Bob replied with a twinkle in his eye.

That was music to Nancy's ears. She had worked so hard to get herself back into shape and appreciated feeling desirable once again. She was also ready to add to their family. As athletic people, sex had always been a big part of their lives and now was one of those few times recently when both were at home and Scott was in bed. Although Bob was tired because of a lack of sleep, the sex was as good as he could ever remember. Whether it was because of the favorable solution to his earlier problem, a few too many beers, the length of time since their last endeavor or all of the above, Bob and Nancy made up for lost time and ended up falling asleep in each other's arms.

What a difference a day makes. Bob was up at the break of dawn feeling rested and relaxed. Work could wait. He was determined to spend the early morning hours with his wife and son. Scott was growing by leaps and bounds and Nancy proved every bit as good a mother as expected. Scott was nearly ten months old and beginning to walk and get around on his own. Bob was fascinated with the mobility of his son.

Bob needed to be careful not to act like he was overcompensating for the way he had acted the previous couple of days. What the future would hold for the Girards was still unclear, but Bob was determined his wife and son would have more opportunities made available to them than he had while growing up. Part of his philosophy centered on the extra money he was making and investing from the point-shaving scheme.

As basically his own boss, Bob was late for work but no one really noticed or questioned when he arrived. Regardless, Bob did not want to bring attention too himself or take advantage of the situation. He felt it would leave the wrong impression with his fellow workers and they would either lose respect for him or try to take advantage of his example. That was highly unlikely since Bob was perceived to be a hard worker and excellent leader, but this thought process spoke volumes to his work ethic and belief in what was the right thing to do.

The corporate basketball season was to begin next week and Bob still had to find his team a coach. He knew quite a few men from his involvement with his own summer camp and two phone calls netted him a volunteer to run the team. Having discretionary funds available, Bob promised his new coach a small stipend but unlimited pizza and beer for him and the team after each game. The games were supposed to be played for fun but there was always some coach or group of players that were infected with extra testosterone and played like each game was the seventh game of the NBA finals. But there was no national championship at stake and Bob assured the coach he would be at the first couple of practices to introduce him to the players and make sure things ran smoothly. The regular season lasted only ten weeks plus a week for the post-season tournament. The teams would be seeded in the tournament by record and it would be single elimination. As a hook, Bob also threw in a free dinner for the coach and his wife at Randall's, one of the top restaurants in Coral Gables, at the end of the season. Ironically, Bob's company should have a pretty good team but that was the furthest thing from his mind at the moment.

Chapter Twenty Four

Bob suddenly realized it was three days until Christmas and he had yet to do his shopping. With Scott about to experience his first visit from Santa Claus, this would be a holiday season to remember. Because the twenty-fifth fell on a Friday, Bob and his fellow workers would have a long weekend to celebrate Christmas.

Bob's parents were scheduled to arrive on the twenty-fourth to spend three weeks. They enjoyed getting out of the cold weather up north and had not seen Scott since his birth. Tom and Ella Girard were easy to entertain and got along extremely well with Nancy. They were also doers and would help Nancy with Scott as well as with things around the house. Nancy could hardly wait for the relief this visit offered.

Nancy's mom, on the other hand, would not arrive until after the first of January. She had planned a trip to a friend's home before arriving in Miami. Marty Champion was widowed and just recently decided to live her life to the fullest. She had a heart as big as all outdoors, but was much different than Bob's parents in that she wanted things always to be a certain way. There was not much flexibility in her actions or schedule and usually after a few days things got quite testy between her and Nancy. If hope springs eternal, the hope was she would be tired from her previous visit and Bob's parents would serve as buffers. Aside from all the potential problems, Nancy and Bob were grateful they could still enjoy their families while everyone could enjoy and appreciate Scott.

Taking Nancy and Scott from store to store during the festive holiday was such a treat, although the stores were too crowded to really enjoy shopping. Just watching Scott take in all the sights was satisfaction enough, regardless of the presents. Scott wasn't quite sure whether he liked sitting on the lap of the man with the white beard and red suit, but if pictures were worth a thousand words then Nancy and Bob had a best seller.

They had gotten in line at Macy's Department Store more than an hour early just to have Scott meet Santa. It seemed like there were a thousand other kids and their parents with the same idea. Scott was mesmerized with the lights, the Christmas decorations and the other children. His head looked like it was on a revolving neck. Much to Bob and Nancy's surprise, many of the children cried or tried to get away from the jovial man with the big tummy. How Scott would react was anyone's guess.

"We're next," explained Bob. "I just hope Scott doesn't go off on this guy. He's liable to grab his beard."

"Give your son some credit," Nancy responded. "He's so wide-eyed and scared he probably won't know what to do."

"Well, here goes," Bob muttered as he set Scott on Santa's knee. Scott looked over his shoulder for his mom and dad but settled in once Santa began to talk.

"Ho! Ho! Ho, little boy!" Santa exclaimed. "And what do you want for Christmas?"

Scott was not old enough to speak in sentences so he just stared at the jolly man with the white beard. As Bob took pictures Scott was oblivious to his surroundings. He was still trying to figure out what was happening.

"Santa, he doesn't talk much but he's excited about Christmas," Nancy added. "This is all new to him."

"He's really well behaved," replied Santa, making Nancy and Bob throw out their chests with pride. "Many of the children start crying and try to get loose. He seems very well adjusted and content to just sit here and look."

"Hopefully, that's a good sign," Bob interjected.

"Usually it is," Santa said. "It usually indicates love on the parents' part and self-esteem on the part of the child. They go hand in hand. You can be proud of your son."

About that time Scott became restless and wanted his mom. Santa gave the young boy a bag of candy and wished the entire family a happy holiday. The Girards continued shopping while thinking of the many blessings they had as a family.

Tom and Ella Girard arrived safely and, as has been a tradition since Bob was a little boy, the entire family went to dinner and then to church on Christmas Eve. Although it was late, Scott slept on his mother's shoulder and did not make a sound. Lighting the candles at the end of the service took on special meaning this year and once again Bob could not help but think how fortunate he was. This became quite evident when he began purchasing presents for his wife and son. It was just two years ago the Girards had struggled with their Christmas expenses, and now the extra money meant they could enjoy Christmas and their new son the way Bob had always planned.

Christmas Day was a blast. Scott couldn't tear open his packages fast enough and both Nancy and Bob seemed to have more fun with Scott's gifts than he did. Nancy was shocked by her new emerald ring, as was Bob with his new watch. In the euphoria of the moment neither bothered to question where the money came from. Bob's parents couldn't have been any better. Tom Girard dressed up like Santa Claus and entertained the neighborhood children while Bob's mom baked cookies for the adults. Ella's cooking was unsurpassed and yet she was able to help without making Nancy feel threatened. Bob's only regret was there was no snow. Growing up in the Midwest, a white Christmas was always one of the highlights of the season. It would have been great to take Scott for a sleigh ride or build a snowman, but with love and hope in the air it was impossible to be disappointed.

Over the next few days Bob was able to get through the University of Louisville at University of Kentucky game, with the Wildcats once again prevailing. It felt good to work a big game without having any distractions, more specifically point-shaving concerns. Mario had advised Bob there would be no mob involvement with that game. The betting was even and very heavy and the game was rated a toss-up, thus too much scrutiny, too little control of the outcome and a chance to lose too much money.

Competition between these two schools was a happening. Two superbly coached teams with limitless basketball traditions and both determined to be the king of the Commonwealth. Over the last couple of years Dick Galino's Wildcats had gotten the best of the battle. The Louisville Cardinal fans would fuss about their coach during the season, but come tournament time be supportive as Benny Doggett once again took his team to the Super Sixteen and often times the Four Final. It was the entire atmosphere of packed arenas, mascots, pep-bands, national television, national rankings and the fast paced style of play that made this rivalry so enjoyable from a fan an official's point of view. It just didn't get much better in sports.

At the same time, Chad was also doing well as Duke rushed to a nine and zero record, including a recent impressive win over a good University of New Mexico team. He had continued to improve and was leading the team in scoring and assists. Bob had the opportunity to watch him play a couple of times on television and the way he handled himself and ran the team was a source of great pride. All those years of camp and tireless practice were beginning to pay off and there was no one more deserving. Bob was relieved he had limited the number of Duke games on his schedule. After all, watching was a lot less stressful.

For the second year in a row Chad would not have the opportunity to get home for Christmas, but his mother made plans to see him play during the holidays in their last game before the conference opener. This game was scheduled for December twenty-eighth in Durham and would give Betty and Chad a chance to visit and celebrate a late Christmas together. Betty was thrilled and Bob helped make the hotel and flight arrangements. This would be her first game at Duke, although she had driven to Tallahassee, Florida to see Chad play his freshman year against Florida State. Chad was excited and could hardly wait until his mother would be with him. As independent as he was, he continued to realize just how supportive and important his mother had been throughout his life, especially those early years when his father was not around. Christmas was never the same without mom.

Betty's trip and visit went smoothly and she and Chad spent quality time together between practices and the game. Although not the wealthiest family, they thoroughly enjoyed shopping and purchasing each other small but meaningful gifts. Betty also visited the Pankowski's and appreciated their attention and interest in her son.

The game itself had been a blowout over an overmatched Harvard team of the Ivy League. Betty would for the first time get to appreciate the atmosphere of Cameron Indoor Stadium. Chad got to play more than usual in a game of this type because Coach P knew how special Betty's being there was to him. Chad did not disappoint his mother. He was the leading scorer in the game and also the best-behaved player on the court. Betty was to find out Chad had been elected captain of the team, which as only a sophomore was literally unheard of at Duke, and had also made the Dean's list. As proud as she was of Chad as a player, Betty was even more proud of him as a person.

What few realized at this time was how well Chad was playing and the interest beginning to develop amongst the NBA coaches and scouts concerning his abilities. At 6'3" and 190 pounds, Chad had a pro guard's body type, and his decision-making and ability to lead were exceptional traits for one so young. How he played the remainder of the year would determine his options and next possible course of action. With the number of scouts in attendance at Duke's games, Chad had become more aware of the NBA's interest.

Although it was Christmas break, Betty was astounded at the crowd excitement and for the first time could genuinely appreciate why the Duke fans were called the "Cameron Crazies." What an atmosphere for college basketball and what a wonderful opportunity for Betty to see her son. They would have a wonderful time during her visit.

As much as Betty hated to leave Durham and her son, she was excited that Chad was so happy and could appreciate his affection for Duke. Everyone from the University Chancellor to the basketball trainer made a favorable impression. More so than any time in the past her thanks for all Bob and Nancy's help in this decision was greatly appreciated. She returned to Miami feeling happy and pleased Chad was in such a great situation.

It was during her visit that Betty informed Chad she was dating someone but led her son to believe it was nothing serious at this point. Chad could not wait to talk with Bob and Nancy to find out more about this relationship. The Girards knew very little about the man but everything Betty told them seemed to be very positive. His name was Jim and he worked as a FBI agent in the Miami office. Betty was anxious for Jim and the Girards to get together, but this was a busy time of the year with games, the holidays and Betty's trip to Durham. Dinner and drinks would have to wait until after the first of the year.

Chapter Twenty Five

With their parents in town, Nancy and Bob decided to jump on a three-day cruise from Miami to the Bahamas. Carnival Cruise Lines had specials this time of year, and with the grandparents to care for Scott this would be a good time to get away and have some long over- due time to themselves. They would leave on the twenty-eighth and return on the thirty-first, in time for New Year's Eve. The trip should be another positive experience in a wonderful holiday season.

The cruise proved invaluable. Nancy was able to get away from Scott for her first extended time since he was born and loved just lounging around the boat and reading. Bob wanted to relax but also took advantage of the computer classes offered on the cruise. He continued to develop a financial plan and was able to read up on the latest business news.

Island hopping, quiet dinners, unlimited drinking, gambling, late shows, watching the stars from the ship's deck and primitive lovemaking proved very therapeutic for both. Emotions ran high as they stayed much to themselves throughout the trip. Both Nancy and Bob worked at devoting this time to making each other happy. There was no arguing or bickering, only caring and affection for each other. Although three days was much to short, both were glad to get back home. Not having Scott around was a big part of their homesickness.

Prior to the cruise, Bob and Nancy had been invited to a New Year's Eve party sponsored by Bob's company. It proved to be quite an event. Three circus-sized tents were erected behind the company's headquarters. One tent featured several bars, another housed the food and the third was set up for the entertainment. Bob had never seen so much booze or so many people working at getting drunk. The food was sensational featuring crab claws, lobster, pasta, roast beef and barbecued chicken. The desserts looked like they were right out of a bakery advertisement and the Amaretto, Bailey's Irish Whiskey and Cuban coffee added a nice touch. But the real kicker was the entertainment featuring The High Street Five, a fifties and sixties group, as well as a disc jockey that filled in on the band's breaks. Bob had never been to a party with so many people, many of whom he didn't recognize. The really neat part was each employee was allowed to bring another couple so Bob and Nancy elected to take his parents. Even at their age they could still dance up a storm and both had a great time.

Early in the evening Bob recognized a familiar face. Mario was in attendance with a lovely lady by his side and Bob wasn't sure whether it was his wife, daughter or just a friend. Bob realized for the first time how little he knew about Mario. Although their eyes met, Mario gave no indication he knew Bob. Bob interpreted the look as a warning to avoid each other, which is precisely what he did. Yet he couldn't help but wonder why Mario would be at this party, although it should have been very apparent he and the Mafia were heavily involved in the company. How else could one explain Bob's good fortune in landing his job, his promotions and subsequent pay raises.

The evening culminated with a fireworks display that would shame most Fourth of July celebrations. Before anyone realized, it was two o'clock in the morning and time for everyone to go home. Fortunately, Bob and Nancy lived close to the office and mom and dad were sober enough to drive.

The next morning came entirely too soon. One thing about Scott, he didn't know or care how anyone else felt the day after or how late each stayed out the night before. He just wanted to be fed and played with. So at eight in the morning the day began ready or not.

"Honey, I hear Scott," Bob mumbled, "don't you think you should feed him?"

"It's not my turn," Nancy responded as she rolled over.

"Come on, you're not going to pull that crap on me."

"What crap? We both got to bed at the same time and it's your turn."

Rather than try to pull a power play by saying it was his company party Nancy had been invited to, Bob decided to bite the bullet and get up. After all, one of his New Year's resolutions was to be more caring and helpful with both Nancy and Scott. He realized what he said was a lame argument and knew it wouldn't do him any good to look for help from his parents since they were tired and sound asleep. Bob was on his own and only two aspirin and calming Scott could help him survive this crisis.

"Up you go little guy," Bob whispered in Scott's ear as he lifted him from the bed. "Let's get you cleaned up and some breakfast before you wake everyone." What a way to start the morning, cleaning a diaper, nursing a headache and making breakfast while your wife stayed in bed. How come he didn't remember any of this in the wedding vows?

"Oh no," Bob exclaimed as Scott hit him with a stream of urine during the diaper change, "I can't believe you just did that! You keep this up and it's going to be a long day, buddy."

While fixing breakfast, Bob remembered he and Nancy invited Betty Payne and her new boyfriend to join them for the traditional New Year's Day pork and sauerkraut dinner. As everyone sat around and watched the afternoon football bowl parades, Bob took a brief nap and was actually feeling pretty good by evening.

At about seven o'clock Betty and Jim arrived, thoughtfully bringing a nice bottle of white wine. Bob was impressed with Jim's young, athletic good looks and derived very quickly Jim was very much in love with Betty. The Girards discovered Jim was a former football player at the University of Alabama and had grown up in Montgomery. After graduating from Preps High School, he had been recruited by and selected Alabama because of its legendary Coach Paul Allen. Back in the sixties and seventies Allen and the Crimson Tide had run roughshod over the Southeastern Conference and most of the good Alabama players went on to play in Tuscaloosa. That Alabama had a law school was an added bonus since Jim knew he wanted to be a lawyer, following in his father's footsteps. Everything had gone pretty much as planned with the Crimson Tide winning the Southeastern Championship three of the years Jim played. Then it was on to UA law school where he graduated number three in his law class. Jim had then joined his father's law practice in Montgomery, married his college sweetheart and seemed to have a promising future.

His good fortune took an unexpected and tragic turn when Jim's wife, father and mother were killed in a senseless automobile accident on the way to Tuscaloosa to see a football game. Jim had gone ahead the day before to take part in an alumni reunion party, and found out the bad news an hour before the game was to begin. Having talked with his wife just the night before, Jim came to realize how precious and yet how fragile life was. Things were even worse when he found out the kids who caused the accident were high on drugs.

Overcome with grief, Jim made a career decision to leave Montgomery and all the haunting memories. It took him almost a year to wrap up his business, advise his clients of his intentions and clear his legal docket before he could make the move. During that time he was able to soul search and think about the direction he would like to take with his life. Part of his decision would be influenced by the soft sentence administrated the kids who were responsible for his family's deaths. Jim was bothered further by the accessibility and ease with which people, especially teenagers, could procure illegal drugs while the dealers seemed to operate above the law.

He decided to leave the courtroom and get in the trenches with these scumbags. As a result, he used his law background to join the FBI. After a number of years as a distinguished field agent in Denver, Colorado, he was promoted to Assistant Supervisor in Charge of FBI for South Florida. Jim had no problem moving to the nice weather and sandy beaches of Dade County and the city of Miami.

It was a number of years before he began dating and only recently had he met Betty through a friend. They seemed to hit it off well and Jim asked her out for dinner and a movie. This all happened at the end of the summer after Chad returned to college and Jim and Chad had yet to meet. Neither Jim nor Betty thought it would be appropriate for him to accompany her on the Christmas trip to Durham. The relationship was not far enough along and the holidays were a time for Chad and his mother to have together.

Bob and Nancy had to admit they liked Jim and at first glance thought he would be good for Betty. Only time would tell how Chad would feel. Fortunately for Jim, Betty warned him the Girards were like family and to expect the third degree. But being a first meeting, and with the grandparents still in town, this was not a good time to probe into Jim's past.

After drinks and small talk, everyone sat down for dinner. The attention now turned toward Betty's trip to Durham. She could not thank Bob enough for helping make the arrangements. The flights proved uneventful and the hotel accommodations were excellent and conveniently located to the campus and where Chad lived. What little transportation they needed for shopping or eating, Chad was able to borrow a car from one of his teammates. Betty couldn't get over the beauty of the school, especially the chapel. The weather had been cold but not as bad as usual. The biggest problem was Betty didn't own winter clothes and had to borrow some things from Nancy for the trip. Also, Coach Pankowski's wife had been very generous and helpful with clothes during her stay.

After dinner, the conclusion of the Orange Bowl game and a nightcap, Betty and Jim left and Bob and Nancy had a chance for the first time in over a week to sit back and regroup. Sure the cruise had been relaxing, but with Christmas, the parents, getting ready for their short excursion to the Bahamas and the company party they were both exhausted. Right on cue the grandparents agreed to bathe and put Scott to bed. Cleaning the table and washing the dishes would have to wait. Bob and Nancy could not get to bed fast enough and to think this was just the beginning of a New Year.

The next day Bob was back at his job and in a couple of days the SEC league games would begin. There was little for Bob to do at the office since the last week before Christmas was designed to prepare for the company party as well as the usual small office celebrations. The company had closed down its operation between Christmas and New Year's Day and most of the employees were in no mood or condition to return to work that first day back. Outside of the start of the corporate basketball season, Bob was in a period of the year where things were slow. Most of what he did this time of year was organize activities for the spring season and prepare his budget for the fiscal year.

On the other hand, Nancy was following through on her intent to increase her work hours. Not only did she feel this would be a way to make extra money, but also a chance to eliminate some of the boredom as a result of staying home with Scott. She wasn't going to do anything until after Bob's parents left, but their being able to watch Scott would enable her to interview some other health clubs. As good as the people on South Beach had been, she wanted to find something much closer to home. Also, in two more days her mother would be arriving. Things would get interesting then.

With the arrival of Nancy's mother, the atmosphere in the house changed. Nancy's father died while she was in high school and she lived with her mother until she went off to college. Nancy always elected to stay at college during the summers, thus contact with her mother was very limited and usually confined to the Christmas holidays.

As an only child Nancy was spoiled, but had worked hard throughout her life. She was very independent and this caused her to clash with her mother whose personality was similar. Bob tried to stay out of the middle of things and would only once in awhile make the mistake of acting as a mediator. Bob's parents got along nicely with Nancy's mother, as older people often do, and this acted as a buffer for everyone.

Scott also played a big part since Marty Champion loved her grandson and was careful not to do anything to jeopardize that relationship. When push came to shove, Nancy had the trump card and both of them knew it. Things went amazingly well during the visit because Nancy was gone quite a bit interviewing and Bob was either in the office or officiating games. Bob liked Marty but felt Nancy's mother thought her daughter could and should have married better. After all, her husband had been a very successful doctor and Nancy and her mother had lived quite nicely. Yet everyone could see Nancy was extremely happy and what more could a mother want for her child than happiness, security and a safe environment. Scott was merely icing on the cake. One could sense Nancy's mother was just waiting to say "I told you so," but for the present Bob was someone she would have to tolerate.

Chapter Twenty Six

At the beginning of January, Bob got back in the swing of things. With conference games beginning, teams seemed to step up their play a notch. There was now a conference championship, conference tournament seeding and post season tournaments for which to play. The Big East and SEC were once again very strong. Bob was fortunate to work in leagues where there were good teams, great fan interest and national implications surrounding almost every game. Just like the players, the officials wanted to be involved in meaningful contests.

An example was Miami University games. Since they did not have an on-campus arena, the Hurricanes were forced to play downtown. This was the home of the NBA Miami Heat and the location made it inconvenient for the college students. College basketball had not really caught on in Miami and with a lack of student support the games were often uneventful and lacked enthusiasm. There was talk of a new campus arena but that had been the case for years with no results. There was also no guarantee the new arena would solve the problem. South Florida had a professional sports mentality with the football Dolphins, basketball Heat, baseball Marlins and the hockey Panthers. These sports coupled with dog racing, hi-lai and the beach pushed college basketball to the back burner.

Although the Hurricane games lacked a certain amount of fan interest, they were easy for Bob since he could be at the arena in less than thirty minutes and back home before eleven o'clock. He never had to skip work and the pay per game was the same as for any other games. Bob was also not asked to control the points in any of these games. Whether it was because Miami University not involved in many national games, the betting was slow or it was too close to home, Bob did not know. Actually, it was probably a combination of all three.

Ironically, Bob's first involvement of the conference season was the Notre Dame Fighting Irish in Miami, although he was not assigned to work the game. Gary Branson, with whom Bob had not talked since last season, called to see if Bob could pick him up at the airport the day before the game. Bob said he would be more than happy to do so and saw this as an opportunity to visit with Gary concerning the point-shaving operation. He found it strange that Mario would not be escorting Gary during his trip to Miami. Could they be up to something?

After Gary checked into the Airport Marriott, they decided to have dinner at the hotel at which time the conversation quickly turned to Mario and the betting. Both men were somewhat hesitant about their involvement in the operation but once they began probing each other the conversation opened up. Gary indicated he had not been used much in the non-conference season but tomorrow's game was on the board. Over the past two years he had supplemented his salary nicely with the extra money from working with Mario and the mob. He was curious as too how much involvement Bob had in the operation and Bob assured him it was minimal. What Gary didn't know wouldn't hurt.

Bob knew the Mafia took precautions to keep the various participants isolated and uninformed about each other's activities. This eliminated leaks, jealousy and knowledge of who else was involved. Both men spoke enthusiastically about the program, but Bob wondered if maybe this wasn't a cover-up for their real concerns. How far would the mob go with this plan, how much more of a commitment was expected from the participants and when and how would this scheme come to an end? These were some of the concerns and questions both men shared. But not knowing whom to trust, these were not things they could openly talk to each other about. What would Mario think if he found out two of his guys were discussing the operation, let alone if one of his guys was having second thoughts about his involvement? Bob left shortly before midnight and told Gary he would pick him up for the game the next afternoon.

Both Notre Dame and Miami had done well in the non-conference season and this was to be a breakthrough year for the Hurricanes. The Irish arrived in town sporting a seven and zero record and a number nine national ranking, while Miami had an impressive six and one record, although their schedule had not been nearly as challenging. Coming off a reasonably successful season the previous year, the administration at the Coral Gables school had hoped for renewed interest in the basketball program. This game should give an early indication if their wishes were to be realized.

This would be a big early test for both teams and go a long way in determining the outcome of the Big East Conference race. The game was hotly contested throughout with the Hurricanes forcing a turnover with less than ten seconds remaining to get a chance to tie the game in regulation and send it into overtime. As they set up for the last shot, the Notre Dame players did a great job defensively and with three seconds on the clock the Miami guard found himself taking a desperation shot off the dribble, lunging toward the basket somewhat out of control. As the off-balance shot went up there was a late whistle and the trail official, Gary Branson, signaled a foul on the Miami player for charging. The ball rimmed in and out but the points would have been disallowed anyway because of the player-possession charging call. At this point Len Washington, the Miami coach, went wild on the sideline with a resulting technical foul. With the two free throws and ball possession, the game was now over for all practical purposes. Notre Dame inbounded the ball and time expired.

With the circumstances surrounding the score and time, Bob was a little surprised at the charging call and shocked by the technical. Usually in that kind of a situation the official would disregard what appeared to be minimal if any contact and allow the players to decide whether the game was won in regulation or went to overtime. The officials' post-game meeting seemed normal, but Bob had already guessed why Gary had made such a call.

On the way out of the arena, Bob thought he saw Mario talking with a couple of people courtside. He was shocked to see the lady Mario was visiting with go over to meet Gary when he came out of the locker room. Were Bob's eyes playing tricks on him? When Bob left Gary last night it was late and Gary was alone. Who was the lady and what did this mean?

Bob didn't have to wait long to find out. In taking Gary back to the hotel, he could not help but satisfy his curiosity. Why the call and who was his lady friend? Gary explained Notre Dame was favored by one point in a game considered a tossup and the mob's money was on Notre Dame to cover the spread. When he saw that last shot heading toward the basket, all he could think about was a possible Notre Dame loss. He knew there was minimal contact to merit a call but he wasn't about to take any chances the ball would go in. Even if he had called the foul after the ball left the Miami player's hand, the Notre Dame shooter would still have had to make both free throws to ensure the bet if the original shot had tied the game. Gary explained he could not take a chance the Irish player would miss both free throws resulting in overtime, or make only one free throw resulting in a one point win for Notre Dame. Failing to deliver on the bet was not good for business and Gary did not want to have to face one of Mario's thugs. Bob need only recall his own situation in Salt Lake to understand what Gary was saying.

But what about the lady he saw Mario with after the game. Gary could only smile as he explained she was one of the fringe benefits of working with the Mafia. Gary basically had a gal in every city where he worked games and no one enjoyed more the pleasures of such an arrangement. In fact, she would be joining Gary for dinner later that evening.

Bob dropped Gary at the Marriott and both agreed to stay in touch, although neither truly thought that would happen. The less they knew about each other's activities the better Bob felt as he drove home under a cloud of self-doubt and concern about his activities with the mob. He was also beginning to wonder what else Mario had in store for him in this point-shaving plan. It would not take long to find out.

The next morning at work Bob received a note to call Mario between noon and 12:30 at a designated number. He was also instructed to call from a pay phone outside the company complex. During lunch Bob walked to the nearest gas station and placed the call at 12:15. Mario answered the phone and much to Bob's surprise proceeded to discuss the situation the night before at the game.

Mario went so far as to confirm the Mafia had bet money on Notre Dame and Gary Branson was involved in the operation. As they talked, Bob was relieved to find that Gary had not told Mario of their earlier conversation. Mario had seen Bob at the game and wanted him to do a favor. Bob needed to understand Gary was nothing more that a bit-player in the mob's long range plans. Although Gary had been involved since the conception of the plan, he had not progressed like the Mafia hoped. His officiating was marginal at best and he was not going to be placed in many important games. Bob must always remember the bottom line was getting national games with great fan interest and thus heavy betting.

What Mario wanted Bob to do as an observer and respected official was to contact the Big East Conference office and talk with the supervisor of officials, explaining the last-second call in the previous night's game. Knowing there was always a report to the league office regarding any game where a technical foul was administered, Bob would appear to be merely helping report and resolve the situation as it had occurred. Bob was not to question the integrity of the official but just make mention the charging call was not the best under the circumstances, thus justifying the actions and post-game remarks made by Coach Washington. This not only would show genuine concern on Bob's part as it related to the officiating, but would also illustrate compassion concerning the coaches under difficult circumstances. As an afterthought, this action would help place Bob above reproach and further endure him with the league administrators. His sincerity and honesty would be looked upon as a positive.

After returning to his office, Bob again wondered what he had gotten himself into. The whole thing now seemed to be spiraling out of control. Each time he thought he had things figured out something new was added to the mix. He did not know who else was involved, what games would be selected, where this plan was headed or when it would end. Bob began to realize there might not be an end to his involvement. He even began to wonder if retirement from this operation was an option. He was building a nice nest egg, but he didn't want to officiate or look over his shoulder for the rest of his life.

When faced with a situation that has no concrete answers, it is easy to rationalize you are still in control. After all, Bob had done his job effectively if one should look closely at the results. But he was not at a point where he had enough money and could afford to call it quits. Only time would tell how much longer he could continue this life of crime, and for the first time Bob was beginning to formulate a plan as to how he might bring this activity to an end.

Meanwhile, things were going smoothly at home. Nancy's mother was scheduled to stay only a week, and Bob's parents would stay a little longer but would be in and out as they mapped out a trip to see some of the sights of South Florida. A couple of days in the Florida Keys, a brief trip to Busch Gardens in Tampa and some time learning more about the Everglades were all a part of their plans.

Nancy had pretty much decided to work at Silver's Gym as an aerobic instructor. She could control her hours, preferring to work in the morning, and was able to bring Scott with her since the gym offered daycare. This would enable Nancy to get in a good workout, make some money, catch a break from Scott and get everything done early in the day before Scott became fussy. She would also have afternoons and evenings free for quality family time, shopping and any unexpected events. Scott, on the other hand, continued to adjust well with minimal maintenance. He was far beyond his age in maturity and seemed very content to spend time with himself and his toys. Part of this had to be a result of the stable and calm atmosphere surrounding the Girards' family lifestyle.

The next week was big since Bob not only had a game Saturday afternoon in Gainesville with the University of Florida and the Tennessee Volunteers, but also Scott's baptism. He would be able to catch an early evening flight after the game back to Miami and Nancy had made arrangements to have Scott baptized Sunday morning while each of the grandparents were still in town. The game went without a hitch and Bob was impressed with both teams. If their play gave any indication, the SEC would be very competitive during the season and have several teams in postseason play.

The next day the sun was shining, the church was full and the grandparents stood as witnesses to the baptism of Scott Robert Girard. The ceremony went without a hitch until the minister touched Scott's head with the water, sending him into a screaming fit. If it were not for Nancy, Scott would still be bellowing the roof off the church. After the service everyone, including the minister, went to brunch at the Cheesecake Factory in Dadeland Mall. What a special day as life's good fortune continued to smile down on the Girards. The next morning Bob took Nancy's mother to the airport at about the same time Bob's parents took off for Key West. With the relatives gone, things would be strangely quiet. Little did Bob know this was but a temporary lull in what would prove too be a very exciting and wild year.

Chapter Twenty Seven

The remainder of January and early February proved rather uneventful. Nancy liked her new job, and Scott seemed to enjoy his new friends at the day care center. Bob continued to work two to three games a week, but also found time for his business and family.

He could not help but keep an eye on Chad and the wonderful season he and the Duke Blue Devils were having. The more Bob officiated, the more he heard Chad's name. Being in a high-profile league, Bob had gotten to know many of the NBA scouts from officiating and at times would get to visit with them briefly at the press table before the games. Sometimes the scouts would ask Bob his opinion on a player knowing Bob called a lot of games involving the best players. Much of what they asked pertained to the player's conduct on the court. The scouts could evaluate his abilities, but with the dollars involved they wanted to be sure as to the character and attitude of their investment. It was unusual a player was such a problem Bob would bad-mouth him. Yet it was nice to know there was still a place in the sport's world for good and descent people.

Whenever the ACC was brought up, Chad's name would surface. Bob would basically treat him like any other player but was pleased to hear Chad was one of the top pro prospects at his position. Not a lot was said about him early in the season because he was only a sophomore, and Coach P had a great reputation for keeping his players at Duke for their four years of eligibility. You only had to look at the former Duke pro players to see the closeness and commitment the players had to Coach P and the program. Chad appeared to be no exception. Most of these guys had stayed the course, which was truly remarkable since each one could have been a high draft choice if they had chose to leave school early.

The NBA scouts thought Chad would stay in school, but Bob was not so sure based on discussions with him over the past summer. It was Bob's hope that whatever decision Chad made, it would be one well thought out and not just a knee jerk reaction to the moment or his mother's situation. Chad was mature enough to sort things out for himself but who could ever predict what young people his age would do especially when looking at the lure of the pros and big dollars. Immediate financial security was not easy to turn down.

Speaking about Chad, Bob and Nancy had not visited much lately with Betty although they were led to believe her time was well spoken for. Jim Stanton had been tied up with some big cases involving drug money laundering across state lines but still found time to be with Betty. They both agreed to drive to Tallahassee to watch Duke play Florida State. With the game scheduled for Saturday night, they would get in on Friday and have a chance to spend time with Chad both on Friday night as well as after the game on Saturday since it would be too late for Duke to fly back to Durham.

Betty was apprehensive about approaching Chad concerning Jim but felt it was time to get their relationship out in the open. Bob and Nancy had helped relieve some of Jim and Betty's anxiety over dinner and drinks one night, convincing both that Chad was mature enough to understand his mother would have relationships and did not particularly want to spend the rest of her life by herself. Bob also relayed his previous conversation in which Chad expressed optimism his mother would find someone to be involved with. Chad was away at school and could only expect something like this would and should happen. The important thing was convincing him this was a serious relationship and not some fly-by-night affair. Bob and Nancy were convinced Chad would not only understand but also approve of Jim and welcome the relationship.

During the same get-together, Jim mentioned to Bob he was now working on an organized gambling scheme with possible ties to sports. This came as a surprise since FBI agents seldom discussed business with outsiders, but Jim had developed a sense of trust with Bob. He went on to briefly explain there had been an unusual amount of betting on various sports events and Jim and a small task force were looking into the nature and origination of the bets. With what little Jim would reveal, Bob got the distinct impression this investigation centered on a money-laundering operation. Bob did not attach much significance to what Jim was really talking about since there was no specific mention of college basketball.

The latter part of February Bob was involved in a series of big games in all three of the leagues he worked. First was an ACC match-up between North Carolina and the North Carolina State Wolfpack, a bitter rivalry but one the Tar Heels pretty much controlled since Dean Thomas began coaching at Chapel Hill. The second big game was between the Georgetown Hoyas and the Syracuse Orangemen, two teams nationally ranked and since the formation of the Big East the two dominant programs in the league. Both had played in the final game of the NACA Tournament, with the Hoyas winning the national championship behind the marvelous play of then All-American Pat Feldon, and Syracuse falling in the final game on two different occasions. Both programs had sent large numbers of players to the NBA in recent years. The third game was the University of Tennessee versus Kentucky in Rupp Arena, one of the great venues for basketball. There was no love lost between those folks even if the game was marbles. Bob always enjoyed travelling to Lexington because it gave him a chance to visit Pat Garren's Rib Shack, possibly the best rib restaurant in the Southeast. He also marveled at the beautiful horse farms.

You could always anticipate the unexpected in the Wildcats/Tennessee Vols match-up and this would be no exception. Playing at home and with its recent success, Kentucky was a five-point favorite. Not only were SEC bragging rights on the line, the two coaches had endured a lot of media scrutiny concerning their jobs. That made officiating that much more difficult because every official knew the questionable calls could lead to a loss and key losses led to coaches getting fired. Any official who said he was not aware of those situations was less than honest, but could not allow problems beyond his control to get in the way of working the game. Everyone, especially coaches, acknowledged job security was not a guaranteed part of the profession.

The day before Bob was to leave for Lexington, he received a message from Mario indicating this game would be on the book. Most of the early betting was on Tennessee to beat the point spread, but the Mafia would be placing their money on the Wildcats. Any rivalry of this nature could turn ugly since both teams would not only try to win the game but also try to embarrass the opponent at the same time. That would keep the alumni happy and improve recruiting in the area. Bob knew he had his hands full and could be in for a long day if he did not take control of the game early.

With the start of the game, Bob could sense the pressure the Tennessee coach was feeling by his activity on the sideline. This was a huge game and he was wired from the opening tip. He was normally one of the easiest guys to work for but today he was questioning every call. Bob was a very tolerant official but also had a line drawn in the sand that coaches knew not to cross. After a number of vocal exchanges, Bob, positioned as the trail official, discreetly advised the Vols' coach to coach his team and leave the officiating to the guys in the striped shirts. Bob had a way of saying things to not embarrass the coaches, yet they would know it was time to stop the bantering. The coach got the message and amazingly his demeanor changed as quickly as the change of possession of the basketball. From then on Bob as well as the other two officials had no problems with the Tennessee bench.

The game was reflective of the competitive nature of the players and coaches. In spite of the physical play, the game was well played and very clean, although at times extremely rough. Kentucky was able to escape to the locker room at half with a three-point lead. Neither team had foul problems but both teams were shooting the ball poorly. Tennessee relied on its inside game with a huge and athletic front line, whereas the Wildcats lived on the perimeter with three-point shooting. The Vols dominated the boards, but Kentucky made up for that with solid, full-court pressure, forcing Tennessee into numerous turnovers resulting in easy baskets.

Halftime was normal as the officials went over what happened in the first half as well as what to expect in the second half. All agreed to let the two teams play and not call any touch fouls. The style of play and officiating was well established and now the officials needed to let the players and coaches decide the outcome of the game.

The second half was as exciting as the first as the two teams made adjustments but basically played to their respective strengths. Throughout much of the half the Wildcats continued to go one-on-one and shoot the ball well on the perimeter, while Tennessee continued to force the ball inside and pound the boards for second-chance opportunities.

With less than two minutes to play, Kentucky had a six-point lead and had temporarily gained control of the game. Not only were they able to control the tempo, they had also exposed the Vols lack of quickness defending the perimeter thus forcing Tennessee into foul trouble. On the flip side, the Wildcat players were showing fatigue from pressing and therefore not able to shoot the three-point field goal as effectively as earlier in the half.

The next Tennessee possession would be critical if it was to have any chance to win but also a concern if Bob was able to cover the points. The Vols were not a team that scored a lot of points and at the end of close games became very conservative. If they could score and make the game competitive, they could turn to their zone to eliminate having to foul and thus prevent Kentucky from building an insurmountable lead from the free throw line. Should Tennessee cut the lead to three or four points in the last minute, the game could easily get away from both the Wildcats and Bob.

Just as Bob was mentally going through the various scenarios during this trip down the floor, the Tennessee point-guard drove the ball to the basket and shot a layup, surprising the Kentucky players who were convinced the Vols would be looking for the three-point field goal. With the Vols now down only four points and less than a minute to play, things would really heat up. Part of being a good referee was anticipating what might happen in a game, especially in the last few seconds. Assuming all three officials were on the same page was generally an invitation for failure. Bob, as the referee, conferred with the other two officials during the Tennessee twenty-second timeout and emphasized the time, score and timeout situation for both teams. There would be nothing left to chance in these final seconds.

Kentucky came out of the timeout with a four-point lead, the ball and forty-five seconds left in the game. It was the Wildcats' intention to hold the ball until the thirty-five second shot clock was about to expire before taking a shot, thus virtually eliminating any possibility Tennessee would have enough time to catch up. On the other side, it was a virtual certainty the Vols would immediately trap and even foul if necessary to get the ball back. With less than eight seconds off the game clock, the Tennessee guards were able to force a trap and seemingly strip the Kentucky guard of the ball. But as the ball came loose there was a whistle, Bob indicating a foul on one of the Vols' guards. Much to the delight of the crowd the fouled player made both free throws giving the home team a six-point lead. With full court pressure the Wildcats were able to make Tennessee work the ball down the court, thus utilizing precious seconds. With an off balance shot in the last ten seconds, it appeared the game was over as the Kentucky center rebounded the miss. But suddenly and unexpectedly there was another whistle and a foul called on a Wildcat player away from the ball. Bob almost shit his pants realizing the two free throws could impact the bet. What could that idiot official be thinking? No one made a call like that in the last few seconds of a game that was already decided.

As the Tennessee player went to the free throw line for a one-and-one, Bob never felt more helpless. Would he ever learn? He had promised himself he would never allow a game to get to this point again. Yet here he was standing in the middle of a nightmare, hoping almost against hope this kid would miss his free throw and the game would end. Call a time out and ice this kid Bob thought as he stood helplessly watching. But that wouldn't happen since Coach

Galino just wanted to get the game over and go home with a win. Bob watched as the first free throw hit the front of the rim, bounced off the backboard and fell into the hands of a Kentucky player. Bob could only breathe a sigh of relief as the horn sounded ending the game.

Although the situation seemed beyond his control, Bob knew he could have whistled a lane violation disallowing the basket if the player had made the free throw. Fortunately, he was not forced to make such a call since it would surely look suspicious and possibly compromise an otherwise well-officiated game. Covering the bet by one point was as good as a hundred.

What a great college game, but what a wakeup call for Bob as he realized again what little control he had over these games. He was beginning to think this would be his last year under these conditions and for sure the last season of officiating if he could not extricate himself from the point shaving-scheme. Bob did not feel bad about what he was doing because in every situation both teams had chances to win the games and he had not been forced to determine who won or lost. But at times he felt so helpless in covering the bet. How much longer would it be before he would have to blatantly alter the outcome of a game and possibly impact a coach's job? As a former athlete, he had tremendous compassion and respect for both the coaches and players and how hard they worked.

On the other hand, this turned out to be a big payday. Many people were not aware the Deep South was one of the largest betting areas in the country and the Vols and Wildcats were naturals for big dollars. On Monday Bob received his normal envelope but this time the amount was a staggering $20,000. It was inconceivable to Bob he could make that kind of money when in fact he was being asked only to determine the point-spread and not who won or lost. Mario called to confirm Bob received the money and to congratulate him on a job well done.

Mario also advised they would need to meet soon in regards to Bob's postseason officiating, beginning hopefully with the Big East Tournament. With the season drawing to a close, the teams were posturing for seeding in their respective league tournaments and this was the time of the year when the real fun began. Rated as one of the top officials from the previous year and having the Big East as his number one league, Bob was reasonably assured of working the Big East Tournament, which this year was again being hosted by Madison Square Garden. Assuming he didn't do something crazy, Bob also knew he would in all likelihood work through the finals. But first he had to wrap up the regular season of which he had five more games. Two games in the SEC, two more in the Big East and a single game in the ACC were all that remained before postseason play.

Chapter Twenty Eight

Betty and Jim were scheduled to travel to Tallahassee to see Chad play. Duke was in second place in the ACC and the Florida State game was big for their seeding as well as a chance to win the league. Chad continued to have a banner year and Coach P couldn't say enough good things about him. Betty and Jim flew up Friday after work and stopped by the hotel where the Blue Devils were staying.

The players had just checked in and were scheduled to have a light workout at the arena. Chad confirmed with Coach P that it would be okay for Jim and Betty to watch practice. They followed the team and sat in the stands after saying hello to coach and Chad. This was Chad's first meeting with Jim and it was way too early for either one to formulate an opinion.

After practice Betty and Jim were invited to dinner with the team. The Duke basketball program was truly a family affair and it was nice to see kids dressed nicely, well mannered and interested in being a part of something larger than any one person. Betty and Jim were also able to visit with Coach P's wife since she accompanied the team to most of the games. The evening was an enjoyable one, and as a former athlete Jim was able to communicate and relate well to Chad. Although this was not an appropriate time to discuss the future, Jim made a good impression and everyone seemed relaxed and comfortable with this new relationship.

As the night concluded, Jim and Betty wished Chad the best of luck and told him they would not see him until the game. The team would hold a shoot-around the next morning, but Jim and Betty did not want to distract Chad and decided instead to go shopping and spend time together. They made arrangements to meet after the game since the team would not be able to get out of Tallahassee until Sunday morning. This would enable them not only to see Chad after the game but also enjoy an early breakfast with him before his return to Durham. Now if only Duke would win the game this would be a wonderful weekend for everyone concerned. Chad was also glad Coach P had a chance to meet Jim since next to Bob he was the closest person Chad had as a father figure. Although this was not the time, Chad would be sure to check with coach concerning his impressions of his mother's boyfriend.

Duke won the game and Chad, Betty and Jim were able to enjoy the post-game celebration. It was very evident to Chad that Jim and his mother had developed a special relationship. Chad would be sure to talk with Bob to find out more about this new guy that had entered their lives. On first impressions Chad must admit he was comfortable with Jim's presence. In actuality, he was glad his mother was involved with someone since this would enable her to have someone to be with while he was away at school. Chad never had any intentions of seeing his mother grow old alone, but he also wanted to be sure her future partner was worthy of such a wonderful woman. One bad experience was more than she deserved.

Back on the home front, Nancy continued to work at the gym while Scott grew and learned new tricks. Besides walking and talking, he was very active and curious. Nancy already noticed he was dominant and aggressive with his day care group. This was not of concern since he was also very gentle and loving with these same children. Nancy proved to be every bit the model mother as she not only spent time with Scott but made sure it was quality time. Whenever possible she would read to him and rent educational tapes for him to watch.

Scott loved to watch the programs featuring animals and Nancy was beginning to make noise about owning a dog. Bob and Nancy both grew up with dogs but Bob realized how demanding and time consuming they could be. As both got older, the dog would require more care than their son. In any case, the timing was not right and it was something they would not consider until a later date. Bob's biggest concern was Nancy would say something to the grandparents and the next thing you knew there would be a puppy in the house.

Chapter Twenty Nine

With the completion of the regular season, the league confirmed Bob would be working the Big East Tournament. He would have a game in a preliminary round plus the final. This assured him he would be recommended as an official for the NACA Tournament. As he promised himself last season, he was determined this would be the year he would work the NACA final game. The big thing now was to avoid controversy and be lucky enough to work solid games with other good officials.

His first game in the tournament was West Virginia against St. John's University. This was an interesting match-up with contrasting styles of play. West Virginia relied on three-point shooting, taking care of the ball and zone defense, whereas the Redmen liked to get the ball up and down the floor, punch it inside and guard aggressively in their man-to-man defense. There was very little interest nationally in this game, and both teams were in a situation of having to at least make it to the finals for a chance to be invited to the NACA Tournament. But a win in this game would go a long way in insuring a NIT appearance. The game was close and yet easy to officiate with the Redmen holding off the Mountaineers to win by five points.

This catapulted Bob into the finals with a day in between games to rest. Everyone felt like the final game would pit the Providence Friars against the University of Connecticut, a heated rivalry between schools in bordering states. Both teams had been dominant in their respective divisions and true to expectations the Huskies and Friars made it to the final game. Both teams were assured a birth in the NACA Tournament but this was for bragging rights and a very high seed in post-season play.

The night before the game Bob received a message to call Mario. The number was not familiar to Bob so he assumed Mario was calling from a different location. As instructed, Bob called Mario from a pay phone in the hotel lobby and upon reaching him was informed the next day's game was on the betting line. The odds-makers installed Connecticut as a seven-point favorite, and even with the large spread the big money was on the Huskies. UConn was having a great season much to the surprise of most basketball experts because of their previous year's player losses, but Providence was also strong and had a history of playing the Huskies very tough. Mario instructed Bob the mob's money would be on the Friars to cover the spread. Six became the magic number for Bob to work with.

Because of the styles of play this game could get away from either team. Both teams played up-tempo basketball and relied heavily on defensive pressure and the ability to convert easy baskets in transition. Whichever team took care of the ball, shot it with respectability and controlled the boards would win the game. Bob knew this would be a tough game to call and even more difficult to affect the outcome.

The atmosphere could not have been better. The fans for each school were some of the best and followed and supported their teams unlike most. The crowd would be evenly split between the two schools, and with a national television audience the game would be electric. This is what all officials hoped for and few had a chance to experience. This meant for a restless night for Bob. Could he control the flow of the game and ensure the outcome and do it in such a way it would not negatively impact his opportunity to get to the NACA Tournament?

There were no surprises the next day as the arena filled and the teams warmed up with a high level of intensity. All players and coaches knew there were very few opportunities to play for a championship, especially one of this stature. You could feel the tension in the air, and the coaches although friendly already had on their game faces. For Bob, the one thing that changed the semantics of the game was the presence of the Big East supervisor of officials. Unlike game film or a written report at the end of a game, the supervisor would have a chance to witness first-hand the officiating and the way the game was played. This only added to the already immense pressure the officials would feel under normal circumstances, let alone a game where Bob was being asked to shave points if necessary.

The game started as expected with both teams tight and not shooting the ball particularly well, but both playing with tremendous intensity. It was a game of runs as Providence jumped to an early eight-point lead only to see UConn answer with a twelve to two run of its own. Nothing out of the ordinary happened in the first half and Connecticut went to the locker room with a slim three-point lead. Pete Malone, the Friars coach, had been warned about his conduct by one of the other officials, but both he and Jim Smith of Connecticut had spent most of their time coaching their teams, not trying to officiate and keep score.

With the start of the second half, the Providence point-guard picked up his third foul on a needless reach-in call and was forced to leave the game. It was too early in the half for Coach Malone to leave him in the game and risk a fourth foul. During his absence the Friars did not have a good ball handler in the game and UConn utilized its press to force turnovers and lengthen their lead. With twelve minutes to go in the game, and the Huskies comfortably ahead by eleven points, the Friars' coach could feel the game slipping away. Unfortunately so could Bob. Malone called a timeout and inserted his point-guard back into the game, and in an attempt to protect his players as well as slow and control tempo, he also went to a half-court, trapping, 2-3 zone defense. This coaching adjustment seemed to disrupt UConn's rhythm and Providence closed the gap to five points with six minutes left to play.

Bob realized he was in a dogfight and a game that would test all of his abilities to control the final point spread. He also knew, unlike the Syracuse game at Utah fiasco earlier in the year, this was not one he could afford to let slip away. As much as officials and coaches dislike judgement calls in any sport, this was one time Bob was glad to have some flexibility.

At approximately the five-minute mark, Bob had a loose ball scrum that could have resulted in a foul or a jump ball. As the whistle of one of the other officials sounded in concert with Bob's, both officials moved toward the pack of players indicating different calls. The other official had a jump ball but Bob indicated he had a foul before the jump ball. After a brief conference among the officials, Bob's call stood. Because of the mass of humanity, it was difficult to question the call but it was significant since it was a fourth foul on Connecticut's best perimeter player. Coach Smith's backup at this position was a walk-on player with limited ability. This would prove to be a critical call since the Huskies not only lost possession of the ball as a result of the foul but they also lost the services temporarily of their best three-point shooter and floor leader. One thing about Jim Smith, he may disagree with the call but he always moved on very quickly to the next play. Bob got an ear full but nothing he had not heard before or anything that would merit a technical foul.

Once the ball was put in play everything returned to normal and the game continued to play itself out. Inside the last two and a half minutes the score favored Connecticut by three points, and Coach Smith made the decision to put his shooting-guard back into the game. Once again Bob sensed the problem in this particular game was not the score as much as who was winning. Providence would have to get the ball, and with the Huskies ability to take care of the ball and make free throws the Friars would be forced to foul and the score could get away from them very quickly.

It was at this time Bob got some unexpected help from one of the other officials. On a power move to the basket his partner called a charge on the UConn center, thus negating a sure two points and causing a loss of possession. The call was questionable but not out of the realm of possibility, although you could not convince Coach Smith and the Connecticut faithful of such. With just more than one minute to play, Providence had the ball needing three points to tie and knowing they would still have at least two possessions under normal circumstances to force overtime or win the game. The Friars called a twenty-second timeout and returned to the court thinking they would look for the three, but take anything easy and rely on their defense to get another possession to win the game. UConn wanted to play solid defense, overplay the three- point line and utilize the clock regardless of what Providence tried to do. Both teams had a time out left and both were in the double-bonus free throw situation. That meant any foul other than a player possession foul would automatically be two shots. As many times happens, Connecticut surprised the Friars with a half-court trap, forcing a turnover and a subsequent foul. Making two free throws with just under a minute to play, the Huskies seemed destined to win another Big East championship since the point spread was now five points.

But forty seconds is a long time in basketball, and no sooner had the fans settled back into their seats when the Providence shooting-guard made a NBA range three-point field goal, cutting the lead to two. Now the question for the Friars was whether to play out the shot clock, hoping for a good defensive stand and a chance for a final possession to win the game, or foul quickly and hope UConn would miss its free throws. Using its last timeout, Providence elected to press the Huskies in the backcourt in an attempt to force a turnover or ten second violation and then foul one of Connecticut's poorer free throw shooters if the ball came into the frontcourt. Malone did not think enough time remained to get a good shot if he let the shot clock run down. UConn was successful in getting the ball across the ten second line and the Friars fouled with about thirty seconds to go. The Connecticut player made both free throws giving them a four-point lead. In a rush and with no timeouts left, Providence pushed the ball into the frontcourt only to miss a short jump shot with about ten seconds to play. A UConn player rebounded the ball and was fouled immediately.

Suddenly, with eight seconds to play Connecticut had a chance to increase its lead to six points, and Bob was beginning to have some second thoughts about the point spread. It was doubtful after the free throws a UConn player would foul, but was there enough time for the Friars to have a legitimate chance to score again. As the Connecticut player missed the first free throw, Bob breathed a sigh of relief that was short-lived with the next turn of events. The second free throw rebounded long and the Huskies maintained possession. As the clock wound down and Connecticut apparently content to run out the clock, one of the UConn subs decided he wanted to get into the box score. With two seconds on the clock, this young man launched a deep perimeter shot that hit nothing but the bottom of the net. As the underneath official, Bob felt entirely helpless and could feel his throat drop into his stomach as the ball went through the net for what appeared to be a seven-point victory for the Huskies.

Just as the horn sounded Bob looked to the trail official, only to see him turn up court without signaling a three-point field goal. Had the shooter stepped on the line? Bob was in no position to see but he could only hope what just happened was not too good to be true. As the scoreboard recorded the two-point field goal, Bob and the other officials ran off the court and into the dressing room. For the record, the first thing Bob did when entering the locker room was dry heave. At no time in his life did he feel more ill and yet more relieved.

The officials conducted their normal post-game meeting and were joined quickly by the Big East supervisor of officials. In reviewing the game, everyone was in agreement the game had been well played and officiated although Bob was surprised no one mentioned the last shot. Bob became nauseous replaying the last shot and how close he had been to not covering the Mafia's bet. He could only ascertain the call was correct but was paranoid because of the situation. Although a tie did not lose, the mob was interested in winning and not just breaking even. Once again Bob literally dodged a bullet and he could only put this behind him and enjoy the end result. But was there more to the story?

Upon his arrival home, he found Nancy had taken Scott to the store to pick up some things but had left him a note concerning the game. Whenever the opportunity presented itself, Bob asked Nancy to tape his games so he could later evaluate his performance and clarify any questionable calls he made during the game. With the tape still in the VCR, Bob's curiosity got the best of him and although normally he would view the game in its entirety later that week, he could not wait to see the last minute of the game, more specifically the last shot.

As Bob keyed up the tape, he watched with astonishment as the Connecticut player stepped up for the last shot and was clearly behind the three-point line. In running the shot through slow motion, it was obvious not only were his feet behind the line but the official on the call was clearly looking at those feet. How could anyone make that kind of a mistake? Then it hit him like a ton of bricks. Bob could not rewind the tape fast enough to the two-minute mark of the game. Something stuck in his crawl and he wanted to see if what he thought was correct. Sure enough, the same official had made the critical call at the one minute and fifteen second mark regarding the charge on the UConn postman.

Was this a coincidence or was something going on Bob did not know about? Regardless of the consequences, Bob was going to meet with Mario and ask what was happening. That night Bob reviewed the entire game but could not keep his mind off his suspicions. Was it possible the other official in the game was involved in the point-shaving plan?

Bob checked the answering machine and recovered two messages, one from Mario and the other from a representative of the NACA Tournament Committee. The message from Mario, disguised as just a basketball fan, was nothing more than congratulations on a well- officiated Big East final game. The message from the NACA Committee was to inform him he had been chosen to referee the Midwest Regional of the first round of the tournament.

Meanwhile, the ACC Tournament had concluded the same weekend as the Big East Tournament and the Blue Devils were champions behind the brilliant play of Chad Payne, the tournament's most valuable player. This helped secure a number one seed for Coach P's team in the East Regional. Chad was just short of sensational as the second leading scorer in the tournament, the leading assist man while committing a tournament low of just seven turnovers in three games. What made the tournament victory even sweeter was the title came at the expense of their arch- rival and ACC regular-season champion North Carolina.

There was nothing quite as exciting on Tobacco Road as a match-up between the Blue Devils and the Tar Heels in basketball. This year was no exception as both teams won a championship, and because of the strength of the league both gained a number one seed in the NACA Tournament, with North Carolina going to the Southeast Regional. Many thought the ACC Tournament final was a preliminary look at the national championship game to be held in less than a month.

Once again, Bob could not have been more proud than when Chad accepted the MVP trophy on behalf of his coaches, teammates, Duke University and his mother in Miami, Florida, who he credited for his success. Bob could only wonder how one so young as Chad could act so old and he looked forward to the day his son might be as mature and wise. Fortunately, the Blue Devils would not be in the same regional with Bob so there would be no conflict of interest in his mind. But for the first time, Bob wondered what would happen if they should both make it to the Four Final to be held at the Superdome in New Orleans, Louisiana.

The next day at the office Bob received his normal envelope, but instructed the messenger to have Mario call him. He needed to set up an appointment for that evening at Korbit's sports bar. The payoff was another $20,000, and Mario made contact shortly before noon. They agreed to meet that evening at 8:30. Bob arrived a few minutes early only to find Mario already sitting in one of the booths. As instructed Bob sat at the bar and ordered a beer, waiting for a nod from Mario to join him. He also noticed Mario's bodyguard sitting at the opposite end of the bar. Within five minutes Mario signaled for Bob. As he sat down, Bob could sense Mario wanted to get right to the point.

First, congratulations were once again in order not only for the outcome of the Connecticut/Providence game but also for Bob's selection into the NACA Tournament. Mario then matter-of-factly asked Bob what was on his mind. Bob was not comfortable asking questions but decided he needed to get some answers to some of his concerns. He asked Mario point blank if anyone else had been involved in point-shaving the Big East final game. Mario sheepishly nodded yes, and Bob wanted to know why?

Mario proceeded to explain there were a number of different reasons for the Mafia's action. First, games of that magnitude were often too difficult for one official to control. Too much was at risk for the teams and therefore too many things could go wrong. With the amount of money involved, the mob needed to have a backup plan. Secondly, Bob was now the key guy in this operation and had to be protected. With the limited number of officials involved in the scheme, Bob was the one guy who could consistently get the nationally prominent games resulting in big payoffs. If he had been asked to control the game by himself, he would have had to make too many questionable calls, possibly drawing unwanted attention to his officiating. This would not only endanger Bob but would jeopardize the entire operation. The other official in the game had been involved with Mario in the operation before Bob came aboard, but was only a minor player and not able to consistently get the games the Mafia needed if this was to be a successful operation. He was the sacrificial lamb should something go wrong, which Bob needed to acknowledge almost did. The important thing was to ensure the outcome of the game without endangering Bob's reputation or jeopardizing his ability to move on to the NACA Tournament. Mario felt they had accomplished both goals.

On one hand it was hard for Bob to reconcile what he had gotten himself into, but on the other it was even more difficult to give up the money. That he had become the Mafia's key guy was a form of flattery, but the stress and tension of completing each assignment was nearly unbearable. Upon reflection, how could he justify his involvement and what avenues were available to change any of this? As long as Nancy and Scott were not involved, and he could adequately provide for them, then he would continue to be a good soldier. What Mario had in store for him next, Bob could only guess.

Chapter Thirty

Nancy was once again enjoying her ability to work extended hours, and unlike some mothers found her son to be nothing but a blessing. Granted, her circumstances were different since she had a job that allowed Scott to be with her and a husband who could provide for his family even if she elected not to work. But her life had always been one of activity and she was determined not to allow Scott to alter that. The new job was working out well and she was accomplishing two things, making enough money to help with the family finances and getting back into shape. Sometimes she felt as if the latter was more important and satisfying.

Then one morning something strange happened. Nancy's car had to be serviced and Bob followed her to the shop. She then dropped him off at his office and took his car to work since she went in later and had errands to run during the afternoon.

She was headed to the gym when Scott spit up some milk. She reached into the glove compartment to get a tissue and while shuffling around she came across an envelope with a Homestead bank imprint. Nancy could not understand what an envelope like that would be doing in Bob's car. She also found a bank statement for $20,000. After checking to verify the name on the account was Bob's, she became curious. Why would he have this separate account and where did the money originate? Knowing Bob and the nature of their marriage, she could only guess there was a simple explanation. Yet she wondered why Bob had not mentioned this. They never kept secrets from each other. How and when to approach him about this was the next question, but she then decided to would allow Bob the chance to initiate such a conversation. After all, he had just gotten back from the Big East Tournament and maybe this money thing had slipped his mind. The day was one of mixed emotions for Nancy but she was confident Bob would have a logical explanation for everything.

That evening after they picked up Nancy's car and were finished with dinner, Bob noticed something was bothering his wife. When Scott was in bed, Bob asked Nancy what was troubling her. She handed him the bank envelope she had discovered in his car. While looking at the envelope, Bob went through the range of emotions beginning while questioning where and how she found the statement. Despite being caught off guard, Bob fabricated a story the money was a bonus from corporate profits given to people in administrative positions with his company. The company had a great year and management decided to take a one-time capital gain, sharing the good fortune with the employees. Bob had become the master of his emotions, a trait so important in officiating, and his response to Nancy was very plausible. What Bob was most grateful for was the fact he had invested most of his point-shaving money in mutual funds and kept only his Big East Tournament payoff in the bank account to cover any unforeseen expenses. He knew he could not explain away the whole amount if it was ever detected.

Nancy's next question, why would he have a secret account at a separate bank? Bob scrambled around the answer to this question but soon convinced Nancy he was using this money to save for Scott's college education and wanted it to be a surprise. By having a separate account, they would be less likely to use the money for things they really did not need. It was the old idea of 'out of sight, out of mind.'

Believing Bob had never lied to her in the past and how he felt about their son, Nancy was willing to accept her husband's explanation. There was no reason not to believe the man she dearly loved and had shared her adult life with. Their relationship was beyond the questioning and proving stage. It was built on trust and

Bob knew he had crossed the line. He could only hope Nancy would accept his answer and not ask more probing questions. To Nancy's credit, and the strength of their relationship, that was the case. What a relief to get this behind them, but Bob made a mental note to be more careful in the future. Fortunately, he had made arrangements for his mutual fund statements to be sent to his office and had rented a safe deposit box at the Homestead bank to store those documents.

Chapter Thirty One

Bob's assignment at the Midwest Regional was a Thursday/ Saturday combination and he would have to arrive in Indianapolis no later than Wednesday afternoon. At that time the officials would get together with the NACA Tournament Committee members assigned to their regional and receive their first game assignments as well as review the tournament format. Bob was excited to learn he would be designated the referee for the featured game between eighth-seeded DePaul University of Conference USA and ninth-seeded University of Michigan from the Big 10 Conference.

It was expected to be an extremely competitive game since teams were seeded one through sixteen, with eight and nine being theoretically the closest to each other in ability. Also, because of the seeding and the tradition of the two schools, the game would be one of CBS's (Central Broadcasting System) national television games during primetime. These two teams and coaches gave the announcers plenty to talk about.

Myers Jobe was the DePaul Blue Demons coach, having succeeded his father Rex who was a legend in college basketball circles. Rex, another Hall of Fame coach, had one of the longest tenures in coaching history at one school, and Myers, as an assistant to his father, had been anointed the heir apparent when his father stepped down. At times this had been a tough mantle to carry but Myers had the Demons back in the tournament after a two-year absence. Ron Oars, the Michigan coach, was a unique guy who seemed to have a love/hate relationship with the media but had been extremely successful during his tenure with the Wolverines. Michigan was one of the standard barriers for the Big 10, and its match-up zone defense and controlled offense were legendary. Because of its style of play no one really wanted to play Michigan, but you played the deck you were dealt and DePaul had drawn to a full house so to speak. To Bob's relief, Mario advised he would not be asked to fix any games in the tournament.

The game went well and was easy to officiate. With Michigan controlling the game tempo, the Demons seemed to have a hard time figuring out the match-up zone. Once you missed a few shots and Michigan began to extend their zone pressure, it made for a long night for the opposition. DePaul proved no exception. Michigan gained control of the game at the eight-minute mark of the second half and the Blue Demons never really challenged after that. The Wolverines would move on to the second round and could be a real problem for anyone on a given night.

Although DePaul made the tournament, things had not gone well the last couple of years and with their early exit the media began to speculate about Jobe's future. Bob personally liked the DePaul coach and was terribly disappointed as were most of college's basketball coaches when Myers was fired the day after his team's elimination. People failed to realize only one team could win the last game on the last day of the season. Too many diehard alumni thought their school was the only one giving athletic scholarships and their team should win all the games. If patience is a virtue, sport's fans were not a very virtuous group. Coaching was a tough business and Bob was glad he had chosen another line of work.

Shortly after the game, Bob was advised he would move on to the second-round games on Saturday and the field of thirty-two. He did not know yet who the opponents would be or whom he would be officiating with but should know something by the end of the evening.

One thing nice about Bob's Thursday/Saturday schedule was his games did not conflict with the East Regional's Friday/Sunday schedule. On his day off he could watch Chad play. Number one-seeded Duke would play number sixteen-seeded Alcorn State University. The Blue Devils were obviously one of the pre-tournament favorites, while the Braves were the surprise winners from the Southwestern Athletic Conference. Everyone knew about Coach P, but few people had heard of Dwight Litley, a lifer who had won more games than most coaches had coached in. No number one seed had ever lost to a number sixteen seed since the NACA had adopted the sixty four team format, but on a couple of occasions the lower-seeded teams had made things interesting. On paper this game was a complete mismatch.

The blowout came early as Duke jumped on Alcorn State in the first five minutes. For the Blue Devils it was case of getting the game over without sustaining any injuries. Coach P played his regulars longer than usual to develop a rhythm and familiarize his players with the atmosphere of the tournament, and this easy win also gave them a chance to build some confidence. The last eight minutes were for the substitutes, although because of its depth Duke continued to build on its already insurmountable lead.

Chad picked up where he left off in the ACC Tournament and played another near- flawless game. For the first time the announcers were beginning to talk openly about Chad as an early entry into the NBA draft. Bob had to admit Chad appeared about as ready as one could be to make the move to the next level. He knew it would be a tough decision but something for the kid to think about after the tournament.

Bob learned his Saturday game would pit Michigan against number one-seeded UCLA. Although they lost in their final regular-season game, the Bruins had shared the PAC 10 regular season crown, ranked number three in the polls and were already conceded a number one seed even before the other conference tournaments were complete. One of the problems the NACA selection committee always had was the lateness of the last couple of games on selection Sunday. Barring any major upsets the seeds would not change much with just one game. Since the PAC 10 had no conference tournament, the committee had to determine how UCLA's final game loss to Arizona would impact its seeding. The committee still felt the number one seed was well deserved since Arizona was also a number one seed. But with the Wildcats sharing the PAC 10 title and having beaten the Bruins twice during the regular season, they were allowed to remain in their geographical area and selected the number one seed in the West Region. UCLA was moved to the Midwest for the second time in the past four years.

Steve Platlin and his Bruins had taken advantage of their first-round opponent with a double-digit victory. This also gave Coach Platlin a chance to rest some of his regulars, rest they needed since they had just completed a grueling final week of the season. Bob's game was interesting in that the Big 10 and PAC 10 were the last of the major conferences not to have adopted a postseason tournament. If ticket sales, corporate sponsorships and television revenues were any indication, a tournament for both leagues was just around the corner.

The Michigan game would be a good test for the Bruins, especially in light of their early failures in recent NACA Tournaments. This would be a test of two very physical teams that liked to control tempo, although UCLA relied on its aggressive man-to-man defense while the Wolverines relied heavily on the previously mentioned match-up zone.

Things were now getting real serious for the officials as everyone wanted a chance to move on to the next round. Bob had a good crew and the game was well played, void of any incidences. The Bruins' pressure defense and ability to make the perimeter shot proved too much for Michigan and Steve Platlin's kids would advance to the Super Sixteen next week at the United Center in Chicago. It would be Monday, after the committee had a chance to evaluate all the officials at each regional, before Bob would know if he would advance. Bob felt he had done a good job and would be terribly surprised and disappointed if he did not earn a spot in the next round.

Bob was able to get home early Sunday and found Nancy had invited Betty and Jim to join them to watch Duke's second-round game. Once again, as the favored teams moved through the tournament the competition continued to improve. The Blue Devils had disposed of their opening round opponent with little fanfare and were now pitted against the number nine-seeded University of Texas at El Paso, a small technological school located in west Texas.

The UTEP Miners were coached by the ever-popular Don 'Gorilla' Simpson, who had coached in one of the historic games of all time back in the 60's. His Miners beat the Kentucky Wildcats coached by the legendary Baron Rapp. What made this an important game was the fact El Paso was a predominantly black team challenging the tradition-rich and all white Southeastern Conference champions. The social ramifications were enormous and many people believe to this day that game changed the direction not only of college basketball but college athletics in general. In any case, because of health problems many thought this might be Simpson's last hurrah. If so, what a magnificent ride he had experienced. This year's team was a group of overachievers, and featured a small but quick athletic team that played extremely well together. Duke, and especially Chad, would be sorely tested by UTEP's exceptional guard play and the fans' sentiment for the 'Gorilla.'

Betty and Jim arrived early at the Girards and Nancy had sandwiches and drinks for everyone. This was the first time the Girards had visited with Betty and Jim since their trip to Tallahassee earlier in the year to see Chad play, and it was easy to see their relationship was growing very serious. Jim and Betty apologized for not getting together sooner but Jim's work- load had been hectic to say the least.

After limited small talk Jim told Bob, "I'd forgotten how much fun being on a college campus at an athletic event could be."

"We sure did have a good time," Betty chimed in. "It was especially fun since Duke won and we could spend some upbeat time with Chad."

"So how did it go with you and Chad?" Bob asked Jim.

"You'd have to ask Betty, but I thought we got along great. He sure is a nice young man and I know he thinks the world of you and Nancy."

"Not nearly as much as we think of him," Nancy added.

"So what's next?" Bob asked as he looked at Jim and Betty.

"What do you mean?" Betty blushed.

"C'mon Betty," Nancy said, "you know what Bob means."

"We're just taking it one day at a time," Jim responded as he came to Betty's rescue.

"But I sure do love this gal."

"Well, whatever you decide, you know we want to be included," Nancy added.

"How bout we change the subject," Betty said sheepishly.

Jim then mentioned he watched the Michigan/UCLA game on television and commended Bob on a job well done. He said he would have watched Bob's first game but his work kept him at the office late Thursday as it had most of the past couple of months. Without going into detail he suggested the FBI, in conjunction with the District Attorney's office, was now heavily involved in a suspected gambling ring. Illegal gambling was nothing new to the FBI, but in this case it appeared the mob had infiltrated college basketball or at least that was the rumor on the street. The specifics of the operation were still sketchy.

"You're kidding," Bob responded as he feigned astonishment at such a disclosure.

"I wish I was," Jim responded, "but most people don't realize gambling on sports is one of our biggest problems and one of the hardest to deal with."

"Why is that?" Betty asked.

"Because it's legal in some states and illegal in others, the rules are not consistent across the country and the people involved in illegal gambling are very smart and hard to detect, let alone convict."

"Do you have a direct link with any group so far?" Bob questioned.

"Not really."

"Then how do you know it's really going on?"

In response to Bob's questions, Jim admitted they had not confirmed a direct link with any specific crime family nor did they know the mechanics behind the operation, but their sources were reliable and this was more than casual conversation.

"What happens next?" Bob asked innocently.

"We just keep watching and pursuing leads, hoping to find a leak so we can tie these activities to someone or some group," Jim concluded.

Bob did everything possible to keep from appearing nervous and was never so glad for a game to begin and conversation to end. What could the FBI possibly know and was Jim referring to the point-shaving scheme Bob was currently involved in? It was something Bob would need to check out with Mario at his first opportunity.

The game went much as Bob anticipated with the Blue Devils capitalizing on their superior height and depth. UTEP was quick and tried to push the ball up the floor for early offensive opportunities whenever possible, but without much success. In the final analysis, Chad would be the difference in the game. Not only was he able to score and set up teammates, he was the only Duke player who could consistently handle the Miners' pressure. This was never more evident than when Coach P took Chad out of the game for a breather. The other guards acted paralyzed and the offense became disorganized in his absence. In fact, it became so bad Coach P would take Chad out only before anticipated television timeouts to get him a few extra seconds rest while not losing too much court time.

In the end Duke built a seven-point lead with less than two minutes to play, and it was now a case of Duke continuing to play solid defense, take care of the ball and make free throws to win the game. The Blue Devils were able to accomplish all of the above thanks in great part to Chad. After making two free throws to increase the lead to eight points with less than 20 seconds to play, Coach P took Chad out of the game to a huge cheer from the partisan Duke crowd. What a magical game for a youngster who not too many years ago was a potential juvenile delinquent hanging around Bob's summer camp.

"We're one step closer to New Orleans and the Four Final," Betty said as the final seconds ticked away.

"Chad played awfully well, Betty," Bob responded. "If he and the team keep playing like that, you'll be in New Orleans before you know it."

"Was it my imagination or was that game both well-played and officiated?" Jim asked.

"It seemed to move along so smoothly."

Bob replied, "You're absolutely right. Neither coach can feel bad about how their team played or how the game was called. Duke was just the better team."

"You can be real proud of Chad, Betty," Nancy added. "He not only played well but he conducted himself like a real sportsman."

"With a mother like Betty, what would you expect," Bob added half-jokingly. "After all, fear will do strange things to people."

"Oh, that was cute," Betty interrupted.

"You know I'm just kidding. Any parent would love to have a son like Chad."

"Amen to that," Nancy added.

Aside from Betty, no one could be prouder or more pleased than Bob and Nancy. Jim could sense the special relationship and bond between these people and only hoped he could one day again enjoy and appreciate what family really meant. Bob, on the other hand, could only hope Scott would grow up to be like Chad.

"Well, we need to get going," Jim said as he looked in Betty's direction. "I've got another busy week coming up and I need to do some work before tomorrow."

"Yeah, we do need to get home," Betty responded. "I'm expecting a call from my son later tonight."

"We sure enjoyed having you over and please give Chad our best," Bob added.

"Goodnight and we'll talk soon," Nancy added.

Bob was never so happy or relieved to see people leave. Hopefully Mario could shed some light on what was going on. Tomorrow couldn't come fast enough.

Chapter Thirty Two

The next day two important events took place. First, Bob was notified he would advance to the third-round of the Midwest Regional at the RCA Dome in Indianapolis. Once again, with this being a Thursday/Saturday combination, it would be necessary for him to arrive at the site no later than noon on Wednesday. The second event involved scheduling a meeting with Mario concerning Jim's comments about college betting.

Mario called early Monday as usual and could sense the concern in Bob's voice. Bob told Mario the good news concerning his Midwest Regional assignment, but requested a meeting before he was to leave for the tournament site. Mario suggested Tuesday evening at 8:00 o'clock at a place in Miami Beach called The Pasta Factory. Since Bob was already scheduled to be at one of his company's basketball games, it would be easy for him to swing by on the way home.

As the day of the meeting with Mario wore on, Bob was visibly concerned about Jim Stanton's earlier remarks. Never in his wildest dreams did he think the point-shaving operation could be detected and maybe it wasn't. After all, Mario had assured him the plan was fail-proof. Nancy even noticed her husband's uneasiness, but Bob explained it away as excitement from being selected to continue in the NACA Tournament. Bob's mind was beginning to play tricks on him. How close was the FBI to exposing the operation? Did Jim detect an anxiety on Bob's part the other night when discussing the investigation? Had the FBI been able to identify any of the players, and if so would they be watching Mario? Was this a false alarm and was Jim talking about a completely different operation?

By the time Bob arrived at the restaurant he was a bundle of nerves. As had been the case of late, Bob arrived early only to find Mario already seated at a corner table. Maybe it was his imagination but Bob was convinced Mario was becoming less and less suspicious and careful with their meetings. Mario congratulated Bob on his continued involvement with the NACA Tournament then wasted very little time in asking him what was on his mind. Bob recanted his conversation with Jim Stanton and asked if Mario was aware of any leaks or any FBI involvement in their operation.

"Sure we're aware of the FBI snooping around, but they're always checking on any activity when it comes to gambling."

"So what happens now?" Bob asked, almost relieved to know Mario seemed to be on top of things.

"What do you mean?"

"Well, if the FBI is checking into our operation, what's our next step?"

"Nothing. First off, we don't believe the FBI has identified us. Secondly, we stopped betting since the start of the tournament."

Mario went on to tell Bob there was increased scrutiny around all major sporting events, whether it be the Super Bowl, a college football bowl game, the World Series, the Master's, the NBA playoffs, the NACA basketball tournament, the Kentucky Derby or a myriad of other high profile events. He was adamant there had been no leak and the FBI was on nothing more than a fishing expedition.

"So what you're telling me is there is nothing too worry about."

"What I'm telling you is the mob is not going to risk our entire operation through exposure at the expense of one game or one person."

"How does that affect me?" Bob asked.

"It means not to worry. You're a key guy and we're not going to do anything foolish to expose you. Besides, at this point we've basically shut down for the season."

Mario went on to explain there was only one other official, Gary Branson, who knew Bob's identity and involvement and Gary was in a lot deeper than anyone else from an officials' standpoint. Bob was told to relax, make the best of the remainder of the tournament and not become a private investigator on his own. If he heard anything of substance he should contact Mario as quickly as possible, otherwise enjoy the tournament.

"Oh, by the way, before I leave I want you to have this," Mario said as he slipped Bob an envelope containing $5000.

"What's this for?"

"This is a bonus for the recommendation and doing the groundwork on Bill Duncan."

"You're kidding."

"On the contrary, you did the work so you get the reward. Remember, we don't expect our people to work for free."

Unbeknown to Bob, a representative of the Mafia had contacted Bill Duncan and he was already involved in the point-shaving operation. In fact, his first game had been two weeks earlier in the semifinal game of the Mountain West Conference Tournament and he had performed nicely.

Bob could hardly believe the mob's generosity, but surmised this as a pure and simple business matter and he was being paid for services rendered. Bringing an official like Bill Duncan on board was a major plus for the Mafia. Bob was surprised Mario revealed Bill's involvement but was glad Mario trusted him. He still had mixed emotions about what he had gotten Bill involved in. Oh well, each person had to decide for himself what was best.

Every day there seemed to be more questions and concerns in Bob's mind, but Mario always had a way of rationalizing what was going on and putting Bob at ease. The one saving grace was Bob was finished for the year or so he thought with the point-shaving plan. He would have the spring and summer to decide what the future would hold, little could he know the best and worst were yet to come.

Bob made arrangements to get to Indianapolis and arrived late morning on Wednesday. After checking into the Sheraton Downtowner, he had lunch and then met with the NACA tournament committee and other officials. He would be doing the Thursday game between the number two-seeded Louisville Cardinals and the number three-seeded Iowa State Cyclones. Bob was not surprised he wasn't calling the UCLA game since the committee liked to give officials, coaches and the teams different looks from different people. The second and third-seeded teams were usually very competitive and this would prove to be no exception. At this point in the tournament, and much to the surprise of the fans, the games became much easier to officiate because only the best teams with the best players were left. Like anything else, the higher the quality of the product the better the results. This game went on the board as a tossup much to no one's surprise.

As Bob witnessed in an earlier game during the year, Benny Doggett had one of his better teams. The Cardinals had excellent perimeter play and relied greatly on defensive pressure. Doggett was no stranger to the NACA Tournament and had a brilliant record of making it to the Eight Elite once he advanced to the Super Sixteen.

On the other hand, Tom Lloyd was a bright, up-and-coming coach who had been at Iowa State for only three years. His ability to turn programs around was legendary and the Cyclones were no exception. Lloyd's trademark was his ability to improvise. Just when opposing coaches had studied the videotapes and felt they knew what to expect, he came up with a different defense or something out of the ordinary. It was expected to be a great game, matching one of the real traditionalists against a riverboat gambler. These coaching subplots added color and excitement to the tournament.

The first five minutes of the game was a feeling out process as each team tried to get a handle on the other team's mode of operation. The game went back and forth with neither team gaining more that a five-point advantage, and the teams went to the locker room at halftime with the Cyclones holding a slim, two-point lead. Neither team was in foul trouble, therefore both played with great intensity at a high level of efficiency.

Bob was again the referee and it was the consensus of opinion at half that whichever team could get a solid lead would win. Both teams were too evenly matched for one to make up an eight or nine-point deficit in the last five minutes of the game. The fans and a national television audience were getting their money's worth.

The second half began much like the first ended and at the eight-minute mark of the game Louisville had gained a five-point lead. Equally important, Iowa State's best inside scorer sprained a knee when he came down after blocking a shot and was lost for the remainder of the game. As an official it was tough to see the outcome of a game determined by a bad call and it was just as difficult when something out of everyone's control impacted the end result. With the loss of their center, the direction of the game took a turn for the worse for the Cyclones. Inside the last two minutes, Iowa State was forced to foul and the Cardinals continued to make their free throws. Louisville won the game by eleven points but the final score was not indicative of how competitive the game had been.

Coach Doggett had his team in the Eight Elite, just one game from another Four Final. Who would have thought it? Surely not the Cardinal fans who at midseason were calling for Doggett's head, saying he was too old and out of touch with the players to be effective. As Bob had said so many times, the fans are behind you, win or tie.

The Georgetown Hoyas upset UCLA in the second game, setting up a Midwest Regional final with two legendary coaches, two tradition-rich basketball programs and two of the best conferences in college basketball. A Louisville versus Georgetown game would be a test of two contrasting styles of play.

Bob, as was the case with the other officials, was calling just one game and decided to leave the next day in time to get back to Miami and see Duke on television. His future involvement would now depend on the committee's evaluation and selection after Sunday's games. He felt he had worked a good game and liked his chances to advance to the Four Final. If selected to move on, what a wonderful way to complete the season.

Duke had little trouble in disposing of its opponent in the third round game of the East Regional at the Continental Airlines Arena in East Rutherford, New Jersey. The next game would be much more difficult since the Blue Devils would be matched against the number two- seeded Indiana Hoosiers out of the Big 10.

Rob Day, the coach at Indiana, had an amazing record in the NACA Tournament having won most recently a national championship in 1988 under the strangest of circumstances. That team was not supposed to challenge for the title, but through a series of brilliant coaching decisions and the maturity of a relatively young team made it to the final game. A last-second three-point shot by a substitute clinched the championship against the favored Marquette Warriors. Since then, Day had put together a number of teams considered title contenders but had come up short. Ironically, Duke and Indiana had faced each other only two other times in their long and storied histories, so this game became a big intersectional battle for bragging rights between the ACC and Big 10. Once again everything was in place for a close, competitive game between two college basketball heavyweights.

Bob and Nancy once again invited Betty and Jim over to watch the game. Betty enjoyed the positive reinforcement from the Girards and also enjoyed their acceptance and inclusion of Jim. There was even talk of an impending engagement provided Chad gave his blessing. Betty and Jim were late getting to the Girards' house so there was very little conversation before the game began.

Bob was anxious and apprehensive about the game. That apprehension increased as he watched the introduction of the starting lineups and the officials. He noticed one of the officials working the game was none other than Gary Branson. Bob had a sudden sick feeling in his stomach and could not help but offer an excuse to go to the bathroom. On the way he grabbed the sports section to check the point spread on the game. He became even more concerned when he realized Duke was favored by five points, meaning in all probability the mob money, if the game was fixed, would be on Indiana. Gary would be instructed to keep the game close and in that scenario anything could and usually did happen. Bob wasn't sure if the game was on the take and held on to Mario's guarantee that games in the tournament were not part of the operation. Regardless, there was absolutely nothing he could do, and with Jim in the house he would have to remain calm.

The game progressed normally with neither team gaining much of an upper hand. Chad made a last-second three-point field goal to give the Blue Devils a one-point lead at halftime. Bob did not care if Hoosiers covered the bet as long as Duke won the game. There was no longer ignoring how brutal and unfair this type of arrangement was to the schools, coaches and especially the kids who worked so hard and played the games. As the first half ended, Betty and Nancy retired to the kitchen to fix sandwiches while Jim and Bob discussed the action.

"Tough first half," Jim volunteered.

"I'll say," Bob replied. "I just hope Chad can get more help from his teammates in the second half."

"He's sure playing well."

"Yeah, but the Hoosiers' size is a real problem. Let's hope Duke doesn't wear down from the physical pounding they're taking. By the way, how's your investigation going on the gambling situation?"

"Which one."

"The one you mentioned last time concerning illegal college betting on basketball."

"Oh, we thought we were making progress but things seem to have quieted down. We'll continue to monitor the situation with the Four Final coming up."

"Hopefully you'll nail those bastards," Bob lied. "There's no place in athletics, especially involving college kids, for that kind of activity."

With the start of the second half, Nancy and Betty returned with snacks and everyone focused on the game. Duke gained momentum and stretched its lead to seven points with less than five minutes to play. Then in a quick turn of events, Chad was whistled for his third and fourth fouls within a matter of thirty seconds. The third foul was reasonable as Chad reached in on an Indiana player who had beaten him off the dribble, but the fourth was preposterous, Chad called for a charge the very next trip down the floor. The questionable foul took place at mid-court as Chad reversed dribble to avoid a trap. The defensive player slid in and under and flopped to the floor as Chad made his move up the court.

"That's a terrible call!" Jim shouted.

"You got that right," Bob volunteered, listening to the broadcasters explain how the block/charge call was the most difficult one in basketball. "Get a life guys."

"What happens now?" Betty asked.

"Coach will probably have to take Chad out of the game," Jim answered.

"Not all's lost," Bob replied with little conviction. "Duke still has the lead. They've got to hang in there until Chad returns." Bob did not have to look to know Gary Branson made the call. If Duke lost the game because Chad was on the bench in foul trouble, Bob would see to it Gary Branson never officiated again. He was not sure how but he would commit to making that promise come true.

As anticipated, Coach P took Chad out of the game, electing to save him until the final two minutes. In the next three minutes the Hoosiers closed the lead to three points, and it was now time for Chad to return to the floor and take control of the game down the stretch.

Bob knew from experience Gary did not have much operating room and could easily whistle Duke out of the game rather than risk a last second shot that could cost him the bet. Unfortunately, that appeared to happen as two more borderline calls from him resulted in Indiana gaining a two-point lead and possession of the ball with less than twenty-five seconds left in the game.

After a Blue Devil timeout, both teams resumed play in what would be the most important few seconds in Chad's athletic career to date. Applying a full-court, man-to-man press, Duke forced the entry pass into the corner and immediately double-teamed the ball. As the rover in the press, Chad anticipated the next pass and stepped into the passing lane to make the interception with eighteen seconds left.

Coach P used his last timeout to design a play. All the attention would be on Chad or Duke's postman, both who had played well in this game. The play was designed for Chad to come off a perimeter screen by the shooting-guard, looking for his center in the post or a pass back over the top to the guard who had flared after the screen. As expected, Chad drew a crowd and the pass over the top was wide open. As the game clock wound down, the off-guard shot the ball from three-point range for the win only to see the ball hit the rim and bounce high to the opposite side of the basket. Out of nowhere Duke's postman went up over the defense and tipped the ball into the basket seemingly tying the score as time expired.

"Yes!" Betty and Jim yelled simultaneously as they jumped from their chairs.

"Oh my God! Oh my God!" is all Nancy could say.

"Unbelievable!" Bob screamed. "But wait, somebody blew a whistle."

Sure enough, an official blew his whistle as the ball dropped through the basket. As Bob held his breath, he noticed the foul was not called by Branson but by the middle official. The preliminary indication was a foul on a Hoosier player. As the Duke partisans went crazy, Coach Day challenged whether the tip left the postman's hand before time had expired. After a lengthy delay, at which time the officials reviewed the play on the instant replay monitor, the basket was ruled good and the Duke player went to the free throw line to complete a potential game-winning play. After an Indiana timeout to try and ice the shooter, the Duke player stepped to the foul line and calmly sank the free throw resulting in a dramatic, one-point win and a return trip to the Four Final.

"Can you believe that?" Jim shouted in bewilderment.

"No, I can't!" Nancy exclaimed as she hugged Betty.

"What a way to end a game. I'll bet Coach Day is beside himself," Bob offered. "That's one of those games neither team deserved to lose."

Ironically, it was not too many years ago in this same arena another Duke player had made a miraculous, last-second shot against the Kentucky Wildcats that catapulted the Blue Devils to their first national championship. Would this serve as an omen for another title?

Chad was selected to the East Regional All-Tournament Team, and Betty was already making plans to be in New Orleans. How ironic that she and Bob could both be traveling to New Orleans to see Chad in the Four Final.

"Well Betty, it looks like you're going to get your wish," Bob said.

Betty shouted, "You bet I am! New Orleans here I come!"

"Hopefully, Bob will be joining you," Nancy added.

"Wouldn't that be great," Jim offered. "But what about me?"

"What about you?" Betty asked.

"I was thinking I might need some time off and a trip to New Orleans sounds great."

"You're kidding," Betty replied in amazement.

"My only problem is finding a ticket to the games. After all, they tell me this is the toughest ticket to come by in all of sports."

"Yeah, but you know someone who can help," Bob interjected knowing Chad would receive four tickets to the Four Final. NACA allowed each player on a participating team to get tickets to be used by family and friends.

"What makes you think I want you tagging along in a city like New Orleans," Betty joked. "Not often do I get to let my hair down."

"I always knew you were a golddigger," Jim retorted.

This bantering went on for a few more minutes before everyone began to make plans for the upcoming weekend. Winning sure had a way of making things more enjoyable.

"So, are you really going to take Jim with you or not?" Nancy asked, already knowing the answer.

"I'll see how he treats me this week," Betty joked. "But in answer to your question, I plan to if he really wants to come."

"Sure I do but I don't want to put Chad in an awkward position, especially during such an important time in his life."

"It won't be a problem. In fact, I asked Chad about the possibility of tickets last week if

Duke should make it to the finals and he told me it wouldn't be a problem." Betty went on, "Heaven forbid, but if Bob doesn't make it to the Four Final I'll have two tickets for you guys as well."

"That's really nice but we couldn't do that," Nancy replied.

"Oh yes you can," Betty stated emphatically. "Chad was adamant you come to the Four Final if Duke made it and that's the way it's going to be. Now, I've got to get home for Chad's call. I'll talk with you tomorrow. Meanwhile, thanks for being such great friends."

Chapter Thirty Three

While Betty and Jim were getting ready to travel to New Orleans, the FBI had committed major resources in an attempt to uncover what it felt was a serious illegal betting scam involving college basketball. With the Four Final days away, the pressure increased to bring these suspicions to fruition one way of the other. Jim Stanton was in charge of this case and he and the Miami DA's office were extremely busy.

The bureau had tracked gambling trends for more than a year and there seemed to be a pattern developing with various bookmaking operations in different cities across the nation. The trademark of the operation was the money bet involved selected bookmakers repeatedly betting unusual amounts of money on the same teams. The numbers seemed to speak for themselves when the betting involved big games, but there was no firm link with a specific crime family although some of the activity had been traced to the Miami-based Cuban Mafia

This investigation was a result of an informant within the Miami mob who heard about the scam. As of yet he did not know the exact details, but was led to believe a man named Mario was fronting the operation. How this all tied together Jim did not know, but as special agent assigned to head the operation he was determined to find out. Jim placed a tail on Mario, shadowing his every move and contact.

But just when the FBI thought it was making progress something would get in the way. For example, as a betting pattern developed relating to specific games, a game like Syracuse at Utah would derail the bureau's theory of which games were involved. Was that game just an aberration or an attempt by the mob to throw off any investigation? That was the $64,000 question and Jim as of yet had not found the correct answer. It was doubtful the outcome of that game was a mistake since the mob didn't allow for mistakes and it was also unlikely it would be willing to lose money on a fake bet. Therefore, Jim could only hope the tail on Mario would create a lead in the case.

With the national championship game in less than a week, would the FBI have time to crack the operation and for that matter would the mob be brazen enough to entertain such an event? If nothing developed, it would probably be next year before there would be additional activity, and a delay of that nature would be a setback for Jim and his group.

Early Monday morning Bob received notification he had fulfilled a promise to himself, he would work the Four Final in New Orleans. Surprisingly, Mario sent congratulations shortly thereafter in his weekly note requesting a meeting before Bob left for the tournament. Bob wondered how Mario could know of his selection since nothing had been announced, but was really no longer surprised by anything the Mafia did. Mario suggested they meet Tuesday morning at Wagons East, a breakfast joint on U.S. 1., after the morning rush at 10 o'clock. That would afford them some privacy. Both wanted to get together before Thursday because the officials were due at the Four Final site that day by noon.

The NACA Tournament committee would bring in twelve officials in three groups of four. One member of each crew would be a substitute. The procedure had changed somewhat in the past few years. Before, the officials would arrive at the tournament site, work the semifinal games Saturday and the three highest evaluated officials would move on to the final game. The committee now felt it was in everyone's best interest if a new group of officials did the final game. This eliminated the carryover affect if an official, coach or player had a problem in one of the semifinal games. The officials would get their assignments on Thursday night and prepare accordingly for what would be by far the biggest weekend of their officiating careers. All of the officials were sworn to secrecy once they were selected and security at the sight was extremely tight.

On Tuesday as Bob entered the restaurant, he had a premonition something was in the works although he wasn't sure whether it was good or bad. Mario had secured the back booth and there were only five customers in the restaurant. This place was probably the best breakfast joint in Miami. The assembly line of cooks to put out the food was amazing and there was no skimping on the portions. The waitresses 'took no crap' from the customers and that was part of the restaurant's personality. A couple of the cooks recognized Bob and said hello, but no one seemed to care about what the other guy was doing. Both men ordered a cup of coffee and made small talk until Mario was comfortable Bob had not been followed. The next hour was spent discussing the coming weekend. Mario also explained there had been a change in the mob's plans concerning the NACA Tournament.

"The powers to be decided we should take a chance on the Four Final," Mario stated matter-of-factly.

"But I thought you said there would be no games involved in the operation during the tournament," Bob protested.

"I said we had no plans at the time we talked but that since has changed."

"Why the change, isn't this dangerous?"

"There are actually a couple of reasons for the change. First, the betting on these games is huge and offers an enormous return on our dollars. Second, we don't think there is anything to worry about because no one would ever believe we'd have the balls to bet on these games."

"Doesn't what I told you about Stanton and the FBI concern you?" Bob asked.

"You bet your ass it does, but we feel we can pull this off before they find out who's really involved. Who knows, the tournament may be the last chance for us to make any real money."

"What do you mean by last chance?"

"Must I repeat myself? In case you didn't know, we bet on the Duke/Indiana game last weekend. If you're right about the FBI turning up the heat, then we want to get in a couple of games before possibly having to bail out of this operation, so what better way to go out than with the biggest event of them all."

Bob was getting a sick feeling as he remembered Gary Branson and the Duke/Indiana game. As upset as he was remembering that game, he was wise enough not to show his feelings in front of Mario. After all, Bob, Mario and the Mafia were in this for one reason, to make money. Emotions and guilt feelings were not part of the deal.

"So what happens now?" Bob asked.

"Nothing until I hear from my bosses," Mario replied.

Bob was instructed to contact Mario at a secured number as soon as he arrived in New Orleans and found out his assignment. Mario would then get back to him at a predetermined time with whatever instructions were necessary. What Bob did not know was Mario would actually be in New Orleans for the tournament. He would pick up his messages from the number he gave Bob and then initiate the next contact. By doing it this way, he not only could control what was about to happen but also be in position to keep an eye on the participants. This was to be the big one and Mario's bosses advised him nothing was to go wrong. Mario knew Bob would be staying at the Marriott so he pre-registered under an assumed name at the New Orleans Royal Caribbean, an upscale hotel in the French Quarter. Bob gave Mario his travel plans, then left the restaurant approximately five minutes before Mario phoned his contact in New Orleans to confirm everything was on go.

What Bob and Mario did not notice were the two FBI agents parked in the lot with a high-powered camera taking pictures of the people who entered and left the restaurant. Both agents grumbled about the assignment, chasing Mario around town, especially when they were not privy to what was really going on. Although they were having a hard time making the connection between a guy having a late breakfast and some illegal activity, orders were orders. One thing the agents were schooled to do was to follow directions.

Chad and the team took Monday off as the coaches utilized the time to put together a scouting report on their national semifinal opponent and make the necessary team ticket and travel arrangements. Chad was personally glad for the break since he had been averaging about thirty-seven minutes a game since the start of the ACC Tournament. He was tired and sore from the constant pounding by the opponents. Even with the day off, he still went to the gym to work on his jump shot and free throws. The outcome of games now were often dependent upon one team's ability to make free throws down the stretch and Chad did not want to be the one to cost his team a chance at a national championship. His work ethic was probably Chad's greatest asset and was reflected in his team's respect for him as their unspoken leader, although only a sophomore. It was hard to believe a national championship was now in his grasp.

Good programs were generally a result of having mature leadership and a willingness to set the example. Although young in age, Chad fit the mold well. Yet he could not help but think about what the future might hold since he was not immune to all the talk about him possibly being a lottery pick in the upcoming NBA draft. It would be good to get the season over, but he was also wise and mature enough to enjoy every moment of what might be the most exciting time of his life as it related to sports. This week would be hectic and Chad would have to be the guy to keep his teammates focused on the task at hand.

Besides Duke, with Arizona coming out of the West, Louisville representing the Midwest and Kentucky returning from the Southeast, the field included tradition-rich programs, innovative coaches and plenty of good players. One team would have to play extremely well for two games to take home the title. All had won national championships in the past and were anxious to become king of the college basketball world again.

Back in Miami, Betty and Bob were finalizing arrangements to get to New Orleans. Chad advised Betty he had her ticket and asked if she would need a second one for Jim. Jim was ecstatic he would have a ticket for the games. Chad was pleased Jim would be escorting his mother since this would give her someone to be with

187

so he would not be distracted. He was also pleased their relationship appeared to be growing.

Ironically, Jim had a hidden agenda for making the trip. His boss wanted him to be in New Orleans in case anything broke in the case. If the Mafia was involved in some illegal betting activity, what better place for Jim to be than at the largest and most important college basketball event of the year. Jim had reservations about accompanying Betty under this pretense but felt there was nothing wrong with combining business and pleasure, especially since there was no guarantee anything would develop in the case.

Bob would leave Thursday morning, but Betty and Jim could not get away until Friday evening. Nancy would wait to see what game Bob was involved in before going to New Orleans. She had other obligations with her new job and had to make arrangements for someone to keep Scott. Anyway, the first couple of days Bob would be tied up with the tournament and have very little free time. With Betty and Jim not traveling until late Friday, Nancy did not want to be alone or the odd-woman out once they arrived, especially if Bob was not scheduled to officiate until Monday night. Bob would advise her of his game after Thursday's meeting with the tournament committee. Hopefully, she could get a flight to New Orleans at the last minute.

Bob made sure Betty knew where he could be reached and told her to call if anything came up or she needed help. He did not think that would be necessary since he knew Jim would be escorting Betty and probably knew more about New Orleans than either of them. In any case, Bob was glad to know Betty would get a chance to be with Chad and see him play. He was further comforted by the knowledge Jim would be there for her protection and companionship.

By Thursday, as the FBI continued to follow leads and look at pictures of those people involved with Mario, Jim was feeling frustrated. The wiretaps on Mario's phones revealed nothing and the number of people he came into contact during a day was astounding, most of which could not be linked to known Cuban Mafia types. It required a team of four agents just to identify and screen these people. Jim was busy directing the investigation and therefore was not involved in the "grunt" work. If he had been, he might have noticed the picture of Bob going in and coming out of Wagons East last Tuesday.

"Man, is there anyone this guy doesn't know?" Jim lamented. "Trying to follow up on all the leads is nearly impossible, especially in such a short amount of time."

"Hell, I'm damn near blind from looking at all the pictures," Agent Groves replied.

Agent Mast chimed in, "If we just had a lead or idea of the person we are looking for, it sure would be a lot easier."

"Well, hang in there," Jim said. "You know these mob types, they generally dot their i's and cross their t's but eventually they make a mistake. We'll just have to cross-reference each person with a phone call or some related activity."

The FBI was running out of time and getting no closer to solving the point-shaving scheme than an informant's unsubstantiated opinion Mario was involved and therefore so was the Cuban Mafia. This was compounded by Jim's anticipated departure to New Orleans. Jim could only hope for a break in the case in the next twenty-four hours.

Arriving in New Orleans, Bob checked into the Marriott and prepared himself for what would turn out to be the most important weekend of his life. The other officials had already checked-in, and at three o'clock that afternoon the officials, game personnel and tournament committee representatives met to go over the assignments and tournament format. Bob was told he would be working as the referee in the final game Monday night. He controlled his excitement but couldn't wait to tell Nancy the good news.

What coaches and players did not understand was how hard each official worked to get to this point and how thrilled and excited each one was to be a part of the Four Final. This was the stamp of approval for being the best and a way of saying 'job well done.' Bob's NACA watch, given to all participants in the tournament, was as important and meaningful to him as the watches of the coaches and players. The ultimate compliment and reward was being selected to referee the national championship game and he was having a difficult time containing his emotions.

The game was not unlike the regular season in regards to preparation, but the outside pressure and media coverage was so much greater. The secret to officiating at this point was not to over officiate. Bob once heard a coach say, 'the biggest mistake coaches make in the tournament was they over-coach.' That appeared to be good advice. Don't try to change your approach or technique just because of the emotion and hysteria surrounding the event. Bob was confident he would do a great job and earmarked a couple of hours Sunday to meet with the other officials to review procedures and answer any questions they might have.

Chapter Thirty Four

Sometimes the strangest things happen to break open a case and this case would prove no exception. After leaving the meeting, Bob returned to his room to wait the predetermined time to call Mario. At 6 p.m. on Thursday Bob placed a call to a secured number, and using the appropriate code relayed to the answering machine confirmation of his working the final game. Approximately thirty minutes after Bob's call, Mario retrieved his messages and was thrilled to hear the news. Not only was his man involved in the Four Final, Bob was working the championship game, the biggest prize of them all. Per their original arrangement, Mario then called Bob's room to confirm he had received the message.

"Congratulations on your assignment," Mario started the conversation. "You must be thrilled."

"Beyond your wildest dreams," Bob responded. "To have the national championship game is a dream come true."

"Well, I won't tie you up with small talk. I'll call you between 8:00 and 8:30 p.m. after the Saturday afternoon semifinal games. Be in your room."

"Anything I need to know right now?"

"No, just be by the phone." Mario knew the less said the better, concluded the conversation and hung up. What Bob did not know or anticipate was Mario already being in New Orleans for the tournament.

On the other hand, what Mario did not know was the FBI was monitoring his cellular phone. Mario had been followed from Miami and with help from the local agents his every move was being watched. Advanced technology allowed cellular phones to be tapped and each call was a potential break in the case. Therefore, every call was traced to see the connection. This last call was of particular interest because it went to a hotel housing members of the NACA Tournament Committee, media and other groups directly associated with the games. In tracing the call the local FBI field agent came up with Bob Girard, the name registered to the room where the call was received. Who was this Bob Girard and what was his association with Mario? The answer would be forthcoming and it would change the lives of a number of people forever.

As the New Orleans FBI prepared to fax its list of Mario's contacts to the Miami bureau, it was evident Jim was getting no closer to solving this case. He had names and numbers but no concrete evidence linking anyone, including Mario, with an illegal gambling operation. The name Bob Girard had been circled since it was determined he was from Miami, and the New Orleans Bureau felt it would be easier and save time if the guys in Miami took care of their own background checks. Just before Jim was to leave his office for the evening, the fax came across the line and the receiving agent asked if anyone knew a Bob Girard? Jim nearly leapt from his seat but managed to calmly ask why?

Agent Groves responded, "The guys from New Orleans have linked him to a phone call from our boy Mario."

"What was the nature of the call?" Jim asked.

"They didn't get the particulars because of poor reception but they know the call was made and completed to his room at the Marriott."

"Are they sure of the name?"

"Yes, they confirmed the name and the room through the hotel operator."

"Is there anything else worth noting?"

"No, but they wanted us to check him out since he listed Miami on the hotel registration form when he checked in."

Jim tried to play it straight when he asked, "Does anyone have a connection?"

With no confirmation, Jim asked that all the pictures taken of Mario and his contacts from Monday through Wednesday be placed on his desk for review. Jim bet if anything happened between the two men, it would be from the time Bob found out about his Four Final assignment to the time he left for New Orleans. Jim could not imagine what Bob would have in common with Mario, but he was not about to cast guilt or absolve wrongdoing without checking all possible leads. Then came the link with the discovery of Bob's presence at Wagons East during the same time Mario was there the previous Tuesday. The chance of this meeting being a coincidence was miniscule, and Jim believed for the first time there might be a break in the case.

Although he had mixed emotions concerning Bob's possible involvement in the case, he could not allow his emotions or involvement with the Girards to deter the investigation. He could only hope there was an explanation to all of this and Betty and the Girards would not be impacted. Jim immediately advised New Orleans to monitor Bob Girard, his calls and contacts, while the agents in Miami began to do a background check, all of this while Bob anxiously awaited the most important game of his life.

Meanwhile, Chad and the Blue Devils were putting the final touches on their semifinal game against the Louisville Cardinals. Louisville was a talented team, featuring solid defense that forced opponent's turnovers that resulted in easy baskets. Like the Blue Devils, the Cardinals had won two national championships and had beaten a very good Duke team for one of those championships. It had been a while since Benny Doggett's team played in the Four Final, but you knew they would be well prepared and excited about being in New Orleans.

Both teams would work out at local high schools Friday morning before making a mandatory appearance at the Superdome for the fans and media. Usually those practices were upbeat and fun, featuring a lot of shooting, individual work with players at different positions and a dunking contest. As usual the crowds were large and enthusiastic during the workouts and each team seemed healthy and prepared to play. The serious work had been completed before the teams arrived in New Orleans and now it was just a matter of breaking up the monotony of the day, staying focused and getting plenty of rest. In less that twenty-four hours there would be just two teams left to compete for the national title.

Chad, as Duke's captain and leader, was preoccupied with keeping his teammates focused on the task at hand and not being distracted by all the outside hoopla. They would have dinner at 6:30 p.m., a team meeting two hours later and curfew at midnight. The managers would bring around a snack at 11 o'clock and then it would be time to try to get a good night's sleep. Chad tried to read a book to relax and help him get to sleep but that proved ineffective. He last remembered looking at his clock at 1:15 a.m. before finally dozing off. Breakfast was not until mid-morning so he would still get plenty of rest.

The other game featured two teams with a great history of play in the Four Final. Arizona, under the guidance of likely future Hall of Fame coach Luke Larson, had dominated the PAC 10 since his arrival in Tuscon by winning ten league championships over a sixteen year period, including seven in a row during the late 80's and early 90's. The Wildcats had experienced a turbulent year with the dismissal of their all-league forward at semester as a result of academic problems, but its appearance in the Four Final was testimony to a great coaching job and a bunch of competitive players pulling together.

Kentucky, on the other hand, owned the record for the most wins of any NACA Division I basketball school with most of these victories accomplished under the tutelage of legendary Baron Rapp. The Wildcats had most recently won the national championship in 1994 and had won a total of six in their storied history. Kentucky's Dick Galino had brought a run-and-press style of play to the Bluegrass State, and people from the Commonwealth would accept nothing less than a national championship.

This would truly be a match-up of contrasting styles with a smaller, quicker Kentucky team pressing, running and shooting the three's against the dominant front line and structured Arizona Wildcats. Both teams had placed numerous players in the NBA and the talent on these current teams was no exception.

As tournament preparation continued with the teams and coaches, the information continued to roll in on Bob Girard, although there was still no direct link between he and Mario other than as acquaintances. Bob worked for a suspected mob run company that had ties to Mario but so did many other people not involved in the Mafia. The next step was to draw a link between Bob, Mario and illegal gambling as it related to college basketball. Jim still had hopes Bob would not be directly linked to this case but his experience told him there were too many coincidences for it not to be a reality.

Knowing Bob was an official, Jim ordered a list of games Bob was involved in during the past two years with the results of the games and the point spread. This process would take only a couple of hours since the information requested was easily accessed by the FBI and its division that worked exclusively on gambling in college athletics. Before noon Jim had the information he requested and a pattern was beginning to emerge as to Bob's involvement.

"So what did you find out?" Jim asked.

"It looks like this guy could be our man," responded Agent Groves.

"What do you mean, could be?"

"Most of the games he worked match the unusual amounts of money bet on those games."

"Yeah, so what's the problem?"

"There's one game that doesn't fit the mold."

"What game and what's the problem?"

It was hard to determine the exact games involved in the point-shaving scheme unless you found a constant. In this scenario Bob was the x-factor and the unusual amount of money bet at the last minute by various outside sources on his games created a trail.

"Girard did a game with Syracuse at Utah that goes against the grain. There was an unusual amount of money bet, not as much as some other games, but the betting sources we monitor placed their money on Utah."

"Let me guess," Jim interrupted. "Utah lost the bet."

"Exactly," responded Groves.

"So what are you telling me?"

Agent Groves went on to explain there might be a reasonable explanation since the amount of money bet was not nearly as heavy as other games. Could that game have been a setup to throw anyone investigating off the trail? Jim, as well as the gambling division, thought that was improbable but possible. But how could the Feds tie things together and substantiate the link between Bob, Mario and the Mafia? Without concrete information there was no case and time was running short with the college basketball season about to end.

"Look, it seems like we have some kind of a tie in between these two guys," Jim stated. "But it also appears we need to move in another direction to solidify this link."

"Like what," asked Agent Mast?

"The gambling pattern seems to implicate Girard and the one game may or may not prove to be important. We don't want to get bogged down with one game. Let's explore other possibilities like his employment records, bank accounts and anything else that might show unusual activity or provide a link to Mario and the mob."

It wasn't long before the FBI linked the Mafia directly to the company where Bob was employed. It was determined the company served as a money-laundering operation for the mob. It seemed less than coincidental Bob would begin working there just prior to his involvement with the games the FBI could reasonably determine were part of the point-shaving scheme. But there were still many questions to be answered such as what and how the games were selected, who and how many were involved and how the payoff was handled.

Jim had for all practical purposes confirmed Bob's involvement in the fix but when and where would he be used again? Jim thought it illogical the mob would be involved in the Four Final. After all, the tournament was too high profile an event and viewed by too many people who would question any unusual activity. Yet, what better stage to pull off the ultimate crime, knowing there would be little suspicion anyone would attempt such a blatant and daring act? It was also noted that nothing was beyond the Mafia.

Jim now suspected Bob had alerted the mob to their conversations concerning the investigation into college basketball betting and hoped this would not compromise solving the case. More than ever the problem for Jim was time. Could his staff pull together the pieces of the puzzle in time to prevent what could be the fixing and tainting of one of America's great sporting events? If not, one of the most daring crimes of the decade could go both undetected and unpunished. The window of opportunity to solve this case was rapidly dwindling.

The initial question for Jim became how to approach this problem. Although Betty was indirectly involved because of her relationship with the Girards, could she become a factor in what needed to be done? Could Jim disassociate himself from the emotional involvement with the case considering the cast of characters? Was he willing to risk his relationship with the people he loved or should he excuse himself from the case? Would phone records and home visits link Jim to Bob and how might that impact the final resolution of this case if brought to trial? These were all questions Jim had to resolve in his mind before making a final determination as to the FBI's course of action. Jim was torn by the variables of the case, but in the final analysis it was his case and he needed to professionally see it through.

The big question at that moment was whether the FBI had enough solid evidence to link Bob and Mario with the mob. Should Jim confront Bob with the evidence, and if so would he help or become scared and alert Mario to the investigation? It was agreed arresting Bob on circumstantial evidence was not the answer since this could alert the people at the top, which is who the FBI really wanted. So, how could Jim approach Bob without scaring him off or alerting Mario and his group there was a problem?

Aside from two local FBI agents doing the groundwork, there was only a select group of people handpicked by Jim who knew the identity of the people under investigation. One of the problems in dealing with organized crime was the tentacles the crime bosses had often times reached into law enforcement. The difference in what law officers made in salary compared to what the mob could pay was huge. Much like Bob, people in law enforcement had honorable intentions when they first became involved, but as years passed and their expenses grew they would cave into the temptations of the easy life. The staff Jim brought together to work this crime he had worked with before and knew to be extremely loyal.

Chapter Thirty Five

As information continued to accumulate linking Bob with the point-shaving scheme, Jim became more and more aware of how his trip to New Orleans with Betty had suddenly taken on a whole new personality. By the time he picked Betty up to go to the airport, Jim hoped to have enough evidence and a plan that would enable him to deal with Bob and not bring her into the picture. Still, with their involvement, how could he keep Betty outside the investigation? The trip to the airport was quiet and Betty could sense something was wrong.

"What's bothering you?" Betty asked. "You sure are quiet."

"It's been a hectic week."

"What, my favorite FBI agent is having second-thoughts about taking some time from work?"

"Not really, it's just that I have problems putting things on the backburner. But it's a new project and it can wait until next week," Jim lied.

"Well don't go if you feel guilty. I don't want you ruining my weekend."

"Don't worry, I won't," Jim reassured Betty, hoping she would quit asking questions. "I know how important this trip is to you but it's important for me too."

There was little conversation the rest of the trip. During the flight Betty reviewed the Duke media guide Chad sent her while Jim pretended to read a novel, his mind elsewhere.

Once in New Orleans, Betty and Jim took a cab to the Hyatt where they had reservations. Duke was also staying at the Hyatt and Chad had helped secure the rooms for Jim and his mom. Nothing could be more convenient since the hotel was connected to the Superdome. This location would enable Betty and Jim to see Chad from time to time without traveling all over town. These arrangements were a blessing for Betty since she had not decided until after Chad's last game to make the trip and by then the hotels in New Orleans had been sold out for months. As they arrived at the hotel, Chad and his teammates were just concluding a team meeting and he would have a few minutes to say hi and visit with them.

"Hi mom, hi Jim," Chad said with a gleam in his eye. "How was the trip?"

""Fine," Betty responded. "So, how are you doing?"

"Good, but it's been hectic and this is only the beginning. There are so many people pulling at us, like the media, alumni, our friends and fans. It just seems so overwhelming at times, but I'd rather be dealing with this than sitting home watching the games."

"I'm sure you'll do fine," Jim chimed in.

"Fortunately, Coach P has been through this before and has prepared us for everything. We just have to listen and stay focused," Chad responded as two fans asked him for his autograph. "See what I mean."

Betty could sense the seriousness of the situation and decided not to burden Chad with a lot of small talk. She asked him a couple more questions, expressed her happiness in being here and wished him the best of luck in Saturday's semifinal game. Chad was cordial but it was easy to see his thoughts were elsewhere.

It was time for the players to go up to their rooms. As usual, they would eat a late snack and try to get a good night's rest. Chad's mind was racing and he knew it would be difficult to get to sleep.

At check-in Betty found a message in her box from Bob Girard indicating where he was staying and the number where he could be reached. Before he departed for New Orleans he told Betty he would like to get together with her and Jim if their schedule allowed. Now that he was not working until the Monday game, he suggested they meet for a nightcap if Betty and Jim got in before it was too late.

With Chad already in his room for the night, meeting Bob sounded like a great idea and she suggested they give him a call as soon as they got to their rooms. After getting settled, Betty gave Bob a call and they agreed to meet at the restaurant in Bob's hotel. That way they could talk without being disturbed or have to mingle with the fans that by this time were already beginning to celebrate their journey to the Four Final.

At approximately 11 p.m., Betty and Jim joined Bob in the Marriott restaurant and they talked about the thrill of being a part of such a great sporting event. Jim's updated information now confirmed Bob's involvement in the gambling probe, although the hard evidence was still being assembled. As the three of them talked about Chad and the atmosphere surrounding the NACA Four Final, Jim tried to act upbeat and normal. That was not easy based on his knowledge of Bob's situation. As the evening wore on, everyone decided the next day would be a long and stressful one and they opted to return to their rooms to get a reasonable night's sleep. Jim paid the bill and all three got up to leave.

"I enjoyed visiting with you guys and I hope things go well for you and Chad this weekend," Bob said in a sincere tone.

"I'm sure it will," Betty said emphatically.

"Regardless of what happens, this has been a great year for Chad," Jim added.

"That's an understatement," Bob responded. "Who could have guessed Duke would make it to the Four Final with such a young team?"

"It just goes to show what teamwork and good coaching can do," Jim added.

"I just hope we can win it all," Betty thought out loud.

"When you get to this point anyone can win," Bob replied. "Sometimes it's just the luck of the draw."

"Well, lets hope the Blue Devils draw to a royal flush," Jim laughed.

As they reached the hotel lobby, Jim turned to Bob and asked, "By the way, what's your schedule for tomorrow?"

"Basically, I'm on my own until the semifinal games. I'll probably take my usual morning walk and then relax until it's time to go to the arena."

"I just thought you might want to join us."

"Honey, I don't think Bob is going to want to go shopping," Betty interrupted.

"So that's what we have planned for tomorrow?" Jim feigned surprise.

Bob tried to act diplomatic when he said, "I need to review some things and it would be best if I passed on the shopping."

"Yeah, I know," Jim winked, "you need to look over the rules after all these years of officiating."

Jim asked if it would be okay to join Bob on Sunday since a morning walk was also a normal routine for him and a way to break up the boredom of the day. Bob was delighted to have an early morning partner and they agreed to meet at 7:30 in the lobby of the Marriot. This would give them both a chance to workout before Jim took Betty to late church. Little did Bob know Jim's real intent but it would not be long before he would find out.

Bob retired to his room where he was about to find out from Nancy she could not get to New Orleans until Sunday morning. In fact, she was lucky to get a flight over the weekend with all the cruise line traffic in and out of South Florida, but there was no way she was going to miss the biggest game of her husband's career. She asked Bob to extend her apologies to Betty for not being able to see Chad's semifinal game in person and hoped she and Chad would understand. Bob would have someone on the tournament committee pick Nancy up at the airport since he would probably be tied up with meetings. They also decided they would stay a couple of extra days and enjoy New Orleans after the pressure of the Four Final was over. She didn't think it would be a problem to find someone to watch Scott a few days while they were gone. After all, how many chances did they have to spend time alone?

Upon their return to the Hyatt, Jim escorted Betty to her room before retiring to his own room. They agreed separate rooms would be best since they would be in the same hotel with Chad and neither wanted to be accused of improper behavior. As it turned out, this would also enable Jim to conduct business without any questions from Betty.

Jim picked up a number of messages at the front desk including an urgent return call to his Miami office. Because of the short timeframe, Jim's agents were working around the clock to solidify the link between Bob, Mario and the Mafia. The association between Mario and the mob was already a certainty, but they needed more evidence to link Bob. Upon returning the call, Jim was to find the missing piece to the puzzle.

"So what's the deal?" Jim asked. "The message said this call was urgent."

"We think we've found the missing link," replied Agent Groves.

"Go on."

"In checking around and calling in a few markers, we found our boy Girard has a separate bank account in Homestead."

"A lot of people have separate accounts."

"Not usually with a balance of $25,000."

"That sounds like a bunch of money for a guy in his situation, but maybe he has a weekly poker game that he's been successful at and doesn't want his wife to know," Jim responded, playing the devil's advocate.

"But this account shows nearly $100,000 deposited during the course of this past year."

"Whoa, now we're getting somewhere," Jim continued. "But where's the extra $75,000?"

"That we don't know yet," Groves replied. "Hopefully we'll have that information by morning. Anyway, I just wanted you to know we're making progress."

"Good job and stay on this until you find out where the rest of the money is."

After hanging up, Jim determined he would confront Bob with this new information when they got together Sunday morning for their walk. For the time being Jim still needed more concrete information linking Bob and Mario and advised his agents to work through the weekend. Time was running out and no one was more aware of that than Jim.

Saturday morning was special with all the hoopla surrounding the games and the hotels alive with fans and ticket scalpers. Both Betty and Jim were shocked to find their tickets were worth up to $2,000 a piece or $5,000 for the pair. Pairs were more valuable, especially if the seats were in the lower level and between the foul lines. Not only was it illegal to scalp the tickets, it would have been impossible to get the tickets away from Betty. After all, this was the one chance Betty had to witness something ten years ago she could never have envisioned. It was hard to fathom Chad playing in the national championship game representing one of the great academic institutions in the country. Chad was also on pace to graduate and would be the first on Betty's side of the family to complete college. That was her biggest thrill. Playing basketball and having his education paid for was icing on the cake.

It's amazing how being the parent of a nationally recognized athlete can open doors and introduce one to people in high places. Not only did the Chancellor of Duke University and the head of the alumni association stop by and introduce themselves to Betty, so too did the governor of North Carolina. Basketball on Tobacco Road was big business and it never hurt to be seen at the Four Final, especially by fans, media and a national television audience when involved in politics. Visibility was a key component to winning elections.

Just as Betty and Jim finished talking with the governor, Chad and his teammates walked through the lobby after their late morning breakfast. Amongst the cheering crowd Chad saw his mother and Jim and immediately joined them for a brief chat.

"Well, did you get a good night's sleep?" Chad asked his mom and Jim.

"Not too bad and what about you," Betty responded.

"I guess okay considering the circumstances."

"So what's on tap for the rest of the morning?" Jim asked.

"We've got a brief meeting where we'll look at tape and review our game plan, and then we'll relax until it's time to go to the arena. How about you guys?"

Betty replied, "We're going to get in some sightseeing and shopping and then go to the arena for the first game. You have any favorites to win that game?"

"Not really," Chad replied in a somewhat agitated voice, "all I can think about is our came with Louisville."

Jim, sensing Chad's tension, added, "your mother and I better get going if we hope to get back in time to see you kick the Cardinals' butts."

As they were walking away Betty remembered, "we saw Bob Girard last night and he said to wish you good luck."

Chad nodded as he joined his teammates. Betty and Jim then walked down to the French Quarter for some sightseeing and shopping. Although Betty's primary reason for being in New Orleans was to see Chad play, Jim had much more serious business on his mind. He continued to hope things would come together before it was too late.

Chapter Thirty Five

Saturday morning Bob took his usual walk and would later go to the arena to watch the second half of the first game as well as the first half of the second game. This would enable him to become familiar with the four teams, more specifically the players, coaches and style of play. Yet he did not want to get overly involved or form any preconceived notions that would influence his officiating in the final game.

It was just a year ago he called the regional of the NACA Tournament and made a promise to officiate in the Four Final. How fortunate he had been the past year, but he worked very hard to get to this point. All his thoughts as to how he would prepare and call the final game were now about to come to fruition. This was such a thrill for a former player and basketball junkie. What would happen in the next seventy-two hours he could not imagine.

The first semifinal game was a typical Four Final slugfest. The game played true to form with Kentucky generating offense out of their pressing defense and three-point shooting, and Arizona pounding the ball inside to score or set up its perimeter game. Fourteen turnovers committed in the first half by Arizona was offset only by Kentucky's fouling. The halftime score found the Kentucky Wildcats ahead by five points, but three starters had three fouls. For another team the foul situation would be a real problem but Dick Galino played nine guys, all of who appeared to be clones of one another. On the other hand, Luke Larson's bunch was relatively foul free, but the press and pace of the game had physically taken a toll on an already thin backcourt. Arizona could run five quality big men in and out, but the drop off in guard play was significant with the lack of quality substitutes.

Jim and Betty arrived a few minutes late for the first game because of traffic problems. Jim wanted to enjoy the game but knew he needed to keep an eye on Bob since receiving additional information from his agents. Through non-stop questioning and research they were able to link Mario and Bob on three additional occasions in various bars and restaurants. Bob's secretary mentioned she saw a fellow worker stop by Bob's office numerous times to drop off an envelope. One time as Bob put the envelope in his briefcase, she noticed the envelope contained what appeared to be a large sum of money. She hadn't really thought anymore about the incident since it was none of her business, and she asked the agents not to tell anyone she provided this information for fear of being fired. The circle was beginning to close and it appeared Bob was in the center.

In the second half, Arizona was able to make one last run at Kentucky with about eight minutes to go. They cut the lead to two points, but then fatigue became a factor and the UK Wildcats went on a twelve to two run the next four minutes to gain control of the game. As usual, inside the last two minutes the game became a contest between Kentucky's ability to handle the ball and make free throws versus Arizona's ability to force turnovers and make three-point field goals. In the final analysis, Kentucky was just too quick and deep and won the game by seven points, advancing to the final game Monday night against the Duke/Louisville winner.

Jim observed Bob sitting at the scorer's table and couldn't imagine why he would get involved in such a scheme. Jim had heard nothing but good things about Bob and his passion for the game, and he always enjoyed the Girard's friendship. If and when this case played itself out, how would he explain to Betty and Chad their best friend's involvement in such an illegal operation? Jim knew there was no way they would initially believe Bob was involved and this could adversely affect his relationship with the Paynes. But that problem was down the road, while presently he needed to deal with Bob only two day's before he would referee the biggest college basketball game of the year. There was very little time and Jim knew he would have to get to Bob tonight or at the latest Sunday morning. Whatever was scheduled to happen Jim was convinced would happen Monday in the final game and it was his job to make sure his staff had everything under control.

The Duke and Louisville game began approximately forty-five minutes after the end of the first game and once again the styles of play were quite different. Duke relied heavily on its backcourt, with Chad creating action off the dribble to score or set up his shooting guard for the three-point field goal. The Blue Devils' inside players were athletic but were utilized more for defense, rebounding and finishing plays. Duke was not as deep or experienced as the Cardinals, electing to play only seven players, with Chad and his running mate averaging close to thirty- seven minutes a game. Louisville, on the other hand, looked inside as their first option and complimented their inside game with step-up jump shots on the perimeter. The Cardinals played nine guys and tried to control tempo with their 2-2-1 trademark full-court zone trap on defense and a high-post series offensively.

The game started with both teams feeling each other out like two heavyweight fighters. Coach P had a unique strategy to combat the Cardinals' press. Instead of using Chad to handle the inbounds pass, he instead positioned him in the middle of the zone press near the ten-second line where he could get the ball, turn and pressure the basket. This created some three-on-two situations, with Duke's big men only having to slide in from the wings to finish plays or the shooting-guard trailing the play stepping into open shooting positions on the perimeter. This strategy proved very effective and forced Louisville out of the press within the first six minutes of the game. On the flip side, Coach Doggett changed to a triangle-and-two, half-court defense with the two chasers on Chad and the shooting-guard. This too proved to be very effective by keeping Chad under constant pressure and taking away the easy, step-up jump shots by the other guard in the offense.

As the first half played itself out, it became apparent this would be a closely contested game throughout. Neither team put a significant run together and the score favored Louisville by three points at the half, with Chad making a long, off-balance jumper just before the buzzer to cut into the lead. Neither team had any real foul problems but both teams had expended a lot of energy. On the surface that should have favored the Cardinals because of their superior depth, but both teams welcomed the halftime break.

What a surprise the second half brought. Little did anyone think Coach P would employ a 2-3 match-up zone to rest his kids, and test Louisville's outside shooting. After all, he had always been a hardcore man-to-man coach. Nor could anyone guess Chad would literally will his team to victory. The change in defense worked as Doggett's guards struggled to knock down perimeter shots, enabling Duke to compact its zone even more to deny the ball inside. Chad was playing like a man possessed, and with fresh legs and confidence in his jump shot as a result of a five-for-eight shooting spree he single-handedly took over the game. When he was not pulling up in transition to knock down the three-point shot, he was penetrating the defense and passing the ball to an open man that merely had to complete the play.

In spite of Chad's play, the Blue Devils had the ball and only a three-point lead with less than thirty seconds to play. Then of all things, Chad got trapped in the corner and had the ball knocked out of his hands resulting in three guys diving on the floor to gain possession of the loose ball. In the ensuing pileup Chad cried out in pain and the huge crowd became strangely quiet while the Duke faithful held their collective breath. The end result was a dislocated ring finger on his left hand forcing Chad out of the game and unable to shoot his foul shots.

As he anguished in pain on the bench, Chad watched his replacement miss the front end of the one-and-one free throw and the Cardinals call a timeout after securing the rebound with twenty four seconds to play. When the trainer and team doctor looked at Chad to analyze the extent of his injury they were shocked to see Chad grab his own finger and pull it back into place.

"What are you doing?" the team doctor shouted.

"What's it look like," Chad replied. "I'm putting this thing back in place so I can go back into the game."

"But you're going to permanently damage your hand."

"I don't think so. I've done this a dozen times in the past playing on the playgrounds at home."

"This is real serious Chad," added the trainer.

"Just do me a favor. Wrap these two fingers together so I can't hurt my hand any more."

"Are you sure?" the doctor asked.

"Yes, I'm sure. But let's get on with this so I can get back in the game."

This was something players did in the 60's and 70's but not in the 80's and 90's. An injury like this today would require surgery, or at the very least resetting the finger by a doctor, and then six to eight weeks in a splint. As the trainer wrapped his two fingers together with tape, Chad watched Louisville come out of its timeout and move the ball into position to run their offense.

With the clock ticking down, Louisville's forward and center double-screened on the baseline for their shooting guard, allowing him the opportunity to shoot a three to tie the game. Coach P had covered just such a possibility during the timeout, but one of the Duke players forgot to switch the screen and the Louisville player came open for the shot, which he made to tie the game with eight seconds to play.

Duke immediately called a timeout and Coach P began to diagram a last second play when Chad interrupted.

"Coach, get me back in the game," Chad demanded.

Coach P looked at the trainer and doctor and they gave their approval. Both realized he could not do any more damage to his hand and therefore could play. It was really just a matter of his pain threshold and what he could tolerate. As Chad ran to the scorer's table you could hear the Duke fans roar, and you could see Coach P wipe his board clean of the previously designed play. The bottom line was to get the ball in Chad's hands and let him create off the dribble. As they broke the huddle, Chad gathered his teammates for one last message.

"Get me the ball and get the hell out of the way," Chad demanded.

"But what if you're not open," one of his teammates asked, "you know they're going to be watching you."

"Don't worry about me, I'll get open. You just do what coach said and get me the ball. Big guys get to the low post and you wings set up on the three point-line expecting a pass."

The only question mark was whether he could go to his left hand and control the ball. That question would be answered in the next eight seconds as Chad received the inbounds pass, passed the ball ahead out of a double team and then received a return pass at the ten-second line.

From that point things became a blur for Chad, his teammates, Betty, Jim, Coach P, and everyone watching as he drove the ball to the basket only to be fouled with two seconds to play. There was no question about the call but the official ruled the foul took place on the drive before the shot. Instead of two shots, Chad would be at the line shooting the one-and-one. Coach Doggett called his last timeout, and Chad's finger began to throb as he went to the bench. In Chad's mind this was where all those days playing outside in the hot Florida sun would pay off. He had worked too long and hard to be distracted by a finger injury, a hostile crowd, a national television and radio audience or anything else. The look of determination in his eyes said it all.

Coach P told his players not to enter the lane too soon, keep everything in front of them if the Cardinals gained possession of the ball and not foul in the last two seconds. Little could he know Chad was already thinking one step ahead of him. What Chad was about to do are things that separate the great ones from the good ones. After making the first free throw, he purposely missed the second one. As the ball rebounded off the front of the rim, and before a shot could be attempted, the clock expired and the Blue Devils were on their way to the national championship game against the Kentucky Wildcats.

What a great match-up this would be with the traditions, the coaches and styles of play that in many respects mirrored one another. Betty and Jim were beside themselves, as was Bob who had watched the second half from his hotel room. This was a great moment for Chad, the Blue Devils and their supporters.

At the press conference after the game Chad was asked a series of questions, one of which was what happened on the last free throw? Did his bad finger cause him to miss?

"I missed the last free throw on purpose," he admitted.

"But why?" asked one of the sportswriters.

"Well, another point wasn't going to make any difference," Chad added.

"Two points puts you up a basket and forces Louisville to make a three-point play to win," one of the reporters concluded. "Weren't you worried about that possibility?"

"Yeah, but they have a better chance of making a basket to tie or win if they get to take the ball out of bounds," Coach P interjected. "With the clock stopped until someone touches the ball inbounds, they can throw the ball the length of the court and get a good shot or possibly fouled. With no timeouts and the clock starting when the ball is rebounded, it would take a length-of-the-court, 'hail Mary' shot to win the game. I liked our chances."

Coach P was right. It was highly unlikely anyone could make a length of the court shot under those circumstances. The writers could not help but be impressed by Chad's ability to both think and communicate.

"On another subject," the writer continued, "how's the hand and what happened?"

"During the loose ball I dislocated the ring finger on my left hand but it seems okay," Chad said without any flair.

"Did the doctor reset it during the timeout?"

"Nah, I just pulled it back in place myself. It's no big deal."

"So what's your status for Monday night?"

"Unless something unforeseen happens, he'll be ready to go," Coach P said.

"I wouldn't miss this game for the world," Chad added.

The moderator could sense Chad and Coach P were tired of the questions and announced they would take only one more.

"What happens the next two days?"

"For Chad a lot of treatment," Coach P answered. "He'll work with the doctor and trainer and I'm sure he'll be fine. The biggest thing now is for all of us to rest and get ready to play a fine Kentucky team."

With that response the press conference was concluded and Chad and Coach P joined the rest of the team and returned to the hotel. Betty and Jim decided, rather than wait after the game in a swarm of people, to go back to the hotel and wait for the team. They knew Chad was okay and saw no reason to hang around the locker room. Betty hoped she could spend a few minutes with her son before he had a meeting.

No one could be happier for Chad than Bob, but with mixed feelings now that he was scheduled to referee the final game. In his own mind he knew once the game started both he and Chad would go about their business without any distractions. Bob believed one of the semifinal games was on Mario and the mob's point-shaving list, but continued to hold out hope they would perceive the final game to be too closely scrutinized and dangerous to get involved with. Not only the magnitude of the game, but the limited turnaround time between the semifinals and final convinced Bob it was all but impossible for the Mafia to set in place everything needed for his game to be on the take. What Bob did not take into account was the mob's determination and lack of fear when faced with such a moneymaking operation. If only Bob could have known how the next forty-eight hours would change his life as well as the lives of those he cared for so dearly.

Chapter Thirty Six

At the scheduled time Mario contacted Bob requesting a meeting with him that night at 11:30. They needed to get together and talk about the tournament.

"So you're in New Orleans?" Bob asked in a surprised tone. "When did you get in and where are you staying?"

"I got in today," Mario lied. "I'm staying with a friend and I'll fill you in on what's going on when I see you later."

"Where do you want to meet?"

"Let's meet at Goodfellows, a restaurant in Metarie about thirty minutes from downtown New Orleans. It's on the corner of Lane and Alamos. Any cab driver will know how to get there."

"See you there," Bob concluded, sensing for the first time the Mafia may be willing to take the next step.

Just as Bob was about to hang up, Mario interjected, "Be sure to be discreet when leaving the hotel. Go out the back way and walk a block before catching a cab. Make sure you're not followed. After all, we can't be too cautious."

Bob was surprised Mario was in New Orleans but knew he was a big sports fan and always talked about attending the NACA Four Final. He was a little concerned about Mario's last remarks, but looked forward to talking with him about the past season and his future in the program. At least that was what Bob wanted to think they would talk about.

By now the FBI had a wiretap on Bob's phone as they continued to monitor Mario's cellular phone. Therefore, Jim knew in advance where the meeting was to take place. Mario's call set the wheels in motion, and by the time Bob arrived by taxi at the restaurant four agents were already at their respective tables on opposite sides of the middle of the dining room. Two men and two women were paired to appear like married couples.

Goodfellows was a well-known local spot that specialized in steaks and seafood. It was a small, intimate restaurant run by John Collini, a third generation Italian whose grandfather had come to the United States back in the 1940's and started the business. There were tables in the middle of the room surrounded by booths along the walls. The atmosphere was low-key but there was enough noise to allow people to talk without concern for others listening to their conversation. John was a man who could be trusted so many mob bosses had visited Goodfellows from time to time. It was also out of the way so Mario was not concerned about running into someone he might know.

Shortly after Bob's arrival, Mario made his entrance with another man and they joined Bob at his table. This was the first time Mario had someone actually sit at the table during their conversation and Bob could tell this guy was Mario's bodyguard. What Bob didn't understand was why Mario would need muscle at a meeting like this. After exchanging pleasantries, Mario once again congratulated Bob on a great year and his selection to work the national championship game.

"So, are you excited about working the final game Monday night?" Mario asked.

Bob thought the question to be trite, but answered, "It's what I've worked for ever since I began officiating."

"What do you think about the game?"

"What do you mean?" Bob asked.

"You know. Who's the better team and what will determine who wins."

"I would have to think Kentucky would be favored. They've played well the last half of the season and seem to have more quality athletes."

Mario then asked Bob if he knew what the spread was on the final game, to which Bob indicated he had no idea. Mario told him the line had just been published and Kentucky was favored to win by three points. Apparently the odds makers felt Duke, while playing only seven players, had the more difficult of the semifinal games and with the uncertainty of their star player's finger injury would be overmatched against the Wildcats. The reason the spread was not greater was due in great part to Duke's past success in the Four Final, Coach P's ability to get the most out of his teams in big games and the effective way Duke had played throughout the tournament in getting to the final game. There was also the outside possibility Chad could be able to play. Because of those factors much of the early money was on the Blue Devils to cover the spread.

"With all you've mentioned, I'm surprised the spread's not greater," Bob responded.

"That's what we thought," Mario replied. "In fact, so surprising we are betting on the Wildcats to beat the points."

Bob looked at Mario in disbelief. How could the mob take on a game of this magnitude and scrutiny? His worst fears were about to be realized. They had picked the national championship game as the prize, and now here he was facing the reality he was being asked, no told, to fix the biggest game of the year and his career. How could he possibly be involved in a scheme so bizarre and what were his options? So many questions ran through Bob's head he just sat there with a blank stare for what seemed like an eternity saying nothing.

Seeing the nature of Bob's reaction, Mario immediately went on the offensive asking Bob if there was a problem. "You look perplexed if that's an accurate word."

"I think that's an understatement," Bob responded.

"You shouldn't be. This can't be that big a surprise."

"I beg your pardon, not a big surprise. Hell, it's a total shock."

"Not so loud. We talked about fixing games in the tournament just a few weeks ago."

"Yeah, but I thought you meant earlier games, not the championship game. Mario, no one in their right mind could risk trying to fix the final game of the NACA Tournament."

"And why not?" Mario smugly asked.

"There's too much attention, scrutiny and security surrounding this game."

Mario smiled and said, "Exactly, no one would ever suspect someone would try and fix a game of this magnitude. It's a no-brainer."

Bob's only response was to ask if Mario and the mob fully understood what they were getting involved in and asking him to do. Mario was emphatic and to the point in answering yes. Then Bob made the ultimate mistake. He told Mario he would need some time to think about whether he could do this. Bob now realized for the first time the severity of his situation. He had up to this point rationalized he had control of the process and could get out of this scam as easily as he had gotten in.

"What do you mean time to decide whether you can do this?" Mario asked as he stuck his finger in Bob's face. "This is not something that's up to you to decide. You've got a job to do and by god you're going to do it. Is that understood?"

"Sure," Bob replied as he retreated from his original statement and opted for time, "I was just surprised and confused for a minute when you told me about the fix."

"So you understand what has to be done?"

"Yeah, you don't have to worry about me," Bob replied in an attempt to bring this conversation to an end.

"Then what you're telling me is everything is on go and I don't have to keep an eye on you and your family. Is that correct?"

"Keep my family out of this!" Bob suddenly lashed out.

"I hope to if everything goes according to planned," Mario retorted without flinching.

Bob needed some relief and a chance to gather his thoughts. He nodded and wished he could take back his original statement questioning his intentions. The last thing he needed was Mario and the mob to be distrustful of him. The idea Nancy and Scott could become involved was almost too much to bear. More than at any other time Bob realized the magnitude of his relationship with the Mafia. They had been very generous and in return all they asked was he deliver on his original agreement. With the mob an agreement was an unwritten contract that only they determined when and how that agreement was rendered null and void.

As the anger built in Bob, he noticed Mario's buddy sit up in the chair and reach inside his sport coat. Bob could only assume he was carrying a gun, and this was not the time or place to make a scene or do something foolish. Bob bit his lip to buy time and think this thing through. If it were just himself, this would still be a difficult decision, but the addition of Nancy and Scott put a completely different light on the situation. Bob could see no real options to what he was being asked to do and reassured Mario there would be no problems with the plan. After all Bob tried to joke, Kentucky should be able to cover the bet on their own.

Bob had trouble finishing dinner. After more talk concerning the game, he was dismissed and returned to his hotel. On the way back to the Marriott Bob pondered his options. He could only conclude he had to carry out the point-shaving plan, only this time it was a different set of circumstances. Not only was this the biggest basketball game of the year, his family was now involved and he was being asked to betray a young man he mentored and loved like a son. In his heart he hoped Chad would not be able to play because of his broken finger and the game would play itself out as many predicted. Saturday night would be a sleepless one.

Bob did not know the Feds had recorded his conversation and taken pictures of his meeting with Mario. Nor did he realize the next day would be a day of reckoning with Jim Stanton. It also didn't enter his thinking that Mario put a tail on him to ensure there were no distractions or sudden problems. Fortunately for Jim, the agents overheard Mario tell his friend to initiate the tail, thus forewarning him not to meet and walk with Bob as previously planned Sunday morning.

Back home Nancy was beginning to have some concerns. Having done business at one bank as long as she and Bob, and being valued customers, she had developed close relationships with most of the people that worked there. She was at a loss when one of her friends at the bank called Saturday morning to inform her a FBI agent had been asking questions about the Girards' banking habits. Questions as to how much money they had in their accounts, what kind of deposits and withdrawals they made during the last year and whether Bob and Nancy were ever seen with unusual amounts of cash. The real concern was the agent had a federal warrant to access their accounts. When questioned, the banker indicated to Nancy most of the questions centered on Bob's activities. What could that possibly mean?

Nancy could only assume the IRS had found something peculiar on their last income tax return or there was a misunderstanding concerning the money Nancy had discovered earlier in Bob's separate bank account. But the question remained, why the FBI? Yet, in Nancy's mind it was nothing to get alarmed about since they always had a licensed CPA from one of the major brokerage firms fill out their returns. If there was a question about their financial affairs, she was sure it could be easily explained. She would be with Bob tomorrow and would ask him if he knew what was going on.

Chapter Thirty Seven

Sunday morning, just prior to their meeting time, Jim called Bob to say he would be unable to keep his walking appointment but needed to talk with Bob as early as possible. He alluded this was urgent and involved Chad and Betty. He gave Bob the number and asked him to stop by his room at the Hyatt after his walk. They agreed to meet right after the walk since Bob was expecting Nancy to arrive early that afternoon.

After returning to the hotel and showering, Bob arrived at the Hyatt where he proceeded to what he thought was Jim's room. Instead, it was a room being used as headquarters for Jim and his agents during their stay in New Orleans. Upon opening the door Bob could sense this was not a typical hotel room setup and entered with a quizzical look on his face. Jim immediately introduced the other two men, identifying them as FBI Agents Groves and Mast, and indicated he needed to ask Bob some questions.

Bob immediately sensed this was the beginning of a horrible nightmare, but knowing Jim he was willing to listen. Jim wasted no time laying the groundwork.

"The reason I asked you here is to clear up some questions we have about your affiliation with a known Mafia member named Mario," Jim began. "But before we get started, let me advise you that you have the right at any time to have legal counsel present."

"Why would I need a lawyer?" Bob asked half-heartedly. "What's this all about?"

"Bob, we have information linking you to this Mario and an illegal gambling operation."

"Get serious!" Bob faked surprise. "You must be kidding!"

"You don't know how much I wish I was," Jim replied. "So, do you want to hear more about this and answer some questions or would you prefer to call your lawyer?"

"I'll listen. I don't have anything to hide but I reserve the right to stop at any time."

"No problem. Now if you don't mind, I'm going to tape these proceedings."

Jim had Agent Groves read Bob his rights. He then outlined the association between him and Mario including the pictures of the two men together, the phone and restaurant conversations last night, the secret bank account in Homestead and the pattern of betting on some of the games Bob had been involved in. As Jim further indicated, if Bob did not want to cooperate, the FBI could easily request through the conference offices and the respective schools videotapes of the games in question. These tapes would substantiate a pattern of illegal activity and combined with the other information presented a strong case against Bob. As Bob listened, Jim could almost sense relief on his part someone had uncovered this horrible secret.

Jim again advised Bob of his right to have legal representation present but Bob waived that request indicating a willingness to cooperate. Bob knew Jim and the FBI had enough evidence to press charges against him if they so desired. Furthermore, Bob was convinced it was just a matter of time before the FBI would discover the other officials involved and the direct link between all of them and the mob. Who would try to cut a deal? He assumed he was the first to be confronted with these charges, so what kind of leniency if any could he expect by cooperating fully in the investigation? Could he trust the FBI to take care of him and his family? How would he deal with Nancy and other loved ones once this was made public? These were all questions that flashed through Bob's mind.

"I'm not about to admit anything although I do have some questions," Bob said. "You need to turn off that tape recorder for a minute."

Jim nodded to Agent Mast to turn off the recorder and then asked, "What is it you want to know?"

"First, if what you say is true, then what are you asking me to do and why aren't you charging me with a crime?"

Jim, realizing Bob was but a pawn in a much larger plan, explained, "Charging you with a crime at this time would probably ruin any chance we have in corralling the guys in charge. We know you're a small fish in this operation but one who can help us bring these guys to justice. To do that you'll need to fill in the holes and give us a complete list of those you're involved with."

"That's asking a lot, assuming, and I repeat assuming, what you say is true and I decide to cooperate, what do I get in return?"

"I'll recommend a suspended sentence and probation with a minimal fine for your full cooperation. But once you agree there can be no turning back and the evidence you present must be accurate and thorough."

"What guarantee do I have that you can deliver?"

"None really but we have a solid case and you have a better chance with us than with your friends. The District Attorney will have the final say and I'm confident he'll go along with my recommendation."

Because of the magnitude of the operation, Jim also assured Bob he would provide him and his family with round the clock protection and even enter him and his family in the witness protection program if necessary. Jim could see Bob start to sweat and wanted him to understand the seriousness of his situation. He was not about to sugarcoat the possible consequences, either legally or with the mob.

Bob asked for a few minutes to think this thing through. Jim and his agents left the room and told him to take his time. The evidence was overwhelming and Bob knew for all practical purposes he had been caught. He could fight the charges but could he beat the rap and what would happen to his family during this process without protection from the FBI? Admitting guilt and participating in this plan would be no easy task but did he really have any other option but to help? In the final analysis Bob knew the answer was 'no.'

Calling Jim back into the room, Bob acknowledged his willingness to cooperate. Jim recorded this voluntary agreement so as to eliminate any future problems that might arise if Bob were to change his mind and claim he had been denied legal representation. With the preliminaries out of the way, Bob began to describe the entire operation and the people involved. He figured his chances with Jim far outweighed his chances with the mob once they found out the FBI knew about their plan.

What was so shocking to Jim was Bob's genuine embarrassment and humility when describing his involvement in the operation. Most of the time the accused rationalized his involvement by saying he was coerced or forced to participate while acting defensive and unforgiving about what he had done. It was as if Bob was ashamed of his actions and relieved and grateful it was all out in the open and about to end.

After listening and recording Bob's story, Jim had to decide how to handle the next thirty-six hours. Things could get dangerous and the whole operation jeopardized with just one mistake. The most pressing question was whether Bob should referee the final game? To the average person the decision should be a simple one, yet this was at best a very delicate and unusual situation. After all, Bob was but a small player in a major Mafia operation. The stakes were high and an underlying theme was the FBI had for one of the few times an opportunity to go after mob personnel at a very high level.

"I've got to referee Monday's game," Bob pleaded.

"It sounds risky to me," Agent Mast volunteered.

"Why?" Bob asked.

"How do we know you won't go through with the fix?" Agent Groves asked.

"Get real," Bob said. "If I was going to go through with the fix do you think I'd be spilling my guts to you guys and volunteering to cooperate? You've taped my confession, but you're still a long way from having this case wrapped up. You need to trust me."

"Okay," Jim interjected, realizing they needed this last game to solidify their case. "It's not going to do anyone any good if we argue about this. I know Bob and I'm of the opinion he should continue to act as if he's going to referee the game. A change at this point would send up a red flag and alert the Mafia to a problem. My guess is they would cancel the entire operation and then where would we be? Back where we started and in my mind that's just not an option. Besides, time is running short and we need to get things in place."

"You're kidding," Agent Groves declared.

"No, I'm not. Do you have a better idea?"

"There has to be a better alternative than this," Agent Mast chimed in.

"If there is, I don't know about it," Jim responded. "Bottom line, it's my call and I say he works the game. If need be we can always make a change even up to game time. I'll assume full responsibility for anything that goes wrong."

After limited discussion it was agreed, with some reservation, Bob should referee the final game. This would not sit well with the NACA, but in spite of what he had done everyone was in agreement Bob was an excellent official and gave the bureau the best chance to carry out its plan. Whether the NACA would even be advised of the problem was yet to be determined. It was also pointed out that Bob had not altered who should win previous games, only the point spread. In fact, the Syracuse/Utah game was indicative of Bob trying to only impact the margin of victory and not the outcome. Just as Bob was a minor player, the FBI also considered Mario nothing more than a smalltime thug. They needed to bait the hook and sink their teeth into the core of the operation so they could inflict irreparable damage to the mob. Now was the time to put the wheels in motion.

Jim also felt he knew Bob well enough and his love of family to trust he would carry out his end of the bargain. There still would be no guarantee concerning the point spread because of how good Kentucky was, but they had approximately eighteen hours to flush out and link to the fix some of the top Mafia bosses. Jim promised he would do everything in his power to protect all parties involved, but reiterated the plan had risks and he could not guarantee the safety of Bob or his family. Even the witness protection program, with excellent results, was not fail-proof. A big key would be for Bob to follow Jim's plan to the letter.

"Look, you've been out of sight long enough," Jim told Bob. "You better get back to your hotel."

"What's the rush?" Bob inquired. "I can assure you Mario and his bunch don't know about this."

"That may be, but after you left the restaurant last night one of my guys overheard Mario tell one of his boys to tail you."

"You're kidding me."

"No I'm not. We don't think they have any suspicion we're as close as we are to breaking this case so we don't want to take any chances now."

"So, what if I run into this guy in the lobby or Mario asks where I've been?"

"Start out with the truth. You went for your daily walk and then you came to the Hyatt to see an old friend of yours who was an official."

"What if they check?"

"That's unlikely but give me the name of a guy so we can register one of my agents in the hotel under his name," Jim answered. "That way if someone should call we'll have you covered and know the mob is getting suspicious." Bob gave the name of one of his buddies and Jim made the necessary arrangements.

"What about Nancy?" Bob asked. "She's due in this afternoon and I need someone to pick her up. I told her it would be someone from the tournament committee."

"Don't worry, I'll take care of it."

Bob was advised to contact Mario and request a meeting about an unexpected development that might impact their plan. Without going into much detail, Bob would explain the NACA Tournament Committee chairman scheduled a meeting with the Four Final officials in conjunction with a request from the New Orleans police. Supposedly some local crime figure was rumored to be involved in an illegal gambling scheme relating to the tournament. Jim hoped this would accomplish two things, divert any possible attention away from the FBI and get the mob involved at a much higher level as it moved to protect its interests. Jim also realized Bob would need access to another phone line and separate room at the Marriott for contacting Jim and his agents since he was not about to take a chance with a cell phone.

"Look, I'll have one of my guys set everything up," Jim explained, as Bob was about to leave. "He'll get in touch with you with the key and the name the room's registered under."

"So why do I need a separate room?"

"In case something comes up unexpectedly. This way you can get in touch with us on a secured line without leaving your floor or the hotel. It will also give us a place to meet in case of an emergency without creating suspicion."

"But how will I know there's a problem if you don't call my room?"

"But we will call. We'll just set up a code. If it's not an emergency use the word 'black' somewhere in the first sentence. If it is an emergency then use the word 'red' in the same way."

Now it was time for Bob to get back to his hotel, contact Mario and set up a meeting for later that evening. Dinner would have to be after six o'clock since his normal meeting with the NACA people was scheduled at three o'clock that afternoon. Bob purposely waited until four-thirty to contact Mario to make him think he had just come from the tournament meeting.

"Mario, this is Bob."

"What are you calling about?" Mario responded in a surprised tone.

"Something's come up and we need to talk but not on the phone."

"You're sure it can't wait?"

"Take my word for it, this can't wait. How about we meet at the same place as last night so I won't get lost?"

"That will work, but what time?"

"Let's make it seven-thirty so I can finish up with my duties here."

"Okay, but this better be important," Mario concluded in disgust.

Bob then went to his second room where he contacted Jim to advise the meeting with Mario was set. Jim explained he and one of his men would meet him at five o'clock in the secure room to work out the details as to what was to be said and how the meeting should be handled. They also agreed Nancy would be taken to the hotel from the airport and told Bob had a meeting with the NACA Tournament Committee that would involve dinner and last minute instructions. She should get together with Betty and Bob would meet her later at the room.

Back at the Hyatt, Chad and the team were getting ready to go to the Superdome for their practice in preparation for Monday night's championship game. Both Chad and Coach P as usual were on the same page. They knew this would be the biggest challenge of the year, not just because it was the championship game, because it was against Kentucky.

Chad's finger was feeling better although still sore. He had spent the past twelve hours in therapy, mostly icing the finger, and was anxious to get to practice to test it and get away from all the questions. This afternoon's workout and the next twenty-four hours of treatment would determine in great part how effective he would be and what chance Duke had of winning.

There was no question in his mind he would play and be expected to perform well. This was no time to let a minor injury to his non-shooting hand get in the way of winning the national championship. No one realized more than Chad how playing for the national championship was a once in a lifetime experience and much of just getting there was luck. An errant pass, missed free throw, foul trouble on the wrong player, fumbled rebound, injury or mental mistake could result in elimination at any stage of the tournament. Now they were in the finals and underdogs to boot, so playing as close as possible to perfection would be a must for Duke to have any chance to win.

Chad and Betty visited briefly after the team breakfast and Chad asked about Jim. Betty explained Jim had an appointment but sent his best and hoped Chad's finger was healing.

"He's at an appointment?" Chad asked incredulously. "Doesn't this guy ever rest?"

"Not often, but this meeting is to see an old friend who's stationed in the New Orleans office so he shouldn't be long. I think he's also worried about being a distraction."

"A distraction, the only distraction I have is when my mom is not being watched after. After all, I did get him a ticket so he could bring you to the tournament."

"I know, but don't be upset. Jim is always there when I need him. Anyway, he knew I wanted to spend a few minutes alone with you this morning," Betty replied, sensing Chad was on edge as a result of the game.

"So how serious are you two?" Chad asked.

"Pretty serious. I really care about him and he's been wonderful to me."

"I must admit he seems like a good guy."

"You don't know the half of it," Betty added. "He's so compassionate, gentle and understanding, and this is the first man since your father and I divorced that I've felt this way about."

"I sensed this was pretty serious but I just want to make sure you don't get hurt. After all, one rotten apple is enough."

"Please don't talk about your father that way," Betty scolded.

"I'm sorry mom but I saw what he did to you and it broke my heart. I don't want that to ever happen again."

"Don't worry, it won't. I've learned a lot from that experience. But you need to understand nothing is guaranteed and I'm a long way from walking down the aisle."

"Well, I just want you to be happy. I hope to spend time and get to know him better once the season is over and school is out."

Chad could tell, as he had sensed the past few months, his mother was genuinely happy for the first time since his father deserted them. Although Chad still had every intention of caring for his mother, he was delighted she had found someone who could possibly share her life and care for her. What little he knew of Jim he liked.

Chad then excused himself to go to a team meeting where they would look at more videotape, discuss the Wildcats and lay the foundation for their game plan. Then it would be off to the arena for a light workout and to walk through the proposed plan. As he got up to leave, Betty said, "By the way, Jim thoroughly enjoyed the game yesterday and thought you played with a lot of courage."

"Tell him I appreciate that but I hope to play even better tomorrow night. Gotta go but I'll try to see you after practice."

As hectic and demanding as this was, regardless of which team won the game, Chad would not trade the experience for anything in the world. All the days hanging around and later working Bob Girard's camp, hours in the weight room and social sacrifices were mere inconveniences compared to the opportunity now before him and his teammates.

Jim returned to the hotel to meet Betty and downplayed the fictitious meeting with his old friend. He perpetuated the lie by stating a couple of things had come up back in Miami but he could handle those things out of the local office. He assured Betty none of this would be serious enough to become a distraction or force him to return home before the championship game was played.

After lunch he and Betty walked to the Superdome to watch Chad workout. Coach P was open minded in allowing the parents to attend practices knowing they would get to spend so little time with their sons during the tournament. A quick trip to the French Quarter and a horse and carriage ride down Bourbon Street before dinner would allow Betty and Jim to spend some quiet time together. Both agreed they were having a wonderful time.

Chapter Thirty Eight

Later that evening as Bob entered Goodfellows and approached the table he could tell Mario was suspicious and impatient. Mario wanted to eliminate the small talk and find out the reason for such a meeting so close to the final game.

"So, what's the deal?" Mario demanded.

"Something came up at our committee meeting today and I think it's something you should know about."

"What the hell is it?"

"The committee chairman advised us there was a rumor to the effect some local, small- time crime boss was trying to fix the NACA Tournament games."

"No fucking way!" Mario blurted out.

"Yes, and in fact the local police were looking into the validity of the rumor."

"Did he say who the guy was?"

"He didn't know but he wanted us to be aware there was a potential problem and be careful who we talked to."

"Now think, this is important, did he tell you how widespread this information was and whether any other law enforcement agencies were involved yet?"

"All he said was it was a rumor and the local police were investigating to see if there was any cause for concern," Bob lied. "It sounded like a small, local operation."

"You're right to alert me to this new development. We'll have to get to the bottom of this as soon as possible. I can't have some pimp ass punk messing up our deal."

Bob went on to say he did not believe their plan was compromised but something had to be done quickly before it was. Time would tell if Mario had taken the bait.

Mario asked Bob to join him in the restroom where he emphasized the problems they would both have if this plan did not work out. He also frisked Bob, indicating the sudden unexpected events meant he could not afford to be careless.

Fortunately, Jim had anticipated such action and wired Bob with a transmitter and microphone named the SX-47. Jim was concerned not only that Mario might check Bob for bugs but with the seriousness of the situation he might elect to leave the restaurant altogether. Knowing this was also a mob hangout, the FBI did not want to risk an agent exposure by again placing them in the restaurant at a time when Mario was on high alert and might be looking for anything out of the ordinary.

The SX-47 was just recently developed by the FBI lab and as yet wasn't department issue. It needed more testing but what better time to check its abilities? This little gadget was at the cutting edge of technology. After numbing the back of the throat with a local anesthetic, the end of a hair size filament was run through the mouth into the throat, up the sinus cavity and into the nose. The filament in the nose would act as a microphone, relaying information to a small receiver/transmitter clamped to the inside of the lower back teeth in the mouth. This in turn would transmit the conversation to a recording machine located in one of the agent's cars as far as a mile away. Although still in its testing stages, the biggest concern was it coming loose when chewing food or the irritation caused by the nose filament. Although they had Bob as a witness, a recording of the actual conversation between he and Mario was far more compelling and substantial, especially when the prosecution's witness had cut a deal with law enforcement. Immunity for a prosecution witness was always addressed by the defense at trial.

No one knew better than Mario if there was any hint of illegal betting the game would be taken off the books and their plan would be destroyed. With the hours of planning, the resources committed and Monday's game being the ultimate payday, the mob could not afford to let that happen. After returning to the table, Mario assured Bob he would get to the bottom of this and have an answer for him in the next twelve hours. Mario, as Jim had anticipated, wanted to flex his muscle and impress as well as intimidate Bob, thus indicating a couple of calls could take care of the problem. To convince Mario of his commitment to the plan, Bob then asked how much a national championship game was worth. Mario was evasive as to the exact amount but indicated it could be big.

"What's big?" Bob persisted.

"Something in the $50,000 to $75,000 range."

"You're kidding."

"No, this is a huge game and one we can't afford to have screwed up. Like I said, I'll have this situation straightened out by tomorrow morning one way or the other."

Mario wanted to quickly review what Bob needed to be concerned with during the game. Bob assured him there would be no problems, and in fact gave Mario some inside information as to the extent of Chad Payne's injury. This further eliminated any questions Mario might have concerning Bob's commitment. The more Bob talked about the game and players, the more confident Mario was their plan was guaranteed and Bob was fully on board.

Mario also surprised Bob when he indicated they both might have to meet with a mob boss if there were any questions or additional concerns about the operation. Mario explained that one of the top guys in the Mafia would be in town to police things and would oversee the operation up until game time.

"So, who is this guy?" Bob asked.

"I can't tell you that, but he makes things happen."

"Well, if we do meet tomorrow we'll have to be discreet. There's already plenty of concern about the game."

"Don't worry," Mario said confidently, "we'll only meet if necessary and we always cover our ass. Now you better get back to the hotel before someone misses you."

Bob took a cab back to the Marriott while Mario placed a series of calls expressing confidence the operation had not been compromised and was still a go. These calls were traced and people on the other end were identified as Mafia lieutenants. Cracking the case and turning one of these lieutenants so as to connect a mob boss with the illegal scheme would be the next step for Jim and his agents. In recent years plea-bargain arrangements had helped the federal government expose illegal activities and indict many principals, but fear of mob retaliation was very compelling and Jim could only hope he would be lucky enough to find someone within the organization willing to cooperate.

As previously agreed upon, Jim had one of his men pickup Nancy at the airport and she joined Betty, Chad and Jim during the early part of the evening. After practice, an early dinner and team meeting, Coach P allowed the players to spend time with their families for the final time until after the game. This was the first real opportunity for Chad to visit with Jim since the tournament began. Chad did not know Jim well enough to sense something was wrong, but Betty noticed a change in him since their arrival in New Orleans. Betty rationalized Jim was feeling guilty about being away from the office.

"Are you ready for the big game tomorrow?" Jim asked.

"As ready as I can be."

"How's your finger?"

"It's okay," Chad responded, trying to change the subject. "Mom tells me you've been busy. Don't you ever get a break?"

"Sometimes, but I guess I'm trying to justify the trip so I don't have to use vacation time," Jim lied. "I don't know if your mom told you but I thought you played one heck of a game yesterday."

"She did and coming from a former college athlete I really appreciate the compliment. Let's just hope we can win one more game."

"You will," interjected Betty.

Chad and Jim seemed to get along well and as athletes had much in common. Chad was pleased Jim thought he showed a lot of class and courage in the last game, and Jim was pleased Chad acted interested in what he was doing.

Even though Chad had set his sights on being a professional athlete and earning a degree in business management, he had not ruled out the possibility of a career in law and maybe someday running for public office. Hopefully with time, Jim could shed some light on the inter-workings of law enforcement. Chad had grown to like the limelight and wanted to remain in the public eye while possibly making a difference for others less fortunate than himself. The law and politics seemed to offer him the greatest opportunity to accomplish that goal.

After dessert Chad excused himself and returned to his room where he reviewed Monday's game plan and watched tape of Kentucky. His finger had improved dramatically and he felt he would be near ninety percent healthy by game time. He was determined to play the greatest game of his career and if he did he would have nothing to feel bad about regardless of the outcome. Sometimes good wasn't good enough but hopefully that wouldn't be the case in Monday's game.

Nancy, Betty and Jim had a nightcap before retiring to their respective rooms. Nancy had gotten Bob's message indicating he would be tied up with the tournament committee and was delighted Betty and Jim had included her in their plans. All three were tired from the day's activities and realized tomorrow would be even more hectic and stressful. Jim was happy for Betty's decision to retire early and Nancy's desire to get back to the room to see Bob.

After escorting Betty to her room, Jim took Nancy back to the Marriott where unbeknownst to her he too would await Bob's return. Jim arrived at the room shortly before Bob and was briefed by his agents to what transpired at the dinner meeting between Bob and Mario. The agents already had copies of the conversations, as well as the numbers Mario called after Bob left the restaurant. The numbers were being tracked but Jim was reasonably sure they would lead to higher-ups in the mob.

Meanwhile, time was running short. Jim knew Bob was caught between a rock and a hard place but this was no time for friendships. The objective was to thwart an illegal gambling activity and bring the perpetrators of the crime to justice. If Bob could help accomplish that end, then 'let the chips fall where they may.' Betty and Chad would just have to understand. Jim could not help but wonder how this would affect all of their relationships. He could only hope for the best because he was very much in love with Betty and truly liked the Girards.

Upon Bob's arrival, most of the preliminary work was already done. In conjunction with the FBI, a New Orleans police spokesman confirmed the word was on the street concerning the local crime boss' interest in fixing the championship game. Jim's buddy at the New Orleans FBI had interceded with a local police captain, a friend of his, to help with the case. The key was secrecy and limiting the people involved to those who could be trusted. The captain assured Jim's friend that would be the case and to this point everything was running smoothly.

"Good job tonight," Jim offered Bob.

"Did you get what you wanted?"

"We sure did and more," responded Agent Groves.

"What do you mean?" Bob inquired.

"After you left the restaurant Mario made a series of calls. Our guess is those calls will lead us to the higher-ups in the mob."

"So, what happens now?"

"We wait and see what direction Mario and his boys take."

"What do you think they'll do?"

"My guess is they'll try to find the local guy and either intimidate him or try to take him out. I don't think they'll cancel the operation since they've already got so much time and resources committed to it," Jim replied.

"You're kidding," Bob responded. "They'll actually eliminate one of their own."

"Welcome to the real world of sleaze, crime and corruption. First off, this local punk is probably not a member of their crime family, and secondly, even if he was, they aren't going to let some two-bit punk get in the way of an operation like this."

"Does this guy even know he's involved?"

"I doubt it," replied Agent Mast.

"What happens if they try to kill him?" Bob asked.

"The police will have a tail on him and try to prevent that from happening. But just short of arresting him, which would compromise the operation, there is only so much that can be done to protect him."

Unfortunately for the local crime boss, he wouldn't know who or what hit him. The Mafia was not in a position time wise to coerce or buy off this guy. They heard from reliable sources he was trying to muscle into something they had worked hard and long to set up and they were not interested in negotiating with some low ranking thug. From Jim's perspective, although he could not openly condone the end result, this was a chance to get rid of a known crime boss while at the same time adding to the building evidence that would hopefully bring down one of the big mob families. Besides racketeering, income tax evasion, etc., it was becoming a real possibility the FBI would be able to add murder to the charges.

Bob was sure he had been trailed back to the hotel and that was confirmed shortly thereafter with the arrival of one of Jim's agents. The agent identified a tail on Bob but the tail disappeared as soon as Bob got on the elevator and punched his floor. Bob rerouted his phone to the FBI whenever he was not in his room so he could be with Jim and still answer his calls. This change could be accomplished by merely flipping a switch. After all, not being in his room after taking the elevator to his floor would lead to suspicions if anyone checked.

But what he didn't know was his phone was continually tapped and his life was now being monitored and controlled by the FBI. The trouble with Bob was he had always been much too trusting. Jim felt what Bob did not know would not hurt him.

Chapter Thirty Nine

It was not long until Bob received a call from Mario indicating they might need to meet early in the morning. This could be the break Jim had been waiting for and he could only hope the Mafia would follow through on its plan.

"What time and where?" Bob asked.

"I'll call by 7:00 and give you the details."

"Can't you tell me what this is all about?"

"No, I can't discuss the details now. Just for your information, there are still some things to be worked out but it looks like the operation will go forward as planned."

"Great," Bob said trying to sound enthusiastic, "but don't make the meeting too late. Remember, tomorrow will be hectic and I don't want to deviate from my normal routine."

Jim realized it would now be a waiting game, and he could only hope the mob had taken the bait and was about to involve higher-ups in the operation. There was not much to decide until they received word concerning the meeting. Jim then confirmed Nancy had arrived and was probably in the room waiting as they talked. He also brought Bob up to speed on Betty and Chad and the excitement associated with their involvement in the championship game. He assured Bob that Chad was fine and would be able to play tomorrow, even if not at full strength. Bob knew at ninety percent Chad was better than the other Duke players at his position.

Bob's questions for Jim were how he was expected to carry out this plan and what protections would be available for him and his family leading up to, during and immediately after the game? Jim could only assure Bob he would do the best job possible, but with the scheduled meeting tomorrow morning he could not guarantee his safety. It was unlikely the mob suspected there was anything amiss with the operation, nor would it risk exposing its prize pupil. The most dangerous times for Bob would be at tomorrow's meeting with Mario and right after the game if it did not turn out the way the Mafia planned.

"We'll have plenty of backup at your meeting with Mario," Jim advised. "If something goes wrong, you just have to say 'this ain't gonna work' and my agents will pull you out."

"Assuming everything goes well tomorrow morning, what about after the game?"

"Depending on the outcome, we'll see what has to be done. Remember, if Kentucky wins by more than the spread, then Mario and his boys won't know anything's wrong and there shouldn't be a problem. Be assured we'll cover every eventuality."

"What about Nancy and Scott?"

"Same thing, I've already placed surveillance on both of them."

"And both our parents?"

"Once again, that's dependent upon the outcome of the game," Jim tried to reassure Bob. "I can only guarantee we'll do whatever's necessary to protect everyone involved."

On that note Jim left Agent Groves in charge and returned to the Hyatt knowing tomorrow would be a busy day. Bob returned to his room where he found Nancy dressed in a very suggestive outfit. Victoria Secret's best had nothing on this gal. It was difficult for Bob, with all that was on his mind, to provide the romantic touch such an occasion called for but it was not long before the lovemaking prevailed. Bob's hope was Nancy would not find out or get dragged into this maize of criminal activity, although he knew that was virtually impossible.

Before dozing off Bob asked Nancy about Scott and if anything was wrong. He could sense a problem in Nancy's voice, and after the usual small talk she explained what had happened with the bank and the FBI agents. Bob assured her he didn't know what was going on and there must be some kind of a mistake. Maybe it was a misunderstanding with the way he reported his income from officiating or the deductions he claimed from the summer camp. In any case, he convinced her there was nothing to worry about. Was that not the reason they always used a licensed CPA instead of doing their own tax returns? Nancy began to feel guilty, especially knowing Bob was involved in the biggest moment of his career. The last thing he needed was a meddlesome wife distracting him with something that probably amounted to nothing. Bob was shocked how quickly and how far along the FBI had moved on this investigation and could only hope the nightmare would quickly come to an end. Lying was something Bob despised, especially to his wife.

It seemed like just a few minutes ago that Bob had gone to sleep when awakened by a ringing phone. On the other end was Mario indicating a meeting would take place in about an hour. The meeting would be held in the parking lot behind the Crossbow Disco, an all-night dance club in Kenner. It would take about half an hour to get there and Bob was to arrive by taxi, walk into the restaurant and wait for Mario. He needed to be there promptly at 7 o'clock, and be sure to exit the hotel by the back stairs and get a cab a block away so as not to call attention to his departure. At this hour of the morning there would be very little activity and it was very unlikely Bob would be seen. Even so, Bob should dress like he was taking his early morning walk.

"Who was that at this hour?" Nancy asked, half asleep.

"One of the committee members who wants to review the events leading up to my arrival at the Superdome," Bob lied. "Go back to sleep."

Bob immediately dressed and ran to the FBI room to report what had transpired, only to find the agent on the phone talking with Jim about what he had just heard. For the first time Bob realized he could trust no one but himself. He felt violated and did not like the feeling.

"What the hell is this all about?" Bob demanded.

"What?" Agent Mast replied.

"You know damn well what I mean. Why the wire-tap on my phone?"

"Look, I just do as I'm told. You need to talk to Jim about this, although I can tell you it's for your protection."

"My ass," Bob shouted, "it's for the FBI's protection and you know it!"

Why the wiretap was a surprise to Bob was a question even he would have a hard time answering. After all, no one needed to know more about what was going on than Jim. From Bob's perspective it was a matter of trust, which was something he apparently had yet to earn.

Jim caught the tail end of the conversation as he walked into the room. He tried to calm Bob down and explained the FBI needed all the information it could get to stay one step ahead of Mario and the mob. Documentation was essential to eventually prepare an airtight case.

"Fine," Bob responded, "but if you want me to continue to help, you better have the decency to trust me."

"Point well taken but we do trust you."

"Like hell you do. The next time you pull a bonehead play like this I'm out of here. Then you can solve this case on your own. See how that works without your star witness."

Jim understood Bob's anger but explained they didn't have time to argue. Both knew Bob had no real bargaining power and he was just letting off steam. The stress was beginning to show and they both agreed they would have to do a better job of communicating with each other. Jim then went on to explain the procedure for the meeting with Mario.

Jim explained there was no way he could place people in the disco on this late notice. It would look too suspicious for people to start showing up at the club at seven o'clock in the morning. Furthermore, they might not stay in the club. Knowing Mario, discovery of Bob's involvement with the FBI would almost surely result in his immediate termination. Bob would have to wear the SX-47 wire again and take his chances. The sophistication of today's equipment was remarkable, but still it was dangerous on Bob's part if he agreed to carry out the plan. Realistically, what choice did he have? Bob should also keep in mind the closer to game time the more suspicious the mob's nature.

For the FBI to build a strong case it would need a recording of the meeting and who was involved. Bob agreed to once again wear the wire. Not only would the FBI have the information on tape, if something did go wrong Bob could alert them to the problem.

Bob was to get the names of the participants, review the plan within reasonable limitations and find out the payoff for the mob. If he sensed things were getting crazy, he was to stop probing and take what he could get without further aggravating the situation. There would be agents in the vicinity and he needed only to use their pre-arranged code to seek help and try to get away. Unfortunately, there were no guarantees nor did Jim imply there was. The best advice he could give Bob was to expect the unexpected.

At about the same time, Chad was beginning to move about after experiencing a restless night. Breakfast for the team was not scheduled until 10 a.m., but Chad and his roommate were already up and headed to the hotel lobby for a bagel and juice. After breakfast the team was scheduled to meet and watch more film as well as talk about its game plan for the Wildcats.

Chad's finger had improved greatly with the continued ice treatment and he was confident the injury would not be a problem for him during the game. The team doctor and trainer were satisfied his finger was back in alignment and if properly taped would offer little concern for additional or permanent damage.

This would be the longest day in Chad's life but he also knew it had a chance to be the most rewarding and special. He could only hope the time would go by quickly and he and his teammates would play their best game of the season. Chad knew they would have to play a near-perfect game if they were to have any chance of winning the national championship.

For Nancy it was not just another day. Her husband was about to be center-stage in the biggest sporting event of their lives. She called home to check on Scott and was told he was doing fine. She also called Bob's parents and her mother to remind them of the time and network the game would be on. This was really unnecessary with Bob's parents, but her mother was oblivious to sporting events and oftentimes forgetful. Nothing had transpired to alert Nancy to any kind of a problem. What a shock she was about to experience in the next twenty-four hours. She would dress and meet Betty for breakfast at the Hyatt and from there they would get in some shopping and sightseeing before the game.

Chapter Forty

After having the SX-47 put in place, Bob left to meet Mario. Taking the cab ride to the restaurant, he began for the first time to try to figure out what he would do when this mess was over. How would he ever be able to look his family and friends in the eyes? What kind of danger had he brought himself and his family? What could he do to insure nothing happened to Nancy and Scott? What and where would he work? Would he and his family have to move and enter the witness protection program? Would he ever have a chance to officiate again? How would Chad and Betty react to him? These were just a few of the questions to be answered, although Bob had more important and immediate concerns. Right now he just hoped to survive the next hour of his life.

Upon entering the restaurant he saw Mario and his friend, both of which approached him and asked him to follow. They moved quickly out the back door of the restaurant and into a small van.

"Sorry partner but you'll need to take off your clothes," Mario instructed.

"You're kidding," Bob said. "After all we've been through and you still don't trust me?"

"It doesn't matter whether I do or not, I've got my orders so strip down."

Bob removed his clothes, and after being searched was instructed to change into shorts, tee shirt and a pair of tennis shoes that were provided. Jim guessed correct when they discussed the degree of

243

sophistication needed with the recording equipment. Jim knew the Mafia lieutenants were very careful, thus the need for something hidden in the body rather than just on the person. Bob was then led out of the van and into a limousine parked on the other side of the lot. Tension was beginning to mount.

Entering the car, Bob noticed a middle-aged man in a very expensive suit sitting next to another gentleman who appeared to be a bodyguard. Bob confirmed for the first time this operation was being directed on site by one of the Cuban Mafia's higher ups. As the conversation began, Bob was introduced to Albert Valdez, a notorious and vicious underworld crime figure, and a member of the Gallibini Family, one of the largest crime families in the country based in New York City. It was apparent the sudden unexpected developments led Mario to ask for help.

Albert arrived in the United States from Cuba with his family in 1959 during the mass exodus from Fidel Castro's dictatorship. His father, Roberto Valdez, had been involved in crime related activities in Havana and continued those illegal ways after establishing himself in the Little Havana area of Miami. Over a short period of time the Valdez name became synonymous with power and greed in South Florida.

At about the same time the Gallibini family was attempting to establish itself in South Florida. As a result, Francisco 'The Boss' Gallibini made frequent trips to Miami combining business and pleasure. On one such trip 'The Boss' met with Roberto Valdez to discuss their mutual interests. As strong as Roberto's hold was on the Miami area, he didn't have the clout of the Gallibini family, and it was made very clear he could either merge or be eliminated by 'The Boss' and his organization. Roberto was smart enough to declare his allegiance to the Gallibini family and that was the beginning of the Cuban Mafia as it came to be known.

It was not long after that Albert, the oldest of three Valdez sons, met Franseca Gallibini, the youngest of the Gallibini daughters, during one of these trips. They connected immediately and after a short courtship Albert and Franseca were married in what many still consider the most elaborate wedding in New York City history. With

Albert's background and his direct link to the Gallibini family, it was only natural he would head up the crime family's interest in South Florida as his father moved into retirement.

As his brainchild, the point shaving scheme propelled Albert to center stage and he was placed in charge of the entire operation nationwide. To Albert's credit, he was not only very successful in conducting mob business in South Florida but had also worked himself into the number three position in the Gallibini family network nationwide.

What Albert wanted to know from Bob was how much the NACA and local police knew or suspected of a possible fix involving the championship game. Bob repeated what he told Mario earlier and what Jim instructed him to say. There were rumors, basically self-contained in nature, a local crime boss was trying to get involved in the game but nothing had been substantiated as of yet.

Albert's next question was very direct. "How hard will it be to ensure Kentucky wins the game by four or more points?"

"Kentucky is very talented and should have very little trouble winning the game."

With a hardened look, Albert corrected, "That's not what I asked."

"Sorry, the Wildcats should easily cover the spread," Bob answered.

"How can you be so sure?" Mario interjected.

"First, they're much deeper and more experienced and secondly, the latest report has Chad Payne still struggling with his injured hand," Bob responded.

Albert interrupted, "Who's Chad Payne and how reliable is your source?"

"He's Duke's best player and my source is someone very close to the team."

"You mean Duke can't win without him?"

"I don't think so."

"Why?"

"Because he's not only the best player, he's their emotional leader and quarterbacks the team," Bob explained. "Duke has no one else to handle the Kentucky pressure."

Sensing Albert's comfort with Bob's answers, the meeting proceeded another fifteen minutes as Albert, Mario and Bob went forward with the plan for the championship game. This was done in great detail so as to eliminate any questions or concerns Bob might have. Lastly, as if to humor Bob, Albert asked what he thought would be fair payment for handling the game. Bob knew Mario discussed their earlier conversation with Albert but decided to make him aware of the importance of this game and his contribution.

"With the visibility, scrutiny and risk involved, I would think $100,000 would be fair," Bob said with a straight face.

"Twenty-four hours ago the game was worth $50,000," Mario volunteered.

"That was before all the problems with the local crime boss."

"Good point," Albert added. "Don't worry about your take. I think $100,000 sounds fair. I like a guy who thinks big. Just deliver the game."

"You don't have to worry about me," Bob replied.

"If that's the case, you should have your money in a week," Albert concluded.

Then the unexpected happened. Bob's nose began to bleed as a result of the wire rubbing the same spot where the previous wire had been. As the first drop of blood fell on his shorts, Bob could sense panic running through his body as well as curiosity on the faces of the other men in the car. Mario handed Bob a handkerchief and Bob laughed off the incident as pre-game tension, explaining he had a bloody nose earlier that morning as a result of picking his nose while reading the paper.

In a desperate attempt to deflect attention from the bloody nose, Bob voiced his concern about the local crime boss making waves and creating a problem just before game time. He indicated he was depending on the money and like the mob did not want anything to queer the deal. This seemed to grab everyone's attention and Albert assured Bob the situation had already been dealt with.

"So was there any truth to the rumor?" Bob asked.

"Yeah, but it's no longer a problem," Mario answered.

"Why, was the guy arrested?"

"He was arrested all right," Mario laughed. "He's now a prisoner of the sea."

"I don't get it," Bob offered.

"Let's just put it this way," Mario said, now bragging, "unless someone is bottom fishing five hundred feet deep in the Gulf of Mexico, or concrete blocks float to the surface, this local punk is not someone to worry about. The dead do not talk."

"Enough Mario," Albert admonished his underling.

Obviously, Mario had said too much. The plan was in place and no further explanation was necessary or forthcoming. Bob would not be privy to the intricacies attached to Mafia business operations. He would later learn the Gallibini Family had crossed over into the Vicini Family's territory, a small mob operation that was well respected by the other major crime families for their operation in Louisiana and Mississippi. The Mafia code required Albert to get permission from Tony Vicini before implementing his plan, and for ten percent of the gross Tony welcomed Albert with open arms. Eliminating some small-time punk who was rumored to be operating on his own received the blessing of the Vicini family boss.

As Bob stuffed the cloth up his nose to stop the bleeding, he knew it was time to bring this meeting to an end. He suggested it would be a good idea if he returned to the hotel before someone noticed his absence. After all, on a day like this one would think the officials would be secluded and resting. Also, Bob indicated he was due at a tournament committee meeting at 10 a.m. and could not afford to be missing or late. Albert seemed to buy into that explanation and advised Mario to have one of the boys give Bob a ride to within a block of the hotel to ensure he would get back as soon as possible.

Everyone bid farewell and Bob changed back into his clothes to return to the Marriott where he would meet later with Jim to verify the conversation had been recorded. They would also need to plan the rest of the operation. But for now Bob needed to try and get a quick nap since he had gotten so little sleep the previous night.

After the incident in the car, he was glad his nap was not of a more permanent nature

Jim was up early to check on how things had progressed and to meet Betty and Nancy for breakfast. As Jim went to the lobby early to get a newspaper and cup of coffee, he noticed Chad and his roommate doing the same. Chad immediately recognized Jim and came over to visit. The two men engaged in small talk before Chad excused himself. Jim wanted so badly to tell Chad how he felt about his mother but he knew this was not the time or place for such a conversation. Chad had enough other things on his mind and the game would be tough enough without any additional distractions.

After reading the paper, Jim called Betty's room to make sure she was up and about. "Did I wake you?"

"No. I've been up for about forty minutes and was just getting ready to call you."

"Unless you have a man in your room, why don't we meet in the restaurant for breakfast," Jim joked.

Betty laughed and joked, "I do have a man with me but I think we can finish what we're doing in ten minutes. Breakfast in twenty minutes sounds reasonable. Has Nancy arrived?"

"Not yet but I expect her any minute. We did tell her nine o'clock."

Betty joined Jim in the restaurant for breakfast just as Nancy was walking through the lobby, and once again he begged off from any planned daytime activities. Jim needed to check in with the local FBI office to see if anything of interest was happening. His rationale was since there were so many overlapping cases with the bureau he needed to be aware of anything the local agents were working on which might impact his work in Miami. Betty could sense Jim's feelings of guilt, being on what many would describe as a bogus case study vacation, and gave him an out when she advised that she and Nancy were invited by some of the other mothers for a day of shopping. Little did she know there was nothing bogus about Jim's visit to New Orleans, in fact, this situation could have as much impact on the mob and illegal gambling as any case in the past half century. Jim was delighted he would not have to worry about entertaining Betty and even asked her to pick up a couple of Final Four tee shirts for him.

After breakfast, Jim immediately proceeded to the Marriott to get updates on what happened with Bob's meeting and what additional information they had on the upcoming game and parties involved. Much to Jim's delight, most of the tape of Bob's conversation concerning the fix was perfectly clear. Unfortunately, the last part concerning the hit on the local crime boss was muffled and unintelligible.

"So what happened to the last part of the tape?" Jim asked.

Agent Mast responded, "As best we can tell in talking with Bob, he developed a bloody nose that we think clogged the ends of the filament."

"Surely you're joking."

"I wish I was, but unfortunately that's what happened. We'll know in the next couple of days if the lab boys can decipher what was said."

. The important thing was Bob obtained the necessary information on the names of the parties involved in the illegal operation as well as an admission of the game fix and payoff. With evidence of involvement as high as Albert Valdez, the immediate concern was how the FBI's plan should be carried out and what protections would be available to the parties involved, more specifically Bob, Nancy and Scott, against a major crime family. Jim was advised Bob had returned to his room for a short nap and decided to wait until after lunch to visit with him.

Mario and Albert had a brief discussion after Bob left. Albert wanted to be sure Bob was on board and he did not have to worry about any surprises.

Are you absolutely sure about this guy?" Albert asked.

"This guys the real deal," Mario responded. "He's been solid all along and would be scared shitless to rat us out or not seal the deal."

"You better be right."

The Gallibini family had placed a lot of faith in Albert and he did not want to disappoint them. Albert was the heir apparent at some point to take over the entire eastern United States Gallibini crime syndicate and very seldom got involved with people like Bob. But this was Albert's brainchild and he was also a close cousin to Mario who he viewed as one of his best and most loyal soldiers. Both men realized the importance of this operation coming off without a hitch, and Mario wanted Albert to give final approval to the operation after meeting with Bob. Mario could be trusted, but with all the complications and magnitude of the plan this call had to be made by Albert.

Everyone has a flaw and many times it's in the people we trust and are closest with. That would prove to be the case with Albert and Mario. The plan was to have Mario and his bodyguard at the game Monday in a prominent place where Bob could see them and be constantly reminded of his commitment. Mario had been brutally straightforward and to the point before he introduced Bob to Albert. He emphasized Albert and the Gallibini family would not stand for any mistakes. They committed a lot of time and resources to this project and expected it to come off without any additional surprises. Bob clearly understood the message and assured Mario and Albert there would be no problems.

Mario maintained the tail on Bob and also continued to research the disposed local crime boss to confirm his involvement as reported in the attempted fix on the championship game. Mario had no reason to doubt his sources, but was always one to be suspicious and thorough. So far everything regarding the events led him to conclude what he heard was in fact true. But he was still glad Albert was making the final decisions up to and through the completion of the championship game.

Chad and his teammates were trying to deal with the anticipation of the game. Duke traveled to the Superdome to have a light shoot around at 11 a.m. Although allotted a full hour, Coach P had limited the workout to forty-five minutes. The game plan was in place and this was merely an opportunity to break up the monotony of the day. Kentucky was scheduled to workout at noon, and Coach P wanted his players to be off the floor before they arrived. Twenty minutes of paired shooting, ten minutes of foul shooting and fifteen minutes walking through Kentucky's offensive plays pretty much wrapped it up for the Blue Devils. Everyone was in great spirits although a little tired. The semi-final game had been a difficult one, and with all the nervous energy being expended it was more mental fatigue than physical exhaustion.

Chad was not overly concerned about his physical condition, knowing when the game started everyone would get a sudden rush of adrenaline and play through whatever problems they might have. What he as the captain and leader tried to do was keep the bench players ready to play since it would be a tough game with a lot of unexpected happenings. Many times in such games an unknown player would rise to the occasion and become a difference maker. Chad hoped that would not be the case, but if it happened he wanted it to be on his team. He was reminded to expect the unexpected, yet only be concerned with those things of which he had control. As a player and coach, you could not help but feel the enthusiasm Chad exhibited and be ready to compete. The responsibility for success would rest with each player's ability to focus and properly prepare for the task at hand. The remainder of the day would be spent resting and mentally preparing for the biggest games of their lives.

Chapter Forty One

Bob was awakened at 1:15 p.m. by a call from Jim indicating a need to meet and put in place the final pieces of the puzzle. Bob walked down the hall to the FBI's room and he, Jim, Agents Groves and Mast began to discuss the plan leading up to and through the end of the game. Jim was out on a limb allowing Bob to work the game but he trusted this man and knew it was the only way they could carry out the plan. After all, Bob had more at risk than anyone. Bob would be expected to referee the game to the best of his ability even if the outcome might work to the mob's benefit.

"Listen," Jim started, "I don't mean to question your honesty but the fact of the matter is your involvement in this operation puts us all at risk."

"I know, but I can assure you I have never decided who won a game by cheating, although I have impacted the difference in the points scored."

"Your Syracuse/Utah game indicates what you say is true but you didn't have as much at stake as you do now," chimed in Agent Groves.

With a scowl Bob retorted, "You don't have to worry about me. Once I agreed to be involved with you guys, I committed myself to do the right thing. Keep in mind I've already put my life at risk. So, what else do you want from me?"

"The right thing is not who wins the game or by how much. The important thing is the game is honestly officiated," Jim interjected.

"We already have the information we need to indict Mario and his buddies."

"Then why keep him on the game?" Agent Mast asked.

"Simple, because if Bob does not show up that would alert the mob and possibly blow the whole deal." Jim emphasized. "I said we have enough info to indict these guys, but we still need to place these guys at the scene of the crime and solidify the betting patterns to put the finishing touches on the case. An indictment is one thing, a conviction is another."

With the present information the Feds had a reasonably strong case, but the mobs reaction to this game could finalize the evidence necessary to expose the operation and get a conviction. If Kentucky covered the spread, nobody outside this immediate group would know anything was wrong and Jim could monitor the payoff to Bob. If the Wildcats did not cover the spread, only this group and the Gallibini family would know something was wrong and the ensuing meeting and possible attempt to eliminate Bob would be documented. Furthermore, Jim needed the extra time to link the betting and influence peddling against the Gallibini family as well as develop a plan for Bob and his family's protection.

Thus, the immediate concern for Jim was how soon he would need to protect Bob. Would it be right after the game or in a couple of weeks when the charges were made public? Jim's actions would be determined in great part by the outcome of the game. He had to assume the worst and thus this meeting to determine what course of action would be taken immediately after the game.

"You realize what might happen if Kentucky doesn't cover the spread?" Jim asked having already determined Bob would referee the game.

"Pretty much," Bob replied, "but do you think they would try something at the arena with all the people, media and security?"

"Didn't you say Mario and his bodyguard were going to be at the game?" Agent Mast inquired.

"That's what he told me after our meeting this morning."

"Then what better place to take you out than right at the arena," Agent Groves volunteered. "With all the people and confusion right after the game, the setting couldn't be any better for those guys."

"But would they risk that with a mob boss like Valdez around?" Bob countered.

"Valdez has already returned to Miami," Jim replied. "We tracked him to the airport right after your meeting this morning. He never hangs too close to the action."

"Well then, I guess I'll just have to trust you guys to get me through this."

Although Bob knew from Mario's conversation he would be at the game with his bodyguard, he was not sure where they would be located. It was decided that before and during the game selected agents would be dressed like ushers and monitor the location of Mario and his friend. Their whereabouts would be determined when they entered the building and went to their seats. There would also be two agents assigned to the locker room to escort the officials to and from the court. Dressed as Superdome personnel, these men would merely carry out a procedure normal to all tournament games. It would be after the game, dependant upon the outcome, when these agents would be called upon to fill their various roles.

Although Jim had all the necessary paperwork from the courts to carry out this plan, the most difficult part would be working with the Superdome personnel in finalizing these necessary changes without alerting the mob or NACA officials. By using only a handful of agents he could trust, the chance of exposure was minimized but still put Bob and the plan at risk. Jim hoped to wait until the last possible minute to involve other agents in the plan to reduce the possibility of leaks. Jim's toughest decision was not to notify the NACA Tournament Committee about a potential problem with one of their officials, but secrecy was paramount to the success of the operation and he decided to risk the consequences and deal with that problem later. And a problem it would surely become.

Fortunately, Jim's friend at the New Orleans' FBI knew and was able to persuade the head of Superdome security into going along with the plan. Because it only impacted a few people at the main entrances and the officials' locker room, the chief of security was able to reassign people without creating suspicion. This was not an uncommon occurrence for events of this magnitude and everyone affected went about their business without asking questions. For the most part the ushers were delighted just to work, let alone get paid, the NACA national championship basketball game. The key element of the plan was to locate Mario and be prepared if the game did not turn out the way the mob anticipated.

With everything seemingly in place, Bob returned to his room while Jim and his agents reviewed the plan. Jim's guys would monitor Bob, and selected agents in Miami were instructed to be on alert and watch the Girard house. There would also be a group ready if necessary to provide security for Bob's parents and Nancy's mother.

"So you think we can pull this off?" Agent Groves asked Jim.

"Yeah, I really do."

"It seems like there are a lot of variables and loose ends," responded Agent Mast.

"With the limited number of people outside our own group, I think we'll be okay."

"But can you trust the Superdome people not to spill the beans?"

"My friend here assures me the chief of security is solid and can be trusted. After all, the ushers won't know or care what's going on anyway."

"Any second thoughts about the NACA people?"

"That's my one concern. I wish I could tell them but they would probably pull Bob off the game and compromise the operation. When the truth is known I'm sure I'll catch hell, but that's just a chance I have to take."

Another question now was whether Jim could deliver on his own promises to Bob. Regardless of the evidence, it was a foregone conclusion Bob would have to testify in court against Mario, Albert Valdez and the Gallibini family for the FBI to get a conviction. Bob wanted to be sure he and his family at the very least would be placed, even if only temporarily, in the witness protection program, and if anything happened to him Nancy and Scott would be taken care of financially for the rest of their lives. Bob had a sizable insurance policy but he wanted the FBI, through its protection program, to commit $500,000 to his wife and son in the form of a mutual fund of his choosing. Normal growth of the fund, coupled with their guarantee of resettling and finding Nancy and Bob a job, would be more than adequate to give his family a new start on life. The money was unacceptable, but Jim assured Bob he would do all in his power to ensure Nancy and Scott's well being if anything happened to him. Jim knew this would be an issue that would have to be revisited.

Another problem Bob wrestled with was what could be done for his parents and Nancy's mom? There was very little doubt the mob would use whatever means available to flush Bob out from hiding. Short-term protection was not a problem but what could be done to protect these loved ones long term? No one could predict how quickly this case would come to trial, let alone reach a verdict. With or without a conviction, the Mafia could be very vindictive.

Meanwhile, Jim could understand the anguish Bob must feel knowing his life was ruined with the hard part yet to come. He liked Bob but made him understand he was still nothing more than a common criminal subject to grave consequences if he did not fully cooperate.

Jim then returned to the Hyatt to change and prepare for the game. He figured Nancy was with Bob and Betty was getting ready for the game, yet couldn't help but wonder how he was going to eventually tell Betty, Chad and Nancy about Bob.

Chapter Forty Two

The game was scheduled for 9:00 p.m. eastern time in an attempt to attract most of the television viewing public. CBS committed millions of dollars to broadcasting the tournament and was bound and determined to capitalize on its investment while making its sponsors happy. Fortunately for CBS and the NACA, the championship game had been the most competitive of all the major sports championships. During the 80's, seven of eight final games were decided by four points or less and most came down to winning plays in the last thirty seconds of the game. On paper this game had the makings of another classic.

Bob and Nancy had shared an early dinner in the hotel. Not much was said and you could cut the tension in the air with a knife. Nancy knew this was the ultimate for Bob in officiating and what he had worked so hard for. She couldn't be any prouder of her husband.

"How soon do you need to go?" Nancy asked.

"We'll finish up and then I need to go to the room to get ready. Are you all set to get to the game?"

"I'm meeting Betty and Jim at the Hyatt at 6:30 and we're going to catch the hotel shuttle for the game. When do the gates open?" Nancy asked.

"Usually about ninety minutes before tip-off."

Bob left for the Superdome at 6:30 to get a feel for the arena and meet with the other officials. Nancy left at the same time and gave him a kiss for good luck. Chad and the Duke Blue Devils would leave the hotel and make the escorted walk to the arena about two hours before game time. This would give them plenty of time to get taped, change into their uniforms and shoot around before tip-off. Kentucky would follow much the same schedule. Jim's small group of agents would be in place by 6 o'clock and the doors to the Superdome would open at approximately 7:30.

Jim would not arrive at the arena until approximately one hour before game time. He would escort Betty and Nancy to the arena and give the appearance of just another fan, not drawing any undue attention to his involvement with the tournament in case anyone should recognize him. Once inside the building he would offer Betty excuses to disappear for short periods of time. All the time he would have access to a beeper and walkie-talkie, both concealed under his sport jacket. He advised his agents not to contact him by walkie-talkie unless there was an emergency.

By the time the teams took the floor for warm-ups everything was in place. Mario had been identified and his seat location was known. Now it was just a matter of playing the game. Jim had mixed emotions since he wanted badly for Chad and Duke to win but also knew that would expose the fix and force him to take immediate action to protect Bob and his family.

Although this would cause a stir, the FBI's position had always been one of secrecy when involved in an ongoing investigation. Dependent upon action taken by Mario and the Mafia, it was possible no one outside the people immediately involved would suspect or identify Bob's involvement in this operation. The hard part was reacting to events out of their control. If Kentucky covered the spread there would be very few initial problems. Jim knew the odds were in Bob's favor, but he was not one to bet against the human spirit and knew no one had a bigger heart than Chad. Wouldn't it be ironic if Chad played just the way Bob had taught him and that would cost Bob his life.

In the officials' locker room, Bob and his two partners reviewed the rules as well as situations that might develop during the game. How would they handle the NACA Rules Committee's points of emphasis, last-second half, game and shot clock situations and television's commercial interruptions? Bob, although nervous about his role in the game, was extremely confident and at ease with himself. It was hard to believe in about two hours he would have fulfilled his dream of officiating the national championship game, but would also become the focal point of one of the biggest investigations in history relating to corruption in amateur athletics. Fortunately, he did not recognize either of the other officials as being involved in the Mafia's point-shaving plan.

After the warm-ups and playing of the national anthem, the teams returned to their respective benches for the introduction of the starting lineups. The atmosphere was electric for all involved and Chad could feel an adrenaline rush as he listened to Coach P's last second instructions. As the players broke from their huddles to start the game, Bob and Chad's eyes met. Chad winked, acknowledging he was ready and this was as good as it gets, and believed there was no one who would work a game in a more honest and straightforward way than Bob. Bob, on the other hand, knew Chad would expect no special favors.

The first half was hotly contested with neither team able to build more than a four-point lead. The officials agreed before the game not to ignore the obvious, but allow the players to determine the outcome of the game by calling only fouls that impacted play. This allowed both teams to gain a rhythm and not have to look over their shoulders for a whistle on every play.

Kentucky tried to take advantage of the loose officiating and its own depth by forcing a fast paced game with good defensive pressure, while Duke tried to slow things down and control the tempo with Chad handling the ball. Coach Galino wasted no time testing Chad's injury by pressing and forcing him to his left hand. Chad was equal to the challenge and scored four points and assisted on another basket in the first two minutes of the game.

The coaches were as focused as the players and offered little problems for the officials. Galino and Coach P were two of the best at working the officials while never losing sight of the ultimate goal. Another championship would only add to their already larger than life reputations. Just as officials respected the coaches who made it to the Four Final, the coaches likewise knew the officials at this level were very professional and capable.

The first half ended with Duke trailing by two points and a chance to tie the game on a last shot, only to lose the ball and watch the Wildcats make a three-point shot at the buzzer. Instead of being tied or up one, the Blue Devils went to the locker room trailing by five points to the hoots and hollers of the Kentucky faithful. It would be interesting to see how this turn of events would affect both teams and the start of the second half.

At halftime there was a lot of activity the average fan could not comprehend. Trainers checked on injuries, managers provided towels and water for the players and the players talked with each other about what needed to be done. The coaches were patient and instructive with little yelling or false hype. While resting, the players gathered their thoughts for what probably would be the most important twenty minutes of their young athletic lives. The officials discussed the first half action and agreed the game had been well played and officiated.

Mario placed a call to Albert Valdez to confirm he was in place and suggest things were progressing just as they had planned. Albert watched the first half and was pleased with the way things had gone. Neither suspected any kind of problems.

Jim excused himself from Betty under the pretense of going to the restroom, when in actuality he needed to check with his agents on the status of the operation and go over any last minute details. At the present time, with Kentucky seemingly gaining control of the game, it appeared they would not have to take any out of the norm post game action.

Outside the locker room Jim asked Agent Groves, "Everything okay?"

"No problems so far and neither of the other officials or the NACA people sense anything is wrong."

"What about the other agents?"

"Everyone's in place and nothing seems to be out of the ordinary," replied Agent Mast. "Mario made a call shortly after the conclusion of the half."

"Probably to Valdez," Jim surmised. "Anyway, I've got to get back to my seat before anyone notices I've been gone too long. Be sure to find out what that call was about."

"What about after the game?"

"I'll touch base with you before the game is over, but for now we'll just have to play it by ear and hope for the best," Jim concluded.

Jim returned to his seat just in time to see Mario and his bodyguard walk down the aisle. What a smug bastard this guy is Jim thought. Betty and Nancy were back from the restroom and the teams were just returning to the court for the start of the second half.

Kentucky seemed to pick up where it left off at the end of the first half. After falling behind by ten points in the first four minutes of the second half, Coach P called a twenty-second timeout and challenged his players. They could either be happy with what they had accomplished to date or they could pull together and make a statement for the rest of their lives. The challenge seemed to work as Duke went on a run, cutting the lead to four points with less than a minute to play.

With fifty seconds remaining and the Blue Devils in possession of the ball, Chad called their next-to-last timeout. Coach P decided there was enough time to score twice and advised his team to look for the quick and easy score, but not pass up a wide open three point-shot. After breaking the huddle, the Duke faithful encouraged their team as it returned to the court. Out of the timeout Chad brought the ball into the front-court, passed the ball to his low post man, flared off a screen set by the forward, received a return pass and knocked down a seventeen foot jumper to cut the lead to two points.

Coach Galino immediately called time out with forty-two seconds to play to set up what he wanted done. The Wildcats would put the ball in the hands of their point guard, work the shot clock down inside ten seconds and let him penetrate to score or create a shot for someone else. Even if the shot missed, it would place the game-clock inside the last ten seconds and make it difficult for Duke to score. He reminded them to take care of the ball, rebound any missed shot, play solid defense and not foul.

Coach P told his team to press and try to force a turnover in the backcourt, but to play solid man-to-man defense if Kentucky got the ball across the ten-second line. There was still plenty of time to win the game and he instructed his team not to foul or take any crazy chances that could result in an easy score or reset of the shot-clock. They had to rebound a missed shot.

Chad had a pretty good idea of what Coach Galino was probably thinking, having watched game tape and playing against the Wildcats' point guard for the last thirty nine plus minutes. As Kentucky broke the press and entered the frontcourt, he sensed the ball would end up in the point guard's hands for the last shot. Chad found himself defending the shooting guard because of a switch during the press. As the shot clock ran inside ten seconds, the Kentucky point guard began a spin move to get by his defender and take the ball into the middle of the defense. When he turned his back to the defender, Chad rotated off his man and slid into position to take a charge on the drive to the basket. As the point guard exploded down the lane, he ran into Chad and the place became eerily silent as Bob blew his whistle.

Video replays would later show Bob's call to be correct, but this was the time of reckoning for everyone involved in the fix. As Mario relaxed in his seat and Jim and Betty looked on, Bob came toward the scorer's table with his hand behind his head.

"Player control foul on white number 20," Bob bellowed.

"Yeah," Chad shouted!

"C'mon ref," the point-guard responded. "That was a block."

"Blue ball out of bounds," Bob signaled.

Although the Kentucky fans were irate, Coach Galino said little knowing the call was a good one. The Duke player made a good play.

"I had the same call," one of the other officials said as he passed Bob to get into position for the last few seconds of the game, which made Bob feel better about his decision.

Mario, on the other hand, nearly came out of his seat and for the first time sensed something was wrong and things might not work out the way the Mafia had planned. Jim now realized it was time to put his plan into action. He would for the first time have to expose himself to Betty as to his underlying interest in this game. Jim pulled out his walkie-talkie and contacted Agent Groves.

"Look, were down to the nitty-gritty and we'll have to act fast depending on the outcome of the game," Jim said.

"How do you want this handled?" asked Agent Groves.

"Move into position, but be discreet. If Kentucky somehow covers the spread, let Mario and his friend alone."

"What if they don't cover?"

"Then arrest them as quickly as possible. Agent Mast will get Bob off the court but we can't take a chance Mario won't try something stupid."

"And if he doesn't want to go quietly?"

"Then use whatever force necessary but be careful with all the people around."

Jim then put his walkie-talkie away and looked at Betty who had a quizzical look on her face. With the excitement surrounding the action of the game, both left well enough unsaid. This was not the time or place to ask or explain what was going on.

As the Duke players jumped up and down with excitement, Coach P immediately used his last timeout to set up what could be the last play. The question was whether to play for a tie and overtime or to look for a three-point field goal to win. Evaluating the fatigue factor as well as mounting foul problems, Coach P decided to go for the win. He substituted Gary, his best shooting guard, for his power forward to get another scorer into the game.

"Settle down, there's still a lot of time left," Coach P advised his team. "Let's put the ball in Chad's hands and run the same play we ran the last possession."

"You mean the flare screen?" a player asked.

"Yeah, only this time make sure to take the shot from beyond the three-point line. If they double team you Chad, then try to penetrate and look for Gary on the backside."

"What if both of us are covered," Chad asked?

"Then drop the ball inside and we'll play for overtime. But remember, we really want to look for the three to win."

"How about the time situation?" another player volunteered.

"With such little time left we'll have to get into the set right away, and with the ball in Chad's hands he can control the clock. We want the shot taken with about four seconds on the clock. This will give us a chance at a put-back basket if we miss, but won't leave enough time for Kentucky to get a shot. Anyone have any questions?" Coach P asked as they broke the huddle. "Also, remember we're out of timeouts."

Everyone seemed on the same page as Duke entered the ball to Chad with fourteen seconds to play. Dick Galino instructed his players to play solid defense, double-team Chad if he had the ball and rotate to any shooters if they got the ball. Everyone on the Kentucky team knew who was designated to take the last shot and wanted the ball out of his hands. As Chad dribbled off a perimeter screen by his shooting guard, he realized the defender had come off the screener to double-team him. Fighting off the pressure, Chad was able to find his shooting guard open just above the free throw line on the backside of the defense. With Chad's size and strength, he was able to split the double team and make a diagonal pass to his open teammate who immediately went up for the shot. The Wildcat players were late to rotate to pressure the shot and the ball passed cleanly through the basket as time expired. The trail official indicated the shot was a three-point field goal. Duke had won the game by a point, 93-92.

At that point the place was up for grabs. As Bob ran off the floor with the other officials, he noticed the Blue Devil players had lifted the shooting guard and Chad on their shoulders and were circling the court with their index finger extended indicating they were number one.

This turn of events caught almost everyone by surprise. Most people thought the game would go into overtime or Duke would miss the last shot enabling Kentucky to carry off the national championship trophy. As the last shot was in the air, the agents escorting the officials were already in position at the end of the court to immediately get them into the locker room. Agent Groves and two other agents had moved into position, and as the ball passed through the basket arrested Mario and his bodyguard indicating to both they could come without creating a scene or be carried out if they resisted.

Jim wanted and needed to get to the locker room without creating a disturbance or upsetting Betty. He knew Betty would be consumed by the post-game activities and was able to slip away while she cheered and watched the celebration. This was not the time for Jim to concern himself with Betty. He had made provisions for Nancy and her safety and the agent in charge explained that Jim would catch up with Betty and Chad later. He would only say something came up and Jim would be temporarily detained. Betty thought that odd, but in the excitement of the moment was preoccupied with joining her son and sharing his childhood dream. The wonderful part was Chad being chosen the most valuable player of the Four Final and she was there to witness the celebration first hand. As she made her way down to the court, Chad spotted her and rushed over to give her a big hug. For this moment in time Betty just knew everything was right with the world.

"Mom, can you believe we did it!" Chad exclaimed.

"Honey, I'm so proud of you."

"This is the dream of a lifetime and I'm so glad you were able to share it with me."

"There's no one more deserving. I'm so happy for you."

"Where's Jim and Nancy?" Chad asked.

"I'm really not sure," Betty replied, as she glanced toward the seats. "Nancy's still up in the stands and Jim said he would meet us back at the hotel. But they both enjoyed the game as much as I did."

Chad thought that to be strange but quickly returned to his teammates who were in the process of cutting down the nets. After accepting the national championship trophy, it would be on to the press conference, a shower and back to the hotel for a wild celebration. It would be at the hotel that Chad would catch up with his mother who, unbeknownst to him, was being escorted by a FBI agent.

Chapter Forty Three

With the sound of the final horn, Jim's plan was put into action. Agents in Miami moved quickly to serve a warrant for the arrest of Albert Valdez. Jim realized Mario and Albert would be out on bond before morning, but with all the protection required he wanted to move decisively and create confusion within the ranks of the mob. Jim also ordered in place protection for Scott as well as provided Nancy's mother and Bob's parents twenty-four hour surveillance. That was the tough part since it would eventually require an explanation, but this was not the time to worry about formalities. Scott was not as big a concern since it would be highly unlikely the mob would know his baby-sitter's whereabouts.

Immediately following the end of the game the FBI rushed Bob out of the arena under heavy guard to a safe-way house in Metarie, not too far from downtown New Orleans. Aside from the NACA tournament officials asking questions as to Bob's whereabouts, since he was supposed to attend a post-game briefing, Jim started receiving information everything had gone like clockwork. Jim was reasonably confident the NACA officials would not announce to the media anything out of the ordinary until they could substantiate what was going on.

Nancy, still unaware of anything unusual, was with Betty under the discreet surveillance of the FBI. The Girards' parents were not as big a concern since Jim knew they would be secondary targets as long as Jim, Nancy and Scott were alive. Since there was yet no formal grand jury indictment, the mob would not risk the problems and bad publicity associated with threatening or kidnapping such people. Threats on Nancy and Scott's lives would come into play only if the case was to be scheduled for trial, while threats on the parents' lives would be a desperate last resort.

Jim could only hope for an early trial date since it would be difficult to protect such a broad based group of people. Hopefully the judges and people in general were fed up with organized crime and a public outcry to get these cases resolved as quickly as possible would be demanded. The evidence was in place and self-explanatory. Except for Mafia politicking, there should be no reason for a delay or continuance. The immediate challenge was to get back to Miami and map out a strategy to bring the case to fruition. Before Jim returned to the hotel to catch up with Betty and Chad, he received word Mario and Albert had already made bail.

At the Hyatt Jim found Betty, Nancy and Chad celebrating with the other Duke faithful, including the coaches and their families. Coach P was about to excuse himself since he would have to be up early to appear on several of the major network's morning shows. Betty had a curious look on her face while Nancy waited patiently on word about Bob and when he would be able to join them. Chad was totally unaware there was a problem and Jim did not think this would be a good time to talk about the case.

"So where did you disappear to?" Betty asked in an accusing tone.

"I'm really sorry I had to leave, but I think it would be better if we talked about this later," Jim replied sheepishly.

"Okay, but I do think I deserve an explanation as to why you left me alone with some complete strangers after the game."

Betty's look indicated she was not very happy about the sudden turn of events but was willing to give him the benefit of the doubt. Jim and Betty had a strong enough relationship to know the truth would eventually come out, probably sooner than later.

After an hour of celebrating and rehashing the game, Chad excused himself to be with his teammates. They were going out to party and Betty could understand and appreciate that. It would not be long before Chad would be home for summer vacation, and she had spent more time with him the last four days, except during one Christmas break, than during the past two and a half years combined while he was away at school. She wished him well, gave him a kiss on the cheek and like any mother told him to be careful and stay out of trouble. They also agreed to meet for breakfast in the morning but not real early.

After Chad excused himself, Betty, Nancy and Jim found themselves alone at the table. Jim felt awkward and unsure about what to say. Betty broke the ice by asking Jim again to explain what had been going on during their stay in New Orleans, more specifically tonight.

"Well, I've been working on an investigation," Jim began.

"What kind of an investigation?"

"Pardon the interruption but I better get back to the hotel. Bob will be expecting me," Nancy said, feeling this was a private conversation she did not need to be a part of. She was mystified when Jim grabbed her arm and asked her to stay.

"This is something you need to hear," Jim directed his comments to Nancy. "It involves an illegal gambling case the FBI has been working on for some time."

"But what docs that have to do with me," Nancy replied.

"The betting was on the NACA Tournament, specifically tonight's game."

"You're kidding!" Betty exclaimed.

"I wish I was since this involves someone all of us know and care about."

"Are we privy to who it is?" Betty asked.

Jim knew to be truthful since their relationship depended in great part on each other's honesty. If it was business and he could not involve her she would understand, but he knew better than to mislead her on what was happening. He made a decision to entrust both women with what he knew, although that flew in the face of FBI policy.

"I really shouldn't tell you but we've never kept secrets from each other and I'm not about to start now, after all, you'll know soon enough," Jim replied. "Bob Girard is involved in an illegal, point-shaving operation."

"No way," Nancy gasped, as she turned toward Betty, "tell me it's not true! My husband could not possibly be involved in such a thing. It's got to be a mistake."

"I wish it was but unfortunately it's true."

"Are you sure? Bob is one of the most honest people I know. I just can't believe it," Betty added.

"Neither could I," Jim responded, "but we have a signed confession from him entailing his involvement."

Betty and Nancy looked at Jim in disbelief. For Nancy, here was a man she loved and trusted, her soul mate and the father of their child. There was no way he could be involved in such a thing without her knowledge. Betty on the other hand looked at Bob like a second father to Chad and the man most responsible for his success. As long as she knew Nancy and Bob, she just could not believe something like this could happen. She could not help but wonder how Chad would react to this revelation.

"Look, there's not much you can do right now," Jim explained. "I shouldn't have told you as much as I did and you need to promise you won't say anything to anyone."

"Excuse me, I think I'm going to be sick," Nancy interrupted, beginning to shake uncontrollably. "I need to get back to the hotel to be with my husband."

"That won't be necessary," Jim interjected. "We've taken Bob to a secret location for his protection and it will be impossible for you to see him now."

"But when will I be able to talk with him?" Nancy asked, now beginning to tear up.

"I hope soon but right now is not a good time. I'm truly sorry about this, Nancy."

"But we can't forsake Bob," Betty interjected.

"Don't worry, that's not our intent. We'll do everything possible to insure he receives fair treatment but all we can do now is offer Nancy and Bob our love and support."

"What about Chad?" Betty asked. "When will he find out?"

"I'm not sure, but soon. You'll just have to trust me on this," Jim concluded.

Jim then asked Betty if it would be okay for Nancy to stay with her under the pretense she would need someone to talk to. He did not mention the safety concerns and there would be an agent watching their room during the night. Needless to say, Betty was in complete agreement with this request.

To say it was a restless night for Betty and Nancy would be an understatement. Both ran the gauntlet of emotions, from the thrill of Chad leading his team to the national championship to the shock of Bob's involvement in a point-shaving operation. Each cried in the other's arms, but nothing they could say seemed to offer any relief for what they were both experiencing. Only time could determine how the case would be resolved but neither would abandon Bob during this time of trial and tribulation. Scott was still too young to understand but Betty was concerned how this would affect Chad.

The next morning Betty and Jim had breakfast with Chad before his return to campus. Nancy was not feeling well and had excused herself from joining them. It was obvious none of them had gotten much sleep, but the joy of winning was still evident in Chad's expressions and mannerisms. The conversation centered on the game and Chad's wonderful performance. Since the team was scheduled to leave shortly, Chad told his mother he would give her a call when he got back to campus.

There had been no leaks concerning the point-shaving scheme and nothing appeared in the morning paper. Jim could not be sure if this lack of interest was because the game was over so late or because there was no apparent link between the arrest of Mario, Albert and the Four Final in New Orleans. After Chad left, Jim advised Betty and Nancy they needed to return to Miami with a FBI agent. Nancy and Scott would be taken into protective custody while he stayed in New Orleans and made arrangements for Bob's travel. Jim could sense the gravity of the situation was beginning to set in with Nancy.

"What are you going to do with Bob?" Betty asked.

"Right now we have him in a secure location but at some point soon we'll have to move him back to Miami."

"When will all this hit the papers?"

"I would guess in the next couple of days at the latest."

"Why the delay," Nancy inquired?

"Well, we haven't charged him with a crime yet. We want to get him back home first so we won't have to seek extradition papers which could delay the process and can sometimes be a problem."

"Is that legal?"

"Legal yes, since this involved federal racketeering, but normal no," Jim replied. "Fortunately, Bob is willing to do it this way. Now I've got to run and I've already told you more than I should."

"Have a safe trip," Betty replied, kissing Jim on the cheek. "You know I love you."

"I love you too. I'll call you later to make sure you made it home okay," Jim concluded. "Oh, by the way, Nancy is going to need your support throughout this."

"I know."

With that Jim left to check out of the hotel while Betty and Nancy finished their coffee and contemplated the last twenty-four hours. He would meet later with the other agents to finalize the plans for Bob's return to Miami and the upcoming trial.

Chapter Forty Four

Bob requested the opportunity to meet with Nancy, Scott and their parents as soon as possible to explain what happened. He did not want them to hear things, mostly rumors, from other sources. Jim realized this would be difficult and somewhat dangerous, but he wanted Bob to have an opportunity to explain himself to those he loved as well as keep Bob in a positive frame of mind for his participation in the upcoming trial. Those arrangements would be made within the week and Jim hoped to go to trial by month's end. The hard part would be the waiting and providing for the safety of the participants.

Two Feds drove Bob back to Miami in an unmarked car while Jim flew ahead to prepare for Bob's arrival as well as the case. The decision was made to keep Bob isolated from his family until the meeting. Bob was able to talk with Nancy, but only to assure her he was okay and would explain what was going on when they met. He tried to convince her things weren't as bad as they appeared but he sensed Nancy knew better. Dependent upon the nature of the meeting and the FBI's concern for everyone's safety, a decision would then be made as to whether the Girards could stay together. Contrary to normal procedure, Bob and Jim agreed it would be in everyone's best interest if formal charges were delayed until after the family meeting. This would enable the transfer of everyone involved while avoiding a news circus. It would also allow Bob to explain himself prior to public speculation of what went down.

The meeting was set at the Drifters, a small hotel in Homestead. On that Friday, with everyone in attendance, Bob walked into the suite to see for the first time those people he loved and betrayed. Jim had instructed the participants to allow Bob to explain what happened before casting judgement or asking questions. Upon entering the room Bob was able to hug Nancy, his parents and Nancy's mom, although Marty Champion was indifferent and cold. As the family sat around the table, Jim excused himself and Bob began describing the odyssey that led them all to this place and time.

"I know you all have been wondering what's going on," Bob began. "Well, I'm the reason everything's happened so I wanted to be the one to tell you what this is about."

"I should hope so," Nancy's mom defiantly interrupted.

"Mom, please let Bob tell his story," Nancy pleaded.

"First, let me tell you how much I love all of you and how sorry I am for what I've done.

"We love you too, son," Bob's mother replied.

"Well, it all began over a year ago when I met a man named Mario," Bob went on to say. "As you know, Nancy and I were expecting Scott and had just moved into a new house. The camp wasn't doing as well as in the past, and with Nancy not working as much things were getting a little tight financially." Bob then spent the next hour explaining the events leading up to his arrest as his family listened in disbelief.

After completing his explanation of the events surrounding the point-shaving scheme, Bob then asked if any of them had any comments or questions. As they all sat in disbelief, Nancy as well as Bob's parents could see that Bob's intent was to make things better for Nancy and Scott while Nancy's mother on the other hand was irate and unforgiving.

"But why wouldn't you come to us for financial help?" Tom Girard asked.

"Oh dad, I couldn't beg from you to take care of my family. After all, you and mom worked so hard and with a fixed income I didn't want you to borrow on your retirement."

"But we would've been happy to help," Ella Girard joined in, "and you could have always paid us back."

"I would have also been happy to help," Marty Champion added, halfheartedly.

"I know all of you would have helped but I guess my pride just got in the way. I didn't want you to think I couldn't take care of my family."

In spite of his intent, Nancy was visibly shaken and Bob could sense her trust in him had been destroyed. There was really nothing he could say to console her. "I know how you must feel, honey," Bob continued.

"No you don't," Nancy retorted. "You don't have the slightest idea how I feel because if you did you wouldn't have done this to us."

"But what I did I did for us, you, me and Scott."

"What you did was betray our trust and put us in a position where we don't know what to expect next. How could you do that, especially to Scott?"

"I'm sorry, I'm truly sorry."

"So am I Bob, so am I," Nancy repeated.

Nothing could lessen the fact he had not been honest with her when trust was always foremost in their relationship. Could he ever bridge that gap? Bob wasn't sure but he sincerely doubted it. As they discussed what was to happen next, all were in agreement Bob had to fully cooperate in the investigation and subsequent trial.

With his return, Jim assured each one of his best efforts to protect them during and after the trial. What he wanted them to understand was he could do everything possible to ensure their continued safety, but nothing was guaranteed. The trial would change their lives forever. After the trial the parents would be at minimal risk, but Nancy, Scott and Bob would always be in danger. The Mafia would not look kindly on this kind of betrayal and was a very vindictive bunch, especially when it came to one of its own. If there were no more questions, he would leave them alone until it was time to go.

"Look, I know this is tough and emotions are running high," Jim added, "but I would strongly encourage you to use the rest of the day to share fonder moments."

"And just how are we supposed to do that?" Nancy's mom chimed in.

"I don't have all the answers, but I've gotten to know Bob and Nancy well enough to know they love one another and all of you. Besides, this may be the last time all of you ever have an opportunity like this."

"What do you mean by that?" Bob's mom asked.

"After we formally charge Bob with a crime, we'll probably not be able to bring everyone together again" Jim responded, "since that would be too dangerous."

"So what happens now?" Tom Girard wanted to know.

"We will place Bob, Nancy and Scott in safe-way houses until after the trial. Ironically, Nancy and Scott will not be with Bob."

"And why is that?" Ella Girard asked.

"Security is the first reason. Also, we can't afford for Bob to have any distractions as we put this case together."

"What about us?" Marty Champion inquired.

"We'll give you and the Girards twenty four hour surveillance, although it would be highly unlikely the mob would make an attempt on your lives."

"And why is that?"

"Because it would cause too much public outcry and the Mafia won't risk bad publicity," Jim concluded. "Anyway, they don't know what we've got and probably think they can only win this case if they find Bob. He will be the focal point of their attention."

With that Jim brought his part of the meeting to a close. All were instructed not to leave the room but they could interact and have dinner together before going their separate ways. It was in everyone's best interest none of them knew where Bob, Nancy and Scott would be secluded or how to contact them.

The rest of the day was filled with stories of better times as well as apologies from Bob to each family member as he visited with them individually. What he could not explain to Nancy was how he could put his wife and son in harms way for the mere lure of money. Had he not thought of the possible consequences and where was the trust?

"Honey, I know what I did was wrong and I can only say I'm sorry," Bob pleaded. "You have to believe I would never purposefully do anything to hurt you or Scott."

"I want to believe you but it's hard to understand how you could get involved in something like this. You had to understand the risks involved and this is against everything you believe in and stand for."

"It just looked so easy and I couldn't imagine it ever getting to this point. Besides, it appeared harmless and a great way to make money for everything we've always wanted."

"Obviously it wasn't as easy and harmless as you thought," Nancy retorted.

"Can you ever forgive me?"

"Right now I can't honestly answer that question. Only time will tell."

"I promise you I will do everything in my power to win back your trust," Bob pleaded. "Please keep an open mind and give this some thought."

"We'll see."

"That's all I can ask," Bob concluded. "I don't know what I'd do without you and Scott. Both of you are my life."

Bob was determined to do the right thing and win back at least to some degree the confidence these people once had in him, but only time would prove whether that was possible.

That evening all of the parties were taken to their respective destinations. Bob was then formally charged with the crimes of racketeering and tax evasion. Jim hoped the delay in charging Bob would help prevent the press from linking Bob with the earlier arrests of Mario and Albert Valdez.

Chapter Forty Five

Over the next few weeks as Jim painstakingly put together the information he hoped would lead to the conviction of Mario and Albert Valdez, Bob provided the times, dates and other pertinent information needed to solidify the case. Loneliness was Bob's constant companion since he was without his wife and son and could only talk with them every other day from a secure phone. Bouncing from one safe-way house to another was unnerving, but not nearly as difficult as reliving the mistakes he made over the past year and a half that cost him his credibility and possibly his marriage.

The press had gotten wind of Bob's arrest and there was a lot of speculation as to who else was involved and the nature of the crime, and the rumors were fueled by both the FBI and DA's offices adhering to the party' line of 'no comment' with an ongoing investigation. Betty and Jim's time together was limited because of his involvement with the case and because he did not want her to be associated with him as the point man. It was highly unlikely Betty would become a mob target but Jim did not want to risk the chance.

As the news made headlines nationally, Jim and Betty discussed the complexities of telling Chad what was happening. Since no additional names had been identified from the prosecution's side of the case, Jim wanted to hold off until just before the trial. He trusted Chad, but knew the fewer people involved the less chance for a leak that might jeopardize the case. Betty was insistent on Chad being told.

"Look honey, we keep having this conversation and I keep telling you I don't think it's the right time to involve Chad," Jim pleaded.

"Why not," Betty asked, "after all, he's already indirectly involved."

"That's not the point. It's more a matter of what good it will do him and whether it will compromise the case."

"That's a copout and you know it." Betty replied.

"And how is that?"

"First, Bob has been his mentor and closest friend since Chad was a young boy. He taught Chad everything he knows about basketball and acted as a second father when no one else would. Secondly, the man who is most involved in this case is the man who may be his next father. And lastly, he reads about the case everyday now that it's out in the open."

"I know but one wrong statement and this whole thing could explode in our face. I just don't want him linked to Bob."

"He already is. Everyone in Miami knows about their association with the camp. If you can't trust my son, then you surely can't trust me," Betty snapped.

"That's not fair so don't even go there," Jim retorted. "I just don't want anyone to get hurt, especially people that I care about."

"Chad's going to be more hurt when he finds out you didn't trust him."

"Possibly, but I don't think so," Jim responded. "Give him some credit for understanding the situation and give me a little more time to think this out."

After agonizing over the problem, Jim agreed it was in everyone's best interest to explain to Chad what was going on and trust his maturity and judgement. It was during spring break that Jim was able to sit down with Chad and Betty and explain the situation. At first Chad's reaction was one of disbelief and denial, but as the case was explained in detail Chad knew what he was hearing had to be true. Coupled with Bob's admission of guilt, there was just too much evidence not to support the accusations. As he openly wept,

Jim could understand the emotion and sense of loss Chad must be experiencing. After all, this was his second father, mentor, role model and the man most responsible for shaping and molding Chad's life.

"How could he have done this?" Chad asked.

"I don't have an answer to that question," his mom replied.

Jim interjected, "only Bob can tell you how and why this happened and at this time I'm not sure he really knows."

"But he was always the one who talked about honesty, integrity and doing the right things," Chad replied.

"Sometimes things just get crazy," Betty added.

"I can still hear him talking about how your reputation was the only thing that counted and the one thing you could control. So how could this happen?"

"It's hard to explain, but if it's any consolation I've worked with hardened criminals all my adult life and I guarantee Bob is not one of them."

Chad had a million questions running through his mind but knew Bob was the only person with the answers. "Is there any way I can see him? He needs my support," Chad concluded.

Jim explained a visit would be up to Bob and whether he wanted to and felt such a meeting would accomplish anything. Before asking Bob, Jim had to be sure Chad really wanted to go through with this. Chad, showing maturity beyond his years, indicated he wanted to see his longtime friend. Jim assured him he would try to make the necessary arrangements before Chad returned to campus from spring break. It was also important to get this done as quickly as possible since the trial was set to begin in ten days.

Bob had mixed emotions about this proposal and was not sure he could face Chad. What would there be to gain? He was still feeling despondent about his earlier encounter with his family. The questions and lack of reasonable answers haunted him, especially since it involved the people dearest to him. Once the trial began and his name linked to this particular crime, the real shame would kick in. Did he want to add to that by seeing and trying to explain to his surrogate son something he knew could not be reasonably explained or understood? Yet, as he taught Chad to be a man and take responsibility for his actions, he knew he could not shun his responsibility to the boy. How Chad would handle the meeting was yet unknown but Bob knew he could not escape seeing him for what may be the last time.

The meeting was set at a nearby hotel and Chad waited anxiously for Bob's arrival. Upon entering the room both men seemed confused as to what to do. It was Bob who initiated the hug, although Chad's response was not as warm as he remembered from the past. As with Nancy, there was a lot of hurt and distrust in Chad's mind. The next couple of hours would determine whether they could work through the questions and have any kind of future relationship. How awkward for two men who had been so close for so many years.

During the meeting it became readily apparent Chad had some very specific concerns based on what he had been told previously by Jim. Chad obviously wanted to know why and how Bob got involved in such illegal activities, and did his relationship with those he loved not account for more than a life as a common criminal? Another key question was whether Bob altered the outcome of any of the games Chad played in, more specifically the national championship game? Bob explained his involvement in much the same way he had to his wife and parents and assured Chad he did nothing to change the end result of any of his games.

"But how can I trust you didn't alter the outcome of some of those games." Chad asked.

"Because I told you I didn't," Bob responded in a hollow way.

"After all that's happened, I don't know if I can believe you."

Although hurt by Chad's response, Bob went on to say, "think of all the games I used to officiate in the ACC before you enrolled at Duke. That used to be my top-rated conference."

"So?"

"Well, after you started playing, I rated the ACC as my third choice of leagues and turned down all the Duke games I was offered even though those were the best-paying and most prestigious games. Doesn't that mean anything to you?"

"I guess, but how about the national championship game?"

"Think about it, if I'd have fixed that game the way I was supposed to, I wouldn't be in the immediate danger I am right now."

"What do you mean?"

"Kentucky was favored to win and the mob's money was on the Wildcats. If they had won as they were expected and covered the spread, you don't have a national championship ring and the Mafia wouldn't know to be looking for me," Bob replied.

Bob could sense a softening in Chad's demeanor but also knew he was terribly disappointed and unsure about their relationship. Like with Bob's family, it would take time and healing if ever there was to be reconciliation on Chad's part. Bob could only hope that would happen, yet realized their special relationship would never be the same.

Unlike the previous meeting with loved ones, Chad seemed suddenly anxious to get his questions answered and be on his way. In some respects, that seemed more disappointing and yet more of a relief for Bob than if Chad wanted to stay.

As both got up to leave, Bob forced a hug and whispered in Chad's ear, "I'm sorry I've disappointed you, but I want you to know how proud I am of you and how much I love you."

Chad returned the hug and likewise said, "I love you too."

Both men could see the tears begin to well in the other's eyes, and the meeting came to an abrupt end. Would this be the last time these two friends would ever see each other?

Chapter Forty Six

Within the next few days the trial of Mario and Albert Valdez would begin. The grand jury had already found enough evidence to refer the case to District Court 13 in Miami and the witnesses were presented for both sides. The members of the jury were finally agreed upon, after much haggling, by lawyers from both the defense and prosecution. Although the mob would try to place one of its own on the jury, Jim's side felt good about the final selections.

Much of what was submitted by the prosecution would be documented by taped conversations and sworn testimony. From its perspective, what would realistically decide the case would be Bob's ability to convince the jury of his honesty and credibility as it related to the evidence, the jury knowing Bob had been offered a deal to turn state's evidence.

On the defendant's side it was readily apparent Albert Valdez and the Mafia would go to any length to discredit Bob and impeach his testimony. One of the early people to testify for the defense was Gary Branson, the official who introduced Bob to Mario.

One thing Bob insisted on before agreeing to help Jim was he would not implicate any other basketball officials. He felt very strongly guys like Gary had made a mistake similar to his, but they were basically decent people who could get out from under the control of the mob with a conviction. Jim agreed in part predicated on his sense they wanted out of the mob's influence, and the assurance they would not participate in any further illegal activities and would immediately retire from officiating. But what Jim could not control was if they perjured themselves during the trial. Then all bets were off. With a guilty verdict, fixing basketball games would be at an end for these guys and if they told the truth they would have a chance to get their lives back. Bottom line, Jim would not give up the prospect of convicting these guys if it was necessary to make the government's case.

Gary was a pawn and wanted a second chance, but was paralyzed with fear of what the Mafia might do if he did not cooperate. Mario had made it clear to him the severity of the punishment if he turned state's evidence. Although appearing for the defense would implicate him with the mob, Gary felt he had no choice but to testify on its behalf. He was obviously called to discredit Bob and refute any knowledge of the point-shaving operation.

"So it's your contention you knew nothing about point-shaving or any illegal activity as it relates to this case? Furthermore, you were not involved in a scheme to fix basketball games, and you are not familiar with either of the defendants?" the defense attorney asked. "Based then on what Mr. Girard told you, please describe to the court his role in this plan."

"Based on what he told me, he was acting with a couple of friends to fix games and make a fast buck."

"And what leads you to believe he actually carried out this plan?"

"He approached me one time and asked me if I would be interested in making some easy money."

"Go on," the defense attorney prodded as they had rehearsed.

"When I asked him how, he told me by controlling the spread on some games," Gary stated while trying to avoid Bob's glare.

"Why didn't you tell someone about this at the time?"

"I just didn't think he was serious and I didn't want to do anything to hurt a good friend. He had helped me during my divorce and I respected him as an official."

"So why have you come forward now to testify against your friend?"

'To protect the integrity of my fellow officials as well as the game of basketball," Branson replied. "Regardless of our friendship, there is no place in our sport for someone like Bob Girard."

Bob looked over his shoulder at Jim and knew there was no way he could save Gary. Gary had crossed the line and Jim would do everything in his power to see him fall.

"One last question, Mr. Branson, again, just for the record, have you ever seen the two defendants before or had any contact with either of them in any way?"

"No I have not," Gary lied.

Gary's problem occurred when Bob took the stand and the DA was able to link Gary with the point-shaving scheme by use of videotape of his games. Furthermore, the prosecution was able to present two other officials who, under the guarantee of immunity, would attest to Gary's involvement with Mario and his attempt to entice them into the point-shaving operation. Three other people substantiated Gary and Mario were close friends since high school. Even the most sympathetic of juries could see through Branson's testimony and the shortcomings of the defense in presenting him as a key witness.

As the trial plodded along, one weekend Bob asked to see Nancy and Scott. They met at a safe-way house in Miami Beach and spent time together. It had been about five weeks since Bob last met with Nancy and their families and he hoped things would be more like normal. This would also be his first contact with Scott. He sensed early on the pent up anger and disappointment within Nancy and accepted for the first time things could never be the same between them. His selfish actions placed Nancy and Scott at risk and for that there would be no forgiveness. Fortunately, Scott was too young to form an opinion concerning the proceedings.

"I wanted to meet with you and Scott without the families," Bob began, as he held Scott for the first time in what seemed an eternity. "I've really missed you guys."

"Are you okay?" Nancy asked in a cold voice.

"Yeah, but it's the constant tearing down of my reputation that's taking a toll."

"Jim says he thinks things are going well."

"I sure hope so. I just can't believe I got myself into this."

"Well, hopefully everything will work out."

"The last time we met you said you couldn't tell me whether you could ever forgive me for what I've done. Can you now?" Bob asked.

"I just don't know," Nancy replied. "I've not had enough time to gather my thoughts."

Nancy could not accept what appeared to be a total disregard for the consequences of Bob's actions. After all, he was her husband and the father of their child. She was convinced they could have worked things out financially without his involvement in this kind of activity. How could he have been so thoughtless and self-indulged?

"I never meant for you, Scott and our loved ones to get hurt."

"I know, but that doesn't change the fact we were hurt."

The problem for Bob was trying to explain something that made no sense even to him. Unbeknownst to Nancy, Bob sensed this could be the last time he would see his wife and son. After a few more hours and much small talk, it was time to say goodbye. Bob picked up Scott and gave him and Nancy a hug and kiss.

As he held both of them close, Bob said with a tear in his eye, "I love both of you more than you'll ever know. I'm so sorry for all the heartache I've caused."

It was all he could do to keep from crying but he did not want to end their relationship with tears of grief. He could only hope Scott would grow up to understand what his dad did was intended to help him and his mother. If only Scott could be like Chad, that was Bob's wish for his son. Bob would never forget watching the two people he loved more than words could describe walk away for probably the last time.

Upon his return to the courtroom, Bob was surprised the defense would call to testify the supervisor of officials for two of the leagues Bob worked in. This proved to be a major mistake for the defense. Although they were there to substantiate the honesty and solid officiating record of Gary Branson, they in fact also supported Bob under cross-examination. They confirmed knowing nothing of any mob related point-shaving scheme, and under cross-examination spoke to Bob's honesty, work ethic and professionalism. They even went so far to say there was no hard evidence to substantiate any wrongdoing on Bob's part.

"So what you're stating is there is no evidence of fixing games?" the DA asked.

"That is correct," replied the supervisor of the ACC.

"Are you also saying there was no apparent point-shaving plan?"

"No, I can't say that. That would be very difficult to determine."

"Then to what extent do you think Mr. Girard was involved?"

"Based on reports from other game officials, analysis of game tapes and evaluations from spotters, it appears highly unlikely he was involved in determining the outcome of games he worked in," responded the supervisor. "In fact, he is one of our top-rated officials."

"Now allow me to ask some questions about Mr. Branson?" the DA asked.

"I object," the defense attorney said as he jumped out of his seat. "Mr. Branson is not on trial here."

"Sustained," the judge ruled. "As you brought these witnesses to comment on the qualifications of Mr. Girard, it would only seem reasonable they should be asked to do the same with Mr. Branson who is a key witness for your side. This moves toward credibility of the two men. Move on with your questioning counsel."

"May I approach the bench, your honor?" the defense attorney asked.

As both the defense counsel and the DA approached the bench, the defense said, "I would like to treat this man as a hostile witness."

The DA responded, "Your honor, you can't allow that."

"Oh yes I can," the judge retorted, showing who was in charge of his courtroom, "but I won't since the witness has not been hostile or made any statements inflammatory to the defense. Let's move on counsel."

During the trial the DA established Bob's credibility, but there was still a lot of work to do. The prosecution's case still hung on the evidence and its ability to prove guilt beyond a shadow of a doubt.

Bob's family, as well as Betty and Chad, followed the trial with great interest. Not a day went by when Chad did not call his mother to get an update on what was going on. Even though this was a case with national implications, the Miami Register newspaper would have more in depth coverage of what was going on as a result of its proximity and daily representation in the courtroom. As the trial wore on, it became apparent the end result would be determined by the juries belief that Bob was trying to save his own skin or the evidence overwhelmingly supported the government's contention Mario and Albert Valdez were part of a conspiracy to fix college basketball games.

The DA's office opted to keep the case simple and not add murder charges against Mario and Albert since there was still no body and the garbled tape prevented clear identification of the perpetuators of the crime. Besides, without a conviction on racketeering and tax-evasion charges, it was impossible to think the government could get a related guilty verdict for murder one. The FBI would have to win this case, show probable cause, substantiate Bob's testimony, come up with a corpse and link the two cases before they could bring murder charges against Albert, Mario and the Gallibini family.

Bob was an excellent witness and was able to cast doubt on Gary Branson's testimony as well as convince the jury of Mario and Albert's involvement in the point-shaving scheme. He was precise in providing names, dates and places that in many instances were corroborated by other prosecution witnesses. Bob and Jim also agreed to make it a point that the NACA Tournament Committee had no knowledge of what was going on with the point-shaving operation. This was Jim's way of attempting to make amends for not having them in the loop during the tournament. On the other hand, the defense determined it was in their best interests not to have Mario or Albert testify.

Word on the street had the mob frantically hunting for Nancy and Scott but to date they had been unsuccessful. Jim determined the time to move Bob's parents and Nancy's mom was now. The case was in its final days and the defense seemed overtly unsure about the verdict.

No sooner were the parents moved to a safe place than Jim received a call at home from Agent Groves, "boss, good decision on the move."

"What do you mean?" Jim asked.

"The mob hit Bob's parent's place."

"Was anyone hurt?"

"No," Groves replied, "and the best part is we caught the guy."

"Any link to the Gallibini family?"

"Bingo and one that's currently on trial."

Often people get involved in things where they have no business and are not needed. In this case it couldn't have come at a better time for Jim. One of Albert Valdez's cousins, a known Mafia member in his own right, elected to take it upon himself to send an intimidating message to Bob to help his cousin with the case. When caught and identified after the bombing, his actions only served to confirm the widely held belief that Mario and Albert were guilty. This was a classic example of how a 'loose cannon' in an otherwise structured and highly sophisticated organization could make a mess of things.

The Gallibini family was outraged but the damage was done. Although the jury was sequestered, news of this nature had a way of finding its way inside the courtroom. Within four hours of the judge's final instructions, the jury returned a verdict of 'GUILTY' on five charges of tax evasion and racketeering in an attempt to fix college basketball games. There was no question the defense would appeal, but the proceedings had followed the letter of the law and there was very little chance an appeals court would find just cause for a new trial. Mario and Albert Valdez could plan on being prison mates without parole for many years and the mob would be wounded although not severely crippled.

For Jim and the DA's office the battle had been won, although the war was still far from over. Jim knew there were others waiting in the wings to lead the mob in Miami, and with each conviction they would be just that much smarter and harder to catch. There was not a lot of celebrating by Jim and his staff since this was just the beginning of a long and difficult process.

"Justice has been served," the DA announced at a victory dinner later that evening.

"The verdict was great new and you did a super job," Jim replied.

"Well, you don't sound very enthused," voiced the assistant DA.

"I am, but the work for us now really begins."

"What do you mean?"

"With the conviction, the Mafia will be more committed than ever to finding Bob."

"Why is that?"

"Remember, Bob not only destroyed their gambling scheme and sent two of their boys to prison, he also knows who was involved in the murder of the crime boss in New Orleans. They never let a snitch go unpunished because it would show weakness and create problems within their ranks. But you can bet the potential for a murder indictment will really peak their interest. Keep in mind, they don't know what we know."

"Let's hope you're wrong," the DA concluded as he finished his glass of champagne. For Bob the battle had just begun. In a separate trial he was found guilty of associating with known criminals in an illegal gambling scheme as well as tax evasion, but the judge suspended his sentence as a result of his cooperation in the Mario/ Albert Valdez case and on the recommendation of the DA. He was placed on three years probation and ordered to repay back taxes plus interest on the money he had not declared with the IRS. Some felt the sentence was too lenient, but on the other hand, except for Bob's confession, many legal experts believed Bob could have beaten the illegal gambling rap altogether. No one was able to directly link him with point-shaving or fixing games and Mario and Albert sure weren't going to admit to his involvement.

Nancy, Betty, Chad and others directly involved with the case received the verdict with a sense of relief but with mixed feelings. For Nancy it was a time to reflect on the damage done to relationships and whether she could ever forgive or trust Bob again. For the parents of Bob and Nancy, it was a time to rally around their children for the sake of Scott. Bob was a loved one who made a mistake and only time and family support could help heal all the wrong that had been done. For Betty it was a feeling of extreme pride for Jim, the man she so dearly loved and respected, and yet a feeling of sorrow for the Girards, people for whom she genuinely cared. And for Chad it was a moment of relief that justice had been served, but mixed feelings as to what the future would hold for the Girards and more specifically his relationship with Bob.

Both trials had received national attention and most people were pleased with the outcomes. That is, those other than the supporters of the University of Kentucky who would always contend the Wildcats were cheated out of the national championship. Yet in looking at tape, it was hard to discredit Bob's officiating in the final game. After all, Kentucky had numerous chances to win the game in the last minute, and it was hard to argue that Bob risked his life in making the call he did near the end. Those who witnessed the game, especially those knowledgeable about basketball, were nearly unanimous about how well the game had been played and officiated. If one positive thing came out of the trials for Chad, it was the reassurance there had been no fixing associated with the national championship game. His championship had been won fair and square on the court and not in the back seat of a Mafia orchestrated point-shaving scheme.

The NACA issued a formal protest it had not been privy to or advised of the problems surrounding its event, but having no legal jurisdiction there was little it could do. As a non-profit organization that often was perceived to act above the law in its own court dealings, there was very little sympathy or support for its position. On a positive note, the case would lead to some revised thinking and new guidelines regarding officiating and game administration, but the less said about the incident the less questions about the autonomous role of the NACA in college athletics. With as much negative publicity as it had received in the last few years, often times it was in the NACA's best interests to take a back seat and let the courts decide the path it should follow. They were wise enough to take that route and accept Jim's public apology.

And lastly, for Bob it was a time to re-evaluate his relationships with his loved ones, put into perspective the hurt and hardship he had caused so many that believed in him and decide what the best course of action would be for everyone involved. Those would be decisions he would have to make in the next couple of weeks. As this process neared an end, Jim was shocked when Bob told him he would not join Nancy and Scott in the witness protection program.

"You're not serious?" Jim replied.

"I'm dead serious."

"But how can you stand not being with your family?"

"It's not easy, but it's what I have to do."

"Why?" Jim implored.

"Because I can't stand to face them after what I've done and I'm not sure Nancy wants me around anyway."

"There has to be more to it than that."

"Yeah, there is. I think my being with them will do nothing but increase their risk of danger. Besides, the mob really wants me and not them."

"I can't argue that but they'll hunt them until they find you. Look, we've had good success with this program and I hate to see you give up your family."

Jim tried to talk Bob into relocating with his family and trying to work things out, but he could sense Bob was committed to this course of action. How had it gotten to this point?

"How will Nancy react to this decision?" Jim asked.

"I really don't know."

"You damn well know she'll be hurt and feel like you've deserted her and Scott."

"Maybe so, but the last time we talked she wasn't sure she could ever forgive me for what I've done."

"But that was during the trial when things were crazy."

"I know, but I also know Nancy and things could never be the same. I broke a trust with her and she will never be able to put that behind us."

"C'mon, Nancy's bigger than that. She loves you and you're the father of her only child. That has to account for something."

"I know and that's a big part of the reason it's better if I allow them to get on with their lives without me," Bob said in a sullen voice.

"Think about Scott."

"I have more than you know and this is the best decision. Scott will have a tough enough time living through the shame I've caused. He doesn't need me there as a constant reminder."

"I wish you'd take some more time to think this over," Jim pleaded.

"I've already taken too much time. Now it's time for all of us to put this behind and get on with our lives." Bob concluded. "Believe me, this is the best thing for everyone."

Bob knew as long as he was alive and there was any chance of an appeal or murder charges being filed against Mario and Valdez, he would be hunted and constantly looking over his shoulder. That was no way for anyone to live, especially innocent people like his wife and son. He was sorry for all the grief he had caused, but knew this problem was of his own making and he needed to be strong enough to do what was right.

As a result of this decision, a plan was put into place as secretive as Jim and Bob's friendship. Jim dealt with many criminals and Bob was a long way from being the hardened criminal the media portrayed. Based on his cooperation during the investigation and involvement with Betty and Chad, Jim was willing to go the extra mile to meet Bob's wishes. After all, Bob helped the government put one of the key crime figures behind bars while putting his life and that of his family at risk. But could the FBI protect the Girards as promised and for how long?

Chapter Forty Seven

Watching all of this from a distance, Chad was finishing up the school year and there was now more and more talk about him declaring early for the NBA draft. His performance in the NACA Tournament only increased his value. Here was a point guard with size, scoring potential, an understanding of the game, a willingness to play hurt and the ability to make those around him better. The professional scouts drooled over guys with half those characteristics. Couple that with his competitive background and cooperative attitude and you had a player who many thought would be a lottery pick. How high a pick was dependent on the order of the draft and which team needed help at his position. In any case, the NACA rule for eligibility was designed so Chad could enter the draft and as long as he did not hire an agent or sign a contract he could return for his junior year at Duke.

The real question was not whether Chad was ready or could play in the NBA, but whether he wanted to leave college at this time. After talking with former Duke players now playing in the pros, it really became a simple decision. Having completed a sensational season while winning the national championship, what did he have left to prove at the college level? The key was whether he would be a lottery pick. If so, what else could he do to make as much as three to five million dollars a year, not counting endorsements, guaranteed for a minimum of three years? He could always return to college and finish his degree but nothing he majored in would afford him that kind of financial stability. Chad could finally realize a lifelong dream to take care of his mother and ensure she would never have to work another day of her life if that was her wish.

Early in May, after returning to Miami, Chad announced his decision. "Today, I'm declaring myself available for the upcoming NBA draft." Also present at the news conference to enjoy the moment was his mother and Coach P.

A sportswriter from the Miami Register asked, "Why at this time?"

"After talking it over with my mom and my coach, we decided this would be a good time to explore the possibility of playing at the next level," Chad responded.

"Did you consult with anyone else?"

"Yes, I talked with a number of former Duke players now in the NBA."

"And what did they say?"

"They told me it was an individual decision, but if I felt ready then I should go for it."

Chad and Coach P then talked about the pros and cons of such a decision and both agreed Chad was ready to play at the next level. Both also cautioned if Chad wasn't projected as a high pick, he could always withdraw his name from the draft and return to Duke.

Jim purposely was absent from the press conference, thinking it was in everyone's best interest he not be publicly identified with Chad and Betty. As glorious an occasion as this should have been, Chad could not help but miss Bob and Nancy. Knowing the heartache he endured as a young boy, he wanted so much to be a role model and father figure for Scott. He realized he may never see them again and he could only hope one day Scott would seek him out and renew their relationship.

During these past few months, even with his hectic schedule, Jim had made his intentions known to both Betty and Chad. Chad and Jim spent some quality time together during spring break and both found the other to be good, honest and sharing in a lot of common interests. Although Betty was at a stage in her life where she knew what she wanted, it was still special to have her son's blessing if there was to be a marriage.

"So how do you feel about Jim?" Betty asked her son one night.

"What do you mean?"

"You know darn well what I mean. You two have spent enough time together, so what have you men talked about?"

"Mom, I really like the guy," Chad replied, "but it's none of your business what we've talked about."

"Are you being a smart-ass young man?"

"Mom, I can't believe you just called your son a bad name," Chad replied in a coy nature. "No, I'm just being honest. So what's the deal?"

"About what," Betty shyly asked?

"Are you two getting married or not?"

"Why don't you ask him," Betty replied in an irritated voice.

"Because I already know how he feels. Now I want to know how you feel."

"I really love the man but I want your blessing before we decide anything."

"That settles it, when's the wedding?" Chad joked.

Shortly after this conversation Jim proposed and Betty accepted his invitation. They would try to have the wedding in early August so as not to interfere with Chad reporting to NBA training camp if he was drafted. It would be an intimate wedding with only immediate family and close friends. The biggest hang up was Jim setting aside time from his busy schedule for the wedding and honeymoon.

Chapter Forty Eight

As the days wore on, it became apparent to Jim and the FBI there would be little chance of a break in the murder case implicating Mario and Albert Valdez. The Gulf of Mexico was a large area and not one conducive to finding a dead body. Furthermore, no one was professing any knowledge of the murder. The tape of Bob's conversation with Mario and Albert was garbled beyond recognition, and it would be hard to go to the grand jury without a murder weapon, a body and only the word of what now was a convicted felon. The Mafia, on the other hand, did not know about the ruined tape and had turned up its efforts to find Bob, anticipating additional criminal charges any day. After all, Albert was more than a Gallibini crime boss. He was family.

"What have you found out so far?" Tony Gallibini, son of the 'Boss', asked his underling. Tony was now in charge of finding Bob Girard and bringing him to mob justice.

"Nothing," answered the man. "No one seems to know where the Girards are holed up."

"You mean after two months we're no closer to finding that snitch and his wife and kid than right after the trial."

"Yes sir, Mr. Gallibini, but don't worry, we'll find them."

"Oh, I'm not worried. Just remember, if we don't find them before Albert is charged with murder it will be your ass," Tony stated in no uncertain terms.

"I understand."

"I hope so. Keep in mind my father is not happy his son-in-law is in the slammer to begin with, but he will not tolerate Albert being convicted of another crime that could result in more serious consequences. Now find that son-of-a-bitch!" Tony concluded, as he slammed his fist on the desk.

Although Albert and Mario were serving the maximum sentence for their crimes, without a murder conviction they would be eligible for release in eight years or time enough for Albert to actively resume his rightful position as head of the Cuban Mafia. With good behavior the time served could be much less. Ironically, many times real jail time added to the reputation and credibility of a mob boss, and Albert's release could fit nicely into the timeframe for him to become the head of the Gallibini family operation for the entire Southeast.

Jim knew the potential murder charge was the only thing keeping Bob's family alive. The Gallibini family was concerned anything they did to his family could result in him coming forward with information to convict Albert. Therefore they had concentrated all their efforts on finding Bob.

Bob, on the other hand, realized the ongoing danger and knew eventually the Mafia would become impatient and strike at one of his family. He requested a meeting with Jim to discuss a proposal he felt could be a final solution to this problem. Realizing how difficult, time consuming and expensive it was to provide protection for Bob and his family, Jim was willing to listen to almost anything.

It was late June when Jim and Bob met at his safe-way house in Boulder, a beautiful community about an hour from Denver, Colorado, to discuss the progress of the murder case and the probability of Mario and Albert being free in another six to eight years. Jim was also able to update Bob on the status of Nancy and Scott, his plans to marry Betty and Chad's selection as a lottery pick in the NBA draft.

Nancy and Scott were living in Dayton, Ohio, a medium-sized city in the southwest part of the state. Dayton was large enough to hide one's identity but small enough not to be infiltrated heavily by the mob. Originally from the Midwest, this was an easy move for

Nancy and one she had requested. For her it meant returning to her homegrown values.

"How are Nancy and Scott doing?" Bob asked

"Actually, pretty well, Nancy just took a position with a local fitness center and seems to enjoy her job."

"And how about my son?"

"You wouldn't know him. He's grown and changed so much," Jim said, realizing the mistake he had just made. "I'm sorry, Bob."

"No, don't apologize," Bob replied, "it's my own fault I'm not able to see him grow and do all those things kids his age do."

"Well, for what it's worth, they both seem to be adjusting as well as can be expected without a husband and father. Are you sure you won't reconsider living with them?"

"Jim, I just can't. You have no idea how much I miss both of them, but my presence would place them even more in harm's way and I'm not sure Nancy would take me back."

Bob went on to mention his enjoyment in watching Chad get selected in the draft, and wanted to know if he and Betty ever asked about him. Jim indicated they did but felt Chad was in denial when it came to talking about Bob.

"I can understand that," Bob responded. "What a disappointment I must be to a kid who trusted me so much."

"I think he'll come around," Jim offered. "He's a bright young man and he'll figure everything out. It's just going to take some time. Keep in mind this has been a terrible shock to all of us."

Jim could tell Chad still had strong feelings for Bob but was having a difficult time dealing with the situation. It was the concept of out of sight, out of mind. Bob understood but could not hide his delight and pride in what Chad had accomplished.

"I'm so proud he's now in a position where he's always wanted to be. Watching him work so hard all those years and then get drafted by the Nets is just great," Bob went on to say.

"Never forget you had a lot to do with his success. If it wasn't for you, who knows where or what Chad might be now. No one can ever take that from you."

"I just hope Scott grows up to be like Chad. Who knows, maybe someday they can get together again."

"I know Chad would like that," Jim replied.

Jim then explained that Chad wanted to make Bob a business proposition. "Chad wants to buy your summer camp."

"How is that possible?" Bob asked with a surprised look on his face.

"The money from Chad's signing bonus will more than cover the value of the camp." As the third pick in the first round of the draft, Chad was now the property of the New Jersey Nets. As a lottery pick, it was just a matter of weeks before he would sign a contract and become a rich young man. Only first-round picks had guaranteed contracts and the Nets needed a point-guard in the worst way.

"But it's not worth anything," Bob responded, knowing there was no one to run it.

"He's intent on making you a fair offer based on the book value of the camp during the last three years."

"But why would he do that?"

"Because it's the one thing that enabled Chad to avoid a life of crime and make something of himself," Jim answered. "He wants it to be a place where kids like himself can go and grow. Also, it will give his mother something to do."

You could see Bob swell with pride. That Chad would elect to continue his legacy with the camp was more than he could have ever anticipated. Bob went on to say, "I'll do it with one condition."

"What's that," Jim asked.

"That the money from the sale of the camp be put in a mutual fund to support Nancy and Scott. With certain limitations they can have access to the money to do with as they see fit, but a part of it must be set aside for Scott's education."

"That sounds reasonable but you're sure you don't need some of the money?"

"No, I've got some money from my investments that Nancy would never accept. The camp money should be substantial enough to meet their basic needs, but will never begin to repay them for what I've put them through."

"I don't see a problem so it appears you have a deal. I'll talk with Chad in the morning and get some kind of an answer," Jim concluded.

Now it was time to get to the real reason for the meeting, which was to provide Bob and his family a cover for the rest of their life and to do so quickly before the mob located his whereabouts or turned their attention to the family. As much as Jim trusted the bureau, he also knew there were bad agents just as there were unscrupulous people in any profession. Determined as the Mafia was too find Bob, both he and Jim knew it was just a matter of time before someone would access his file and track his new identity. Everything had a price and Bob was tired of running.

"So, how serious is it?" Bob asked.

"Pretty serious," Jim said while trying not to alarm Bob. "We know the Mafia has increased the pressure to find you and in so doing they've called in a lot of valuable markers."

"What's your plan?"

"Unfortunately, all we can do is to continue as we have unless you have a better suggestion. Remember, the witness protection program has specific guidelines, but those are regulated to some degree by the will of the people we are protecting."

"What's your biggest concern?" Bob asked pointedly.

"As solid as the people are that work for me, there is always the chance someone in the FBI will go bad," Jim responded. "Money has a way of corrupting people and the Gallibini family would spare no expense to find you, including paying someone on the inside."

"Basically what you're saying is there are no guarantees for me or my family?"

"Not only that, but with every day that passes your parents and Nancy's mom are more at risk as evidenced by what happened to your parents' house. These scumbags will stop at nothing and it appears their patience is about to run out."

Having confirmed what he already thought, Bob revealed why he requested this meeting. He had a plan but indicated there was considerable risk involved. He would cover all angles of the plan and told Jim he needed his help for the plan to work. Bob asked Jim to reserve judgement until he heard him out. Jim's biggest concern was Bob's plan appear manageable, definitive and within reasonable safety guidelines. Both men knew secrecy and attention to detail were the keys. Whether the plan would work was questionable at best, but both men agreed something needed to be done to bring this situation to an end. With that in mind, Bob spent the next hour outlining a plan he thought could bring closure to this miserable existence, even if it was at the expense of his own life. He also wanted to see Nancy and Scott but knew this could endanger their cover. Since the last meeting with his wife and son it was apparent their relationship could never be the same, so why make things any worse?

"Look, I know things are over between Nancy and me but I would really like to see my parents one last time."

"You know that will be extremely dangerous." Jim emphasized.

"Yes, but at this point we both agree they're not at risk like Nancy and Scott and if we're ever going to do it, it has to be now. Do me a favor and see if they want to meet."

Jim knew Bob was still distraught from the hurt and fear he had caused everyone, especially his parents. His dad always preached people are only as good as their name and now he had to live with the embarrassment of his son's actions. Not knowing how much longer he could dodge a bullet, Bob wanted to try and reconcile with his folks.

"I'll see what I can do," Jim concluded.

Chapter Forty Nine

Upon his return to Miami, Jim contacted the Girards to confirm their interest in meeting with their son. As much as one would expect them to jump at the chance, one only had to remember the actions of their son had caused them to lose their home and put their lives at risk. At the expense of his own logistical problems in setting up the meeting, Jim was still delighted when Tom and Ella accepted his invitation.

Jim made the necessary arrangements for them to meet at a small hotel just on the outskirts of Denver. This was close to where Bob was now hiding and where Jim had begun his career with the bureau. He was open with his staff about the concerns surrounding this operation and there were those who felt strongly he should delay or even cancel the meeting. Jim wanted to get this meeting behind him so he could place Bob once and for all in a 'safe environment.' It was apparent to all involved Jim was tired of babysitting Bob and wanted to get on with other cases as well as his impending marriage.

Jim contacted a couple of buddies from the Denver bureau to monitor the meeting. This was uncharacteristic, but Jim advised his own guys he could not justify time away from their current, more pressing cases to transport them to an area where there already were qualified agents who could do the job.

"Are you sure you don't want us to go?" asked Agent Groves.

"It's not that I don't want you to go, I can't justify the expense," Jim replied. "It's already costing the bureau more than I want to spend to get Bob's parents to Denver."

"But we've been with you on this case from the beginning," argued Agent Mast.

"I know, but you're on most cases with me from the beginning. If I didn't know better, I'd suspect you guys are looking for a little rest and relaxation."

Besides, this was not an investigation or a particularly difficult assignment and Jim was scheduled to be back in his office within three days.

Much to Jim's reoccurring nightmare, but unbeknownst to him, one of his new agents was a Mafia plant. Nelson Rodriquez had been with the bureau for five years and proved to be a competent investigator. The problem was he had been stationed in Kansas City and was anxious to return to Miami, the city where he grew up. He, his wife, and two young children missed their families as well as the Miami culture and weather. Agent Rodriquez approached the bureau on a number of occasions and most recently became adamant about either being transferred or quitting the force. Because he was bilingual, a minority and good at his job, the FBI was willing to grant his request rather than lose him to local Miami law enforcement. Nelson had been transferred to the Miami office three weeks earlier and Jim was delighted to have someone of Nelson's background on his staff.

"It's good to finally meet you and I want to welcome you to Miami," Jim said at a monthly luncheon to introduce the new agents to the rest of the staff.

"It's great to be home," Rodriquez replied.

"I'll bet your wife is looking forward to warm weather instead of the bitter cold you've experienced the past few winters."

"That's an understatement, but she's not the only one that feels that way."

"My agents tell me you've developed an interest in the Albert Valdez case. Is there a reason for that?"

"I'm not so much interested in Valdez as I am Bob Girard," Nelson lied. "As a boy I attended his camp and he was very influential in my associating with the right kind of people and turning my life around. At the time I was headed for a life of crime."

"You're not the only one to have that experience," Jim replied, thinking of Chad.

"Anyway, I would like to help in any way I can. We need more people like him to help our young people and keep the streets of Miami safe from gangs."

"If anything should come up, I'll keep you in mind," Jim concluded.

Jim had little further personal contact with Rodriquez but on this occasion was particularly impressed with the young agent. Here was a guy with impeccable credentials and apparently committed to making South Florida a better place to live. Jim was taken by how handsome and smooth this guy was. He was extremely articulate, both in English and Spanish, and knew his way around Miami. Some of the other agents had alluded to his work ethic and diligence and those who partnered with him suggested he was the consummate professional. Jim hoped his early enthusiasm would not wane as he became involved in the everyday struggles of Miami. What Jim did not know was the mob had become involved with Nelson during his college days at Florida International University.

FIU had one of the outstanding criminology departments in the country and Rodriquez graduated near the top of his class. Much like Bob, the mob's involvement with Nelson began in a subtle way and pressure free. It started with summer employment between school sessions and quickly escalated to helping with his family. Under the threat of deportation of one of his brothers who was in the country under an illegal visa, Albert Valdez was able to pull some strings to ensure the Rodriquez family could remain together. Coupled with employment for his father who could speak but limited English, this tied the knot and set the wheels in motion for Nelson's future. As the relationship developed, Nelson Rodriquez had been helpful in a couple of situations with insider information, although being moved to Kansas City limited his effectiveness and contact with Valdez and the Cuban Mafia.

With Albert's conviction it was time to call in favors. Rodriquez was directed, not asked, to demand a transfer to Miami. If he had been in Miami a year earlier, much of what happened could possibly have been avoided as far as the Gallibini family was concerned. Now that he was there he was quickly advised as to his role in finding Bob Girard.

By his good fortune, association with the FBI staff and Jim's trusting nature, Agent Rodriquez found out about and alerted the mob to Bob's meeting with his parents. Now it was just a matter of putting a twenty-four hour watch on the parents and having a hit team ready to react on a moment's notice. Jim had been careless in his security measures and his travel plans were easily accessible.

Jim's arrival at the Denver airport, where he met Bob's parents, was without fanfare and the assigned agents were in place as previously instructed. The trip was an exhausting one filled with fake names and many plane changes, but Tom and Ella were anxious to spend time with their son and relieved to see Jim. Everything appeared to be in place and Jim could only hope things would go as planned.

As the agents moved into position, Jim asked one of the agents to help the Girards with their luggage and escort them to the meeting point. Jim would say hello and then go ahead to meet with Bob and secure the hotel room.

"So, how was the trip?" Jim asked.

"For people our age, very tiring," Tom Girard replied.

"I'll bet. You don't know how excited Bob is to see you."

"Not anymore excited than we are to see him," Ella responded.

"Just to review," Jim went on to explain, "Bob is already at the meeting point and we will give you as much time with him as we deem safe. Security, you know."

"We're looking forward to what little time we have."

"I'm sure you are."

"What happens after this?" Tom asked.

"Bob will be moved to another safe location, and you'll return home where you will have protection as long as needed. Your surveillance is purely precautionary," Jim lied. "We don't feel you're a target at this time."

"Will we ever see our son again after today?" Ella asked with a mother's intuition.

"I won't lie," Bob concluded. "It's very doubtful we'll be able to do this again."

Jim then departed while the other agents helped the Girards. He needed to go over some last minute details with Bob before his parents arrived at the hotel, and Jim could sense Bob was excited and nervous about the meeting and couldn't wait to see his folks.

Once at the meeting site, Jim allowed the family to visit in private and reminded them of the time restriction. Anything longer than three hours would put the operation at risk. As the agents waited outside, Bob and his parents talked about the past, what had happened to them as a family since their last meeting and reminisced about the good times, including Bob's marriage to Nancy and the birth of Scott, the Girard's only grandchild. Bob updated them on the situation with Nancy and Scott and could see the tears well in his mother's eyes.

"Son, I'm sorry things haven't worked out for you and Nancy," Ella said.

"Me too mom," Bob replied in a sad voice, "but I understand her position."

"But it's so unfair with Scott and all," added Bob's father.

"Unfair is what I did to my family dad. He's better off with his mother and only time will tell whether he'll understand everything and why it happened."

As the meeting drew to a close, Bob found loneliness creeping into his very being but gained strength from his parent's forgiveness and understanding. "Mom and dad, this may be the last time we see or talk to each other," Bob said with a crackling voice. "I just want you to know how much I love you and how sorry I am about everything. I know I've disappointed you. Can you ever forgive me?"

"The disappointment will never replace the love we have for you and the pride we share having you as our son," Bob's mom responded, tears now running down her cheeks. "Your dad and I pray every day for your safety and our thoughts and good wishes are always with you."

As Jim entered the room, everyone could sense the conclusion of a beautiful reunion. Jim indicated an end to the meeting and reminded the Girards there would probably be no further contact with Bob. The mob had turned up the heat and any contact would put both parties in severe danger. As long as Bob remained a witness in a possible murder case, the Gallibini family would not call off the dogs. At this point the FBI was reasonably confident Bob was the primary target, but any perceived contact with Bob could place others in real danger as well.

As the Girards were the first to leave, Bob shared a hug with both parents. It was a difficult moment for everyone, but especially Jim who felt helpless.

"Bye mom," Bob said as he gave her a kiss on the cheek, "I love you."

"Goodbye son and remember our prayers are with you," his mother responded.

"I love you dad," Bob said as he hugged his father.

"We love you too son," his dad replied. "God be with you."

With that the parents were escorted to a car manned by two agents. A second car was to follow three minutes later. This was a precautionary move and would alert Jim and the remaining agents to any problems if the parents were followed. The report from the cellular phone fifteen minutes later confirmed there had been no tail and everything seemed secure.

Chapter Fifty

Now it was time for Bob to leave the hotel where he would be escorted to a new location that Jim hoped would serve as a permanent residence. As Bob walked across the parking lot, a car approached from the lobby end of the hotel. Bob who had on a stained Cleveland Indians baseball cap and sunglasses noticed something strange about the Chrysler Town Car with the heavy tinted windows. Just as Bob was about to get into the back seat of Jim's car, the passenger side windows of the Town Car rolled down and guns appeared.

"Get down!" Jim yelled realizing the severity of the situation.

"Hit them!" yelled a man from the car.

Jim and Bob saw the guns at the same time but it was too late. As gunshots rang out, Jim was able to duck into the front passenger seat while the agent driving was opposite the action and protected by the body of the car. Bob was not so lucky, sustaining gunshot wounds to his chest and stomach.

As Bob collapsed on the pavement, the agents near the hotel room opened fire and were able to immobilize the Town Car by shooting out the tires. Two of the hired guns were killed in the shootout while the driver hid on the floor of the front seat until ordered out of the car, at which time he was placed under arrest. The last thing anyone witnessed, as the smoke cleared, was Bob lying motionless on the ground with a blood soaked shirt. Jim was the first to get to Bob and offer assistance.

"No! No!" Jim screamed as he held Bob's head in his arms.

The first agent by his side asked, "Is he still alive?"

"I don't think so," Jim responded as he changed positions to check for a pulse and breathing. "Call 911 and get someone here now!"

"Can I help?" another agent volunteered.

"Yeah, clear the crime scene and see if anyone else was hit," Jim replied.

Jim hovered over Bob like a mother hen and would not allow anyone else to work on him until the paramedics arrived. They administered CPR but to no avail. Bob was pronounced dead at the scene and was transported to the local hospital for a doctor's evaluation and declaration of death.

Meanwhile, the other agents were securing the crime scene and one was reading the suspect his rights. Jim was shocked and irate and it took all the strength the agents could muster to keep him from physically attacking the man now in custody. The suspect had been hit by a bullet and sustained an arm wound so before questioning he would also be transported to the local hospital for treatment.

"You son-of-a-bitch," Jim screamed at the suspect, "I ought to kill you right here!"

"I didn't shoot him," the prisoner protested, fearing for his life.

"You might as well have. You were part of the shooting."

"What do you mean?" the driver asked innocently. "Those guys rented this car and asked me to drive. I didn't know they were going to do something like this."

"Yeah, right asshole," Jim yelled, still being restrained by another agent.

"Really, I've never seen those guys before today. They called ahead to the car rental and asked if the agency could recommend anyone to drive them around Denver."

As Jim reached out to grab the suspect he said, "sure, and I'm the president you no good piece of shit."

"I'm just telling you what happened," the driver lied.

"Well, I'm just telling you what's about to happen if I get you alone," Jim menacingly replied. "I'll kill you!"

In so many words Jim advised the driver he should have sustained a fatal wound to avoid what he had in store for him. He could not wait to get to the station and begin questioning the thug, but first he needed to get Bob to the hospital. Jim and his driver escaped injury as did the other agents, but all shared in the disappointment and grief associated with losing someone under their jurisdiction. It was doubly difficult since the person was Jim's friend and under his personal protection.

Upon their arrival at the hospital, Bob's body was wheeled into the first emergency operating room. Shortly thereafter, the driver of the assassin's car was wheeled into the hospital where he passed by the operating room and heard the attending physician pronounce Bob 'dead on arrival.' Fear crept into his body as he heard Jim ask, "wasn't there anything that could be done?" How would this half-crazed FBI agent react to his friend's death? He was now concerned he might find out.

Bob was covered with a sheet and taken to a room where his body would be held until released to Jim as part of the witness protection program policy. The suspect was treated for superficial wounds and released to the custody of the Denver FBI where he was escorted downtown to be charged with murder and questioned. Jim went with Bob's body to insure everything was taken care of and advised the other agents he would contact the family.

Contacting Bob's family would be one of the most difficult assignments Jim would ever undertake. His sloppy work had led the Mafia to the hotel and resulted in the death of their son. Jim was not able to reach them until later that night upon their return home. Bob's parents were in shock and could not believe they had been with their son less than five hours ago enjoying what little time they had left before he would disappear from their lives.

"But Agent Stanton, how could this happen?" Tom Girard asked in disbelief.

"I really don't have a good explanation," Jim responded with a heavy heart.

"We were just with our son earlier today," Ella sobbed, speaking to no one in particular.

"I'm terribly sorry. I don't know what went wrong. These men just seemed to appear out of nowhere. I don't know what to say."

"It doesn't sound like there is much you can say except you and the rest of the FBI screwed up!" exclaimed Bob's father, now turning bitter at the outcome of their meeting. "You got what you wanted from him so that takes care of everything as far as the bureau is concerned. You should be ashamed of yourselves."

"That's not fair," Jim tried to explain, knowing there was enough blame to go around. "I cared very much for your son and did everything in my power to prevent this tragedy."

"Yeah, well what you did wasn't good enough," Tom concluded and hung up.

As tough as that conversation was, Jim now had to call Nancy. How would she react? Nancy tried to act strong but Jim knew she was trying to hide the hurt. "Oh Jim, I feel so bad."

"I know what you mean. After all, he was a friend and it happened on my watch."

"No," Nancy continued, "I mean about not telling Bob how much I loved him the last time we were together."

"He knew you loved him."

"But I was angry and vindictive and just never really thought it would get to this. If only I could have put my personal hurt behind me and treated him like the loving and caring husband and father he really was," Nancy lamented. "Now Scott nor I will ever see him again."

Through all her disappointments, Nancy always had and always would love Bob like no one else. It was so unfair Scott would never grow to really know his father.

"Do Bob's parents know?"

"Yes, and that's the irony of this whole thing. They had just visited with him earlier that day in Denver."

"How did they take it?"

"Not very well as you can imagine," Jim replied. "They feel like it was my fault and they probably are right."

"No, don't say that. You did everything possible to help Bob and our families," Nancy said, choking back tears. "Don't beat yourself up over this."

"I don't know Nancy, I just don't know. I should have known better."

With Bob gone, Nancy and Scott could give up their hidden identity and resume their previous lives if they so desired. The threat of further retaliation was miniscule since Bob was the only one who could link Mario and Albert to the murder. More killing would be considered extreme and unwarranted by the Gallibini family and not tolerated by the other mob bosses. There was already enough attention being focused on the Mafia, none of which was doing them any good.

Nancy agreed to call her mother and tell her the news. Fortunately, Scott was still too young to understand but someday Nancy would explain his father's death. Bob and Nancy always agreed to be straightforward and not hide anything from their children.

"What are you going to tell Scott?" Jim asked.

"I doubt anything right now since Scott's wouldn't understand anyway. I won't try to explain the situation until he's old enough to understand."

"Well, Betty and I are there for you if you need help. Please keep in touch."

"Thanks for everything, Jim," Nancy said as she began to cry. "I've got to go."

Right now, one of Nancy's biggest disappointments was Bob would never see Scott participate in sports, play an instrument or hold the lead in the school play. On the other hand, she was not sure how forgiving Scott would be growing up without a father. Whatever it was Scott decided to do, Nancy was confident he would be successful if he had his father's determination. The hard part would be explaining how a convicted felon was such a good man.

As far as coming out of hiding, she would have to think on that. Remaining under an assumed name would deflect a lot of criticism from Scott and possibly provide her with a better opportunity to raise her son in a normal environment. He was still too young to know his real name and she would have to convince the grandparents what she was doing was for the best. Who knew, by the time Scott was old enough to understand what had happened she could be remarried and they could both have a completely different name anyway, although that was the furthest thing from her mind at this point.

Jim's last call was to Betty and they seemed to share similar feelings. Jim was terribly distressed Bob's demise had happened under his watch and Betty tried to help relieve Jim's sense of guilt. What more could have been done? He took all the precautions necessary and no one could control the unexpected.

"Jim, you can't blame yourself for what happened," Betty said.

"Well if not me, then who?" Jim asked as he continued to take Bob's death personal.

"It's no one's fault. You followed the book and sometimes things just don't work out. How were you supposed to know the mob would find out about the meeting and execute their plan, especially in broad daylight."

"Betty, you don't understand, that's what I get paid to know."

Betty tried to explain that if it had not happened this time, how much longer before Bob would be exposed and dealt with? This was a risky business and Bob understood the consequences. Everyone who knew Bob would grieve his loss but Jim could not hold himself responsible for the incident. She, more than anyone, knew of Jim's fondness and concern for Bob's welfare. There would be ample time to grieve, but Jim must put Bob's death behind him and get on with his life both personally and professionally. Betty always had a way of making Jim feel better and this was no exception. That was a big part of why he loved her so much and wanted her for his wife and best friend. He vowed to heed her advice as he hung up the phone, but knew that would be easier said than done.

Chapter Fifty One

Jim was tormented not just with Bob's death but the thought the Mafia seemed to know the details leading up to the meeting with Bob and his parents. Only later would Jim find out how this all came about.

As to the matter at hand, the driver of the Town Car had requested and been granted a lawyer, thus limiting some of the questioning by the FBI. In the course of the conversation between client and counsel, the suspect confirmed the death of Bob Girard.

"So you're sure Bob Girard is dead?" counsel asked.

"Guaranteed," responded the driver.

"How can you be so sure?"

"Look, I saw him the hotel parking lot and he was shot all to hell."

"But was he dead?"

"The paramedic took his vital signs and I heard him pronounce the guy dead. Isn't that proof enough?"

Counsel was adamant as to what the suspect knew because he was to report directly to Tony Gallibini. It was in everyone's best interest the information be accurate.

"Then what happened?" counsel persisted.

"They took me to the hospital where I saw this Girard guy again."

"Explain."

"I mean, when I went to the hospital I passed by the room where the doctor was looking at him. He was lying there stiff as a dead mackerel."

"Go on."

"Well, I heard the doctor tell the FBI agent Girard was dead."

"Did you hear anything else, anything at all?"

"Not really. The doctor pulled a sheet over the guy's head and I went down the hall for treatment," the suspect concluded. "Now, is that good enough? The bastard's dead!"

The suspect was advised not to talk to anyone while the lawyer excused himself to make a call, but assured his client he would be out on bail within the next twenty-four hours and rewarded for his role in the killing. The death of Bob Girard would be relayed to the Gallibini family and was a source of great rejoicing.

As Jim reflected back on the events leading to Bob's death, he realized he had not been as cautious as he should have been and had a bad feeling the end result may have resulted from a leak within his office. Jim never had a problem of this nature under his command, but was confident the person guilty would surface as he began to backtrack through the plan. Not having problems in the past did not preclude guilt on the part of his long-time agents, but he was pretty sure a new agent or staff member would be guilty of this crime. With that thought driving him, Jim wanted to quickly tie up loose ends and get back to Miami.

Jim's involvement in Bob's burial was somewhat limited since the Girard's were still upset with the FBI's handling of his protection. They decided to deal directly with the Denver funeral home where their son's body was being held, while Jim on the other hand would have to remain on the road a few more days to ensure Bob's body was cared for.

"I'm sorry to bother you Mr. Girard, but I'm returning your call," the man on the other end of the phone said. "I'm the funeral director involved in your son's arrangements. Please accept my condolences for your loss but I need to ask you a few questions."

"Go ahead." Tom replied, still stung from his son's death.

"How would you like us to handle your son's body?"

"Well, surely we want him shipped back here where we can give him a proper burial. We have a number of plots for our immediate family and we want him buried with us."

"I can understand that," the director replied.

"Will you be able to make those arrangements?" Ella asked.

"If you like, but I must advise you of a couple of things."

"Go ahead."

"First, we are required to identify his body before he is shipped anywhere."

"What does that involve? Do we need to fly to Denver?"

"Not necessarily. Agent Stanton was kind enough to ID the body but we need to verify you're okay with that."

"Sure, that's fine with us," Tom agreed, knowing this would eliminate their spending a lot of time and money unnecessarily. Tom and Ella Girard were just now beginning to realize their son was gone forever, and they were appreciative someone would be so willing to help minimize their grief time.

"And the second thing is to alert you to the condition of the body."

"What do you mean by that?" Ella was alarmed.

"He was pretty badly shot up. Unfortunately his body suffered a great deal of trauma."

"What are you getting at?" Tom interrupted, wanting to get to the point.

"I strongly recommend you have a memorial service without an open casket."

"It's that bad?" Bob's mom asked as she started to weep.

"Ma'am, I'm terribly sorry but it's not something any of us can do much about. If you want people to remember your son as he was, I would strongly encourage you to take my advice. It will cut down on the expense and make it easier for us to transport the body. Everything will already be done from this end, thus eliminating any duplication or confusion, and it will allow us to get you the body for burial much quicker."

Stricken with grief, the Girards agreed. "Please do what you think is best and send us the bill. We appreciate your help and concern."

A memorial service turned out to be the best thing. This gave the Girards time to plan a proper burial and allowed people to remember Bob as a vibrant, athletic guy and not a bullet- riddled criminal. In spite of a lack of publicity, it was surprising how many of Bob's old friends came to the service and gravesite. His former high school coach and a former college teammate eulogized him, and the letters from those that could not be there were too numerous to detail. As so often happens in death, Bob was remembered for all the good things he did and what he meant to the community. Jim went to the funeral and only regretted Nancy elected not to pay her last respects. He believed Nancy still felt guilty but sensed she was there in spirit. She also believed it was too early for Scott to be exposed to all the questions about his father. The Girards, in an attempt to reach out, assured Nancy that if someday she and Scott wanted to join Bob the plots would be available.

After the funeral, Jim's attention now turned to the investigation. Was there a crooked agent in his office? There was nothing more despicable in his mind than a bad FBI agent, especially one tied to organized crime.

Agent Rodriquez, on the other hand, had received word of Bob's death and telephoned his contact to confirm the information already given the Gallibini family. He had monitored Jim's phone call to the office describing in detail the murder, arrest and Bob's burial. Nelson also learned through other agents Bob's tapes were unintelligible, so Jim and the bureau no longer had anyone linking Albert Valdez to the murder of the New Orleans' crime boss.

"So, what you're telling me is there is no way the FBI can link Albert to the murder," Tony Gallibini asked.

"That's right," Nelson replied smugly.

"All this time we thought they had his confession on tape. Can you believe that shit? Now with scumbag Girard dead, they have nothing."

"Well almost," Nelson replied.

"What do you mean, almost?"

"The only thing that could happen is for the FBI to find the murder weapon or if Mario was to sing to cover his own ass."

"Don't worry, the weapon's been destroyed and Mario knows we can take him out at anytime. Besides, Mario has been a loyal friend to Albert and this family."

"Then it sounds to me like you're home free."

Tony then concluded, "Good work Nelson, my dad will be very pleased. By the way, tell your father to look for a package within the next few days. We like to take care of our own. After all, if we don't, who will?"

This was secondary confirmation Bob was dead, and Albert could now count the days until his release from prison without fear of additional, more serious charges. The news spread fast within mob circles and the Gallibini family was relieved one of their own would soon return to the fold. They could now eliminate any further thoughts about harming the Girard family. From now on it was business as usual or so they thought.

Only a few weeks remained before the wedding and Jim wanted to bring to a close any loose ends with the Bob Girard case. At the airport, after the funeral, waiting to board his plane to Miami, Jim called Nancy to tell her about the funeral and ask what she wanted to do now that Bob was buried. Nancy confirmed she would like to maintain her hidden identity. She apologized for not being at Bob's funeral and confirmed Jim's thoughts regarding her feelings of guilt and interest in protecting Scott. Her presence would have lead to too many questions, some of which she was not yet ready to answer.

"Maybe some day Scott and I can visit Tom and Ella and go to the gravesite."

"I sincerely hope so," Jim replied. "Maybe that would bring closure for you."

"There's a lot of explaining to do with Scott before we can take that step. By the way, how are you and Betty doing?" Nancy asked, trying to change the subject.

"Great. This case has been trying but Betty's a great lady and seems to understand the nature of my work. Are you coming to the wedding?"

"I would love to, but with my new job and Chad in preschool I don't think I can get away," Nancy replied. "Anyway, I don't think I can afford it right now."

"I understand, but if you change your mind you're always welcome."

"Thanks but I've got to go, Scott's yelling about something. Give Betty my love and thanks for everything. I know this didn't work out the way any of us wanted, but you did everything possible and I sincerely mean that."

"I just wish I could've done more," Jim said in a humble voice. "Give Scott a big hug and kiss for us, and I hope to see you at our wedding."

Chapter Fifty Two

With Bob's funeral now behind him, Jim turned his attention to what he suspected to be a breach of trust within his own office. Upon his return to Miami, Jim took a calculated risk by confiding in one of his closest friends and fellow agents about his concerns regarding the Girard case. If he was wrong about this individual, the case as well as the identity of the guilty agent would be lost and Jim would personally be in grave danger. Per request, Agent Groves picked Jim up at the airport at a time known only to the two of them. It was actually the night before Jim told his secretary he would return from the funeral.

"Thanks for picking me up," Jim said, as he entered the car. "Does anyone know I'm back in town?"

"Not to my knowledge," answered Groves.

"Good, take me to my office."

Jim was driven directly to his office where he asked his partner to wait outside in the agency parking lot while he went upstairs. Jim needed a witness to these proceedings but also wanted backup in case someone had uncovered his scheme.

"Look, you stay down here with the car," Jim instructed his partner. "I'll call you on the walkie-talkie if I need help, but remember to keep your eyes and ears open."

"You sure you don't want me to come with you?"

"Positive, we don't want to scare anyone off."

Jim could only hope his long-time confidant was not the man he was seeking. He then proceeded to his office where he uncovered two small, hidden video cameras, one directed at his desk and the other at his secretary's desk, the person responsible for Jim's travel and whereabouts. After retrieving the tapes, Jim entered his office only to notice a damp spot on his chair as he sat down. Thinking the night janitor may have spilled some water during cleanup, Jim moved into the video room to view the tapes.

As he watched the tape of his secretary's area, a person appeared on the screen wearing a stocking mask to hide his identity. The intent of the person was perfectly clear as he started the computer, pulled up what looked to be Jim's itinerary and made notes. There were two different nights the room was accessed, the most recent invasion occurring earlier in the evening. It was apparent the intruder did not expect Jim to be back this soon.

The second tape was just as revealing, although the mask still concealed the identity of the intruder. The real horror struck Jim when he noticed near the end of the tape the intruder had inadvertently placed a wet cloth on his seat after wiping the desk clean of fingerprints. Could that person still be in the building?

Suddenly Jim could feel the hair stand up on the back of his neck, sensing another person in the room. As he turned Jim saw the shadow of a person with a gun pointed directly at his head.

"So you slipped back early," the muffled voice said. "Could it have been to try and catch someone who may have betrayed the bureau?"

"Possibly, and it looks like I succeeded," Jim replied.

"Maybe you did, but then again maybe not."

"What do you mean maybe not?" Jim asked, stalling for time. "I've got you."

"Do you," the man responded in a sarcastic tone, "or do I have you?"

Jim had been caught by surprise and was destined to join Bob in a coffin only two weeks before his wedding. The only thing saving him at this moment was this man's confusion as to what to do. Here this guy was with the head of the Miami FBI who surprised him by his early return. What would be his next course of action?

"Look, if you give yourself up maybe things will go easier for you," Jim said.

"I doubt that," responded the man, a stocking shielding his identity.

"You know you can't get away with this."

"And why is that?"

"Because the place is secured," Jim bluffed. "You don't think I would come here looking for you by myself?"

"You sound like some cowboy out of one of those old western movies," the man joked. "If I didn't know you were getting back early, I doubt anyone else did. So don't ride in here with a white hat on and act like you're the town marshal."

As the two stared at each other, the door suddenly opened and the janitor appeared. Jim was convinced this guy slept all night and never cleaned anything but to his surprise here he was ready to empty Jim's waste paper basket. This sudden movement and noise distracted the man with the gun and Jim was able to dive under the table. Pulling his gun, Jim yelled at the janitor to run for help.

Realizing the situation and confidant Jim was still not able to identify him, the intruder decided to run rather than get involved in a shootout. As he bounded down the steps, out the back door and into the parking garage, the masked man ran right into Jim's partner. Jim had already notified Groves on the walkie-talkie to be alert to someone running from the building. Seeing the stocking mask on a man running out of the building, Agent Groves told the intruder to stop. Instead the masked man fired his gun at Groves, only to receive in return a bullet to his leg. As the wounded man fell to the ground he dropped his gun and placed his hands in the air. Jim came running out of the building to join the action.

"I see you got him," Jim yelled. "Good work but be careful, he's dangerous."

"Are you okay?" Agent Groves asked Jim.

"Thanks to the janitor, yes."

"What about the janitor?"

"I'll explain later," replied Jim, "but first let's find out who this guy is."

Removing the mask, neither Jim nor his partner was particularly shocked to find Agent Rodriquez. A seasoned agent, Nelson immediately denied any wrongdoing and defied Jim to link him with any crime.

"But why did you do this?" Jim asked.

"I want a lawyer," Rodriquez demanded.

"Sure, just as soon as we call the local police and have you arrested," replied Agent Groves. "We'll let them read you your rights."

"You'll never prove anything," Nelson said.

"We may not have too," Jim responded.

"And what does that mean?" Rodriquez asked.

"That's for us to know and you to find out," Jim said with a smirk on his face.

Proving Rodriquez guilty would not be too difficult. Jim's secretary remembered Nelson hanging around her desk when she used the password to access her computer files, the night garage camera verified Agent Rodriquez wife's car parked in the garage the nights in question and the office video tapes would substantiate the match between the stocking mask and gloves he was wearing when he was apprehended. He also had a key to access the offices. But the damaging evidence for Rodriquez would come from a thorough background check that would reveal his association with Albert Valdez and the Cuban Mafia.

How much Nelson would expose the Gallibini family would be anyone's guess. On one side he had to worry about the mob and his family, while on the other he had to worry about being in prison with a bunch of guys he put away and who hated law enforcement people. Jim would let Nelson sit in jail for a couple of days allowing him time to weigh his options.

"So, what's it going to be Rodriquez," Jim asked a few days later, "us or them?"

"I don't know what you're talking about," Nelson laughed.

"Laugh now, but even if you beat this rap, who's to say you didn't give up the Mafia?"

"What are you talking about?"

"You know," Jim went on, "there's a lot of information we have the Mafia doesn't know about."

"So, what's that got to do with me?"

"What if we should initiate some arrests linked to work you've been involved in. Do you think your mob buddies might suspect you betrayed them?"

"You can't do that," Rodriquez pleaded as his demeanor changed.

"Oh, we can't. A well-placed rumor sure would add fuel to the fire. If I were you I would give this a lot of serious thought," Jim said in a threatening way.

"You're too much by the book to pull something like that," Nelson replied without much conviction.

"We'll see," Jim said as he got up to leave. "Give me a call if you change your mind and oh by the way, I hope it's not too late when you do. Between the inmates looking for some fresh meat and the mob dealing with a snitch, I wouldn't want to be in your shoes."

With that final comment Jim walked out the door knowing nothing he could do would change the damage incurred by so many innocent people in this case. It wouldn't make Rodriquez an honest agent or absolve the bureau of its failure to follow through on promises made to ensure the safety of those involved. Jim's guess was Nelson would opt to fight the case, hope for an appeal and depend upon the Gallibini family to protect him while he was in prison. The important thing was a bad agent had been exposed and eliminated and another blow had been dealt organized crime. The case had come full circle and Jim could now move on with his life.

Chapter Fifty Three

The wedding proved to be quite nice and a bit more lavish than Betty and Jim had anticipated. Chad was not about to see his mother and her husband have less than the best and insisted on paying for the reception with the money he made after signing his new contract. Jim argued with Chad until they finally agreed to split the cost. The church ceremony was beautiful and Chad was thrilled that Jim would ask him to be his best man.

The wedding was followed by a wonderful reception at Don's Resort and Golf Club in Miami Shores. Jim had forgotten how many serious drinking buddies he had in the bureau, and most of them kept the reception rolling until the wee hours of the morning. Many of Chad's friends showed up but left early to enjoy the nightlife of South Beach. Chad would catch up with them later after driving his mom and her new husband to their hotel at the airport.

The honeymoon was a ten day cruise on Royal Cruise Lines to the east Caribbean, originating out of San Juan, Puerto Rico with stops in St. Thomas, the U.S. and British Virgin Islands, St. Lucia, Grenada and Aruba. The opportunity to get away from the office after all that had happened the past six months was a blessing in disguise for Jim. Finally, both he and Betty would get a chance to relax and enjoy each other minus distractions.

Chad, on the other hand, was about to embark on a brand new period in his life. He was to report to training camp in a couple of weeks and his agent was convinced it was the beginning of a long and profitable career. With Chad's personality and good looks, numerous companies had already contacted him to endorse everything from shoes to cereal. No one was happier or more excited about his good fortune than Jim.

After a wonderful time in the Caribbean, it was somewhat depressing to return home. The honeymoon was wonderful but it was time to return to the real world. Jim was tying up some loose ends at home when Chad called.

"Jim, is mom home?" Chad asked over the phone.

"No, she went to the store to pick up a few things. How's everything in New Jersey?"

"Fine, and how was the honeymoon?"

"Great, the islands were beautiful and the weather perfect. Your mother and I had a great time. So how do you like the NBA?"

"Good so far. My agent is excited about the future, and being in a large market it looks like there could be some endorsements coming our way soon."

"That's great," Jim replied. "How's the team?"

"We're young but athletic and enthusiastic. I just hope we can channel all that energy into wins."

"I'm sure you will."

"Well, tell mom I called and I'll call back later."

"I'll tell her and once again thanks for the wonderful reception. It meant a lot to both of us, but especially your mother."

"Happy to help dad," Chad responded. "No one deserves it more than you and mom. Talk to you soon."

Jim wanted to talk longer but realized he was still making his way with Chad. But to be called 'dad' was almost more than Jim could stand. He couldn't wait to tell Betty.

There were a lot of things for which to be grateful. They had expanded Bob's old basketball camp and it had taken on a positive identity of its own. Chad had already made a significant impact on the inner-city community, and his involvement and popularity caught the eyes of the political heavyweights in South Florida. Who knew what the future might hold after basketball. Politics might still be in the cards.

Chapter Fifty Four

As Chad went through preseason training camp, it became apparent he would be the starting guard for the Nets in their season opener. That would be a difficult task for a rookie, especially against the defending world champion Chicago Bulls in Chicago. Chad made arrangements for Betty and Jim to be at the opener and all were thrilled to have dinner in Chicago the night before the game. They were able to get caught up on things and Betty couldn't be happier or prouder for her son.

Jim and Betty spent the next day looking around Chicago. Chad attended a noon shoot- around and would rest at the hotel until game time. Betty and Jim would enjoy an early dinner so they could get to the United Center in time to watch warm-ups.

As they arrived at their courtside seats, Chad spotted them and walked over. "I just want to tell you again how glad I am you could be here to see my first game. It means a lot to me and I sure hope I don't disappoint you in how I play."

"We wouldn't have missed it for the world," Betty replied, "and you'll play just fine. Don't you have to warm-up or something?"

"I've already done enough shooting. We'll go to the locker room shortly before we come back out for formal warm-ups so I've got a couple of minutes to visit."

"By the way," Jim added, "we sure did enjoy last night."

"Your coach and the other players seem like nice boys," Betty interjected.

"Men, mom, men," Chad whispered. "We're not boys anymore."

"Well they sure seem like nice people. I'm so happy for you."

"Things are really good right now but there is one thing missing from making this a perfect night," Chad said.

"What's that?" Jim asked, somewhat bewildered.

"I wish Bob and Nancy Girard were here."

"I know honey," Betty replied, not really surprised by this statement.

That was the first time Chad had mentioned Bob's name since before the wedding, but it showed how much he still loved the man and appreciated all he had done for a lonesome, wayward kid. Chad was very loyal by nature and could not or would not forget Bob's love.

"You know," Chad went on, "I've had a lot of time to think about Bob and everything that happened and I now realize although it was wrong what he was trying to do, was it really that bad to want something better for his family?"

"No, Chad." Jim went on to explain, "nothing was wrong with the wanting, but nothing can justify the means by which he tried to accomplish that end."

"I know. I guess I'll never be able to forgive him completcly for all the hurt he caused so many people, but I've also come to appreciate all the good he did for so many others, especially me."

"That's a sign of maturity son," Betty added.

"I just wish he could be here to watch and enjoy my success," Chad said as tears welled in his eyes. "I've got to go in now. See you after the game."

"We better get to our seats," Jim volunteered in an attempt to change the mood of the conversation. "Good luck!"

Conclusion

As Betty and Jim returned to their seats, Jim wondered if he would ever be able to tell Betty, Chad, Nancy or anyone the truth about what really happened to Bob Girard. His brief encounter with the unidentified man as he entered the building caused him to revisit the case.

As they stood for player introductions and the playing of the National Anthem, Jim could not help but to think back to that day in June when he met with Bob and listened to a proposed idea that initially was beyond Jim's comprehension. Bob had devised a plan he hoped would not only stop the Mafia's pursuit of him and his family, but would enable Jim to flush out the suspected leak in his organization. Their conversation was still fresh in Jim's mind.

"Bob, I can't put you at that kind of risk," Jim said. "We have guidelines for the witness protection program and to deviate that far from those guidelines would be asking for trouble."

"Look, I can't be at greater risk than I already am," Bob argued. "If we don't try something, I'm a dead man and who knows what might happen to my family."

"Okay, so explain again what you have in mind but I can't promise I'll sign off on it."

"First, you spread the word in your office there is to be a meeting between me and my parents." Bob continued, "if there's a leak like you think, this will give the appearance of one last chance for the Mafia to make a hit on me."

During this proposed meeting Bob would become a visible target, which he had grown accustomed to during the past few months. Use of a substitute would create a possible leak as well as put that person's life in danger, something Bob did not want and Jim would not okay.

"But that's ridiculous," Jim protested, "not only will this meeting put you at risk but your parents as well."

"C'mon Jim, you know I wouldn't do anything that would put my folks in danger. Think about it, they want me, not them. If we set this up right, my parents will be out of harm's way before anything happens, and if we don't do something my parents will become more serious targets as time goes by."

"Go on."

Bob went on to explain that after the meeting with his parents he and Jim would change into full body, bulletproof suits. Bob's suit would be hidden by a long-sleeved shirt and lined with blood bags that would explode on contact to give the appearance of real wounds. Aside from the body armor, Bob would also wear a protective headliner under his baseball cap as well as bulletproof sunglasses. With the exception of limited facial exposure, Bob would appear to be safe from a gunshot.

"But what if they don't make the hit?" Jim asked.

"They will," Bob replied. "Even if they don't, nothing's lost. In fact, that would be a good indication there was no leak in your office."

"So the hit takes place, then what?" Jim asked with renewed interest.

"That's where it gets a little tricky," Bob confessed as he proceeded to outline the plan.

With all the variables, Jim had some reservations about the plan but both men agreed the only way to eliminate the constant fear and uncertainty with so many lives at stake would be for Bob to appear to be dead. One of the key elements of the plan required Jim to be overprotective of Bob once the hit took place. None of the other agents could be allowed to work on Bob or care for his manufactured wounds.

"That shouldn't be that big a problem," Jim said.

"Yeah, but here's the tough part," Bob went on. "Somehow you've got to get me to a hospital and have me pronounced dead. If there is no evidence that I actually died, the mob will assume I'm still alive and nothing will change. They take nothing for granted."

"How in the hell am I going to do that?"

"You're creative," Bob mused, "call in some markers."

Jim thought for while and then remembered two retired FBI agents and long-time friends who lived in the Denver area. He told Bob he would contact them and see if they would help. These were two guys they could trust, and if they were willing to help he would get back to Bob but warned him not to get his hopes up.

Jim made contact with his buddies and asked for their help. He gave them a vague description of his plan, answered their questions and tried not to divulge the people involved. A big part of this exploratory process was based on Bob's belief these guys would do just about anything to punish the mob and uncover a rogue agent. But he also didn't want to expose the operation if they felt uncomfortable about bending the law.

"So, let me understand," said retired Agent Ball, an overweight, middle-aged man with an infectious smile, "we are to locate an ambulance and act as paramedics." Ball had taken retirement early and now spent most of his free time fishing and playing golf

"That's correct," Jim replied.

"Then what do we do?"

"You'll position yourself near the hotel where we're meeting and arrive on the scene when I give the signal. With the possibility of multiple injuries, you must be the first ambulance on the scene so we can ensure you'll be dealing with me and the supposed victim."

"What if nothing happens?" asked retired Agent Edwards, one who could still be an ad for military recruiting. This guy was in great shape and had the physique to prove it. Unlike Ball, he was active as a personal trainer and had a rather large clientele.

"Then nothing happens but I'll bet that won't be the case. The key is your quick arrival, pronouncing the victim dead and getting him to the hospital."

Once they got to the hospital the real fun would begin. They would need a doctor to pronounce Bob dead and sign a death certificate. But who could they get that would risk his license to forge a death certificate? One of the retired agents knew a semi-retired friend who was a doctor he thought would be willing to help.

The doctor had lost his wife and daughter to a gang-style killing as a result of being in the wrong place at the wrong time. The women were walking in front of a store when the hit took place and both received deadly gunfire. The perpetrators of the crime were linked to the Mafia but were never brought to justice. The mob reportedly sent the shooters underground and provided them with new identities. The doctor vowed to avenge their deaths but had never had the chance. This looked like an opportunity to make good on his promise.

Jim would meet with this doctor before flying back to Miami. The outcome of this meeting would determine whether the proposed plan would go forward.

"I'm sorry about your wife and daughter," Jim said after talking with the doctor about the plan. "You don't have to do this if you don't want too."

"I know that Agent Stanton, but I guarantee you I'm looking forward to being able to help in any way I can," the doctor replied.

"You could lose your license and even go to jail."

"I've been in my own kind of jail since the murders of my loved ones and have nothing left but my desire to help put an end to the Mafia. Anyway, I'm done practicing medicine for all practical purposes and only fill in when needed." The key was the doctor still had hospital privileges so the meeting would be set around his scheduled day of work.

It was now time to alert Bob that everything was in place and on go. Both men agreed Denver was an ideal place to carry out the plan. Not only had Jim identified and contacted people there willing to help, the weather that time of year was chilly during the day providing Bob and Jim with a reason to wear warmer clothing to cover the bulletproof gear. Also, this location would enable Jim to work without using any of his own agents from the Miami office, thus isolating the possible leak. Bob was pleased but still wanted to go over some details.

"So the doctor pronounces me dead, but who will handle the body and help make the arrangements for the funeral."

"You're not going to believe this but the doc's son is a funeral director and holds the same hatred for the death of his mother and sister as the father," Jim explained. "If the truth should ever rear its ugly head, the doctor has covered the son's ass by signing the death certificate although I think the son would help regardless."

"I don't get it?"

"Who's to say someone isn't dead if a doctor says he is. The kid's off the hook."

Having had that question answered, Bob went on with the plan. The mob must receive first-hand verification he was dead. For that reason the paramedics and doctor's performance would be critical as would evidence of an official death certificate. Jim assured Bob those things had been taken care of. Little did either man know at the time there would be a witness to the crime that would report Bob's death to the Gallibini family. That would later be seen as 'icing on the cake.'

"No one can be allowed to see the casket is filled with cement bags. Keep in mind this must be a closed-casket memorial service. Once the body is identified and buried there will be no reason to question my death."

"Don't worry, I'll be at the funeral and make sure everything goes according to plan."

According to the plan, if all went well Bob would physically alter his appearance immediately following the funeral and seek a new residence on his own. There should be little concern about his identity if he was believed dead. Never the less, he would take no chances.

Bob realized he would never be able to contact anyone he once knew but that was the price for bringing this nightmare to an end. Most important, Nancy, Scott, Marty Champion, and Tom and Ella Girard would be able to return to normal lives. Bob couldn't thank Jim enough for his involvement in this plan since no one knew better than he the risk Jim was taking with his career. Jim saw the successful completion of the plan as a way to bring this case to a close, uncover a potential corrupt agent and help a friend who had impacted in such a positive way the lives of two people he dearly loved, Betty and Chad. Not to mention the role Bob played in damaging the Mafia's infrastructure.

As Jim and Betty found their seats and stood for the national anthem, Jim reflected back on how lucky they had been in carrying out Bob's plan. He had not heard from Bob since the day at the hospital and had no confirmation as to where Bob had settled. Jim remained optimistic things had gone well and actually hoped one day to see Bob again, although he knew that was at best a remote possibility. In their last conversation, Bob led Jim to believe he would probably locate somewhere in the Midwest in hopes of keeping an eye on Nancy and Scott. Bob preferred big cities and he mentioned the Chicago area as a possibility.

As the singing of the Star Spangled Banner drew to a close, Jim looked beyond the flag into the back rows of the upper deck and caught a glimpse of a man who held his attention. Was it the stained Cleveland Indians' baseball cap, his profile, the sunglasses or just a gut feeling about this guy? Was this the same man Jim saw earlier in the concourse? Could that be Bob Girard? If so, maybe Chad's NBA debut would be more complete than he would ever know.